W9-DIN-395

THE

WESTERN WORLD;

OR,

TRAVELS IN THE UNITED STATES

IN 1846-47:

EXHIBITING THEM IN THEIR LATEST DEVELOPMENT
SOCIAL, POLITICAL, AND INDUSTRIAL;

INCLUDING A CHAPTER ON

CALIFORNIA.

WITH A NEW MAP OF THE UNITED STATES,
SHOWING THEIR RECENT TERRITORIAL ACQUISITIONS, AND
A MAP OF CALIFORNIA.

BY ALEX. MACKAY, ESQ.

OF THE MIDDLE TEMPLE, BARRISTER AT LAW.

IN THREE VOLUMES
VOL. II.

SECOND EDITION

NEGRO UNIVERSITIES PRESS
NEW YORK

Originally published in 1849 by Richard Bentley

Second Edition

Reprinted in 1968
by Negro Universities Press
A DIVISION OF GREENWOOD PUBLISHING CORP.
New York

Library of Congress Catalogue Card Number: 68-55900

Reprinted from a copy in the collections of
The New York Public Library
Astor, Lenox and Tilden Foundations;

Printed in the United States of America

CONTENTS.

Chapter VIII.

Chapter IX.

Chapter X.

THE WESTERN WORLD;

OR,

TRAVELS IN THE UNITED STATES IN 1846-7.

CHAPTER I.

PARTY, PARTY-SPIRIT, ORGANIZATION, AND TACTICS.

Party inseparable from Popular Governments.—Difficulty at first experienced of comprehending the scope or drift of American Party.—Apparent Confusion, and its cause.—Zeal which characterises American Party.—Progressive Career of the American Politician.—The different Political Arenas in the Union—The Township—The County—The State, and the United States.—Politics do not interfere with Business in America.—Party Allegiance.—Political Influence of Young Men in America.—Intelligence of the American Partizan.— Violence of Party-spirit on the eve of an Election.—Peaceable manner in which Elections are conducted.—Division of the Polling Districts.—Relative Position of parties with regard to the Questions at issue—Difficulty at first of ascertaining them.—Party systematized.—Local, subordinate to national Party.—Primary Division of Party.—The Whigs.—The Democrats.—Their Principles and Characteristics.—The different States, the Battle-fields of National, as well as Local Party.—Parties, as connected with the Commercial Question.— Party Names and Nicknames.—Organization and Tactics of Party—Difficulty sometimes experienced in controlling it.—Party Excitements in the Capital.—Different Manifestations of Party Organization.—Party, in its national aspect—Its Machinery.—Mode of Action during an Electoral Campaign.—Party Conventions.—The Dictatorial Attitude which they have recently assumed.—Tyranny of Party.—" Compromise Presidents."—Party Organization in the State, the County, and the Township.—Extraordinary Demonstrations of Party.—Candidates must be nominated, to have any chance of Success.— Conclusion.

To those unaccustomed to look below the surface of things, it may appear singular that, in a

country where the people have it all their own way,
such a thing as party, in its less favourable sense,
should be found to exist, or that violent party feeling
should be permitted to disturb the relations of civil
life. If government is ever really, as it is in all cases
professedly, wielded for the good of the masses, one
would, at first sight, naturally suppose that in the
United States, where the masses have all the departments of the government in their own hands, that
object, and that alone, would be pursued, and that
the multitude, in quest of its own good, would be
led by its own instinct in the right path. Nor would
this be altogether a groundless supposition, were
people as wise as they might, or as patriotic as they
should be. But republicanism, even in its most undiluted sense, is no cure for human folly, nor is the
most ultra-democracy a sovereign remedy for the
selfishness of man. Ignorance finds its ready instruments for mischief, even in the best of institutions; and
self-interest is ever active in deranging the practical
working of what may be theoretically the best adjusted
political machine.

So far from the great modern republic being
the scene of political harmony and unanimity, it
is the most violent battle-field of party that the
world has ever seen. Men are not only led by conflicting interests into antagonist positions, but there,
as elsewhere, they are found taking the most opposite views of matters purely affecting the public
weal. And what gives to party, perhaps, a more
violent aspect in the United States than it assumes
in any other country, is that every man is, more or
less, an active party man, enticed into the political
arena not only by the excitements incident to the
scene, but also by the apparent ease with which his

direct connexion with the machine of government will enable him to subserve his own interests and prosecute his own purposes. He feels that, if he manages well, he can do himself, for himself, what, in most other countries, it requires the aid of the great and influential to secure. Generally speaking, there are no intermediate influences between him and his object, the good offices of which he must purchase with a price, be it in money, in abject subserviency, or by any compromise of his independence. The door is open to him, which he can enter without another's introduction, and once within which, he can play his own game in his own way. With these facilities and inducements, the difficulty appears to be to avoid becoming a partizan. The republic is one universal party field, and the number of politicians keeps pace with the census.

It is extremely difficult for a European, for some time at least, to comprehend the drift or the spirit of party in the United States. Before him is one wide spread field of political activity, where opposing forces encounter each other in singular combination and constant evolution; but it is only after long and patient observation, that he can discern the views and principles which conjure into being the moral phantasmagoria of which he is a puzzled witness. He is like a man looking, for the first time, at a great and complicated machine, with its cranks and wheels and cylinders moving in all directions, and at every conceivable angle; and who, from the intricacy of its mechanism and the complexity of its movement, is for some time at a loss to discover the elementary power from which proceeds the harmonious activity, which transfuses the ingenious arrangement of inert

matter before him. Confused as the political drama
in America at first appears to be, it is not without its
method, its plot, or its cast. The chief difficulty in
the way of its analysis lies in this, that the main
story is generally overcharged with underplot; which,
instead of illustrating and aiding, only serves to
obscure and mystify it. It is after a close and careful
observation of its more imposing movements, as well
as of its constant and flickering evolutions, that the
stranger becomes apprised of its sources, its objects,
and its tendencies, and discovers party in America to
be a great moral banian-tree, with one principal, and
a multitude of minor roots.

One great source of confusion to the uninitiated
looker-on is found in the many divisions and subdivisions into which parties resolve themselves in the
United States. Even on questions of general policy
they are not always found with the same dividing
line between them; whilst they split into sections,
and fragments of sections, on matters of local and
minor importance. Parties are frequently found
battling furiously with each other, in the arena of
domestic politics, who are ready, on a moment's
notice, to combine against a common enemy on a
question involving the general interests of the confederation. One wonders how, in the never-ceasing
mêlée, party allegiance is at all preserved. But, notwithstanding the apparent confusion, the discipline is
very perfect, as will hereafter be shown. It matters
not that both of the great parties may be rent to pieces
on minor points; their different parts exhibit a won-
derfully cohesive power when the struggle is one
which involves, in the remotest degree, supremacy in
the councils of the Union. Domestic quarrels are

forgotten, or put in abeyance, until the common cause is either vindicated or lost. Nay, sometimes a species of double warfare is going on, men fighting side by side on some questions, who are, at the same time, inveterately opposing each other on others; resorting to the same ballot-box in one case, but dividing their votes in another.

But whatever may be the question on the political tapis, whether it be one simply involving the merits of different candidates, or a point of national policy; whether it have relation to the domestic management of a township, or to the foreign relations of the Union; there never seems to be the slightest abatement of the virulence which distinguishes the incessant strife of party. In the old world, where party struggles, generally speaking, turn upon great principles, where the fight is between old systems and new, and mighty moral forces are in the field disputing for the issue, it is no wonder that great passions are evoked, or that the spirit and enthusiasm of the multitudes should sometimes rise to a pitch which is grand whilst it is terrible, dangerous whilst it is sublime. But nothing can be more ludicrous than the contrast, which is not unfrequently exhibited, between the stereotyped zeal of the American politician and the petty objects on which it is expended. The grand principles for which the people elsewhere are still fighting, and which give to political warfare its more dignified and imposing forms, have all been conceded to him, and the greatest range which his political vision can now take is confined to practical questions of domestic bearing. In the part which he takes in reference to these, he exhibits the same energy that is elsewhere displayed in the contest for principles of universal application. In his township, in his county, in his State, and in his more important capacity as a citizen of the United States, he is the same active and impetuous politician, seeming to know but little difference between one question and another, so far as the gauging of his zeal, in respect to them, is concerned. It is not to be doubted but that the contests in which he is sometimes called upon to act his part are, in their results, of the greatest national importance, when the excitement which pervades the country is not altogether disproportioned to the magnitude of the issue: but the eagerness and virulence with which the pettiest points are battled for, is more the result of the constant political skirmishing which is going on, than of the importance which is attached to them. To the commercial man, business occasionally brings its "slack time;" to the farmer, the mutations of season now and then offer repose; but to the American, in his political capacity, there is no rest. From one end of the year to the other, his attention in this respect is never permitted to flag: he is constantly oppressed with the multitudinous duties of sovereignty; and, as he shares the popular diadem with his neighbours, he is brought into daily concert or collision with them, as the case may be, until, at length, political strategy becomes a habit of his life.

In all countries Mammon has his worshippers, of whose sincerity there can be no question. But, as there is no other country in the world where wealth gives such ready distinction to its possessors, or where fortunes can be so successfully scrambled for, there is perhaps none in which it is so eagerly coveted as in America. But it is not the only thing that gives distinction—official position placing its occupant side by side with the man of wealth. In the United States,

particularly in the Northern States, the wealthy
classes are generally confined to the towns; the system by which land is parcelled out and held, preventing the growth of a rural aristocracy. It is seldom,
therefore, that wealth is found concentrated in one
hand in the rural districts. The consequence is that,
to the great bulk of the farmers, this avenue to social
distinction is closed. Not so, however, with political
offices. These, particularly such as are of a local
character, they retain almost exclusively in their own
hands. The first field for the country politician is
the township, which has its own school districts and
its school commissioners; its road and bridge commissioners; its justices of the peace, &c.; which offices
afford the only source of social distinction in the
localities in which they are held. They are all elec-
tive; and if a man does not care for taking the field
for his own purposes, he is dragged into the little contests which ensue at the solicitation of his more ambitious neighbours. Having once taken his place in
the political arena of his township, he can never
afterwards recede,—his vote in the balance of parties
being seldom to be dispensed with. Once a township politician, his views generally expand, so as to
embrace a wider field, and the one next in order—his
county. He may in some instances be very unwilling
to venture on the larger stage, but, in nine cases out
of ten, the exigencies of his party throughout the
county force him upon it. Besides, to the majority,
the county offices are a more tempting bait than
those of the township; and such of the county politicians as are not contending for them on their own
account, seek to confer them on their personal or
political friends. In some of the States, such as New
York, the county offices are of a legislative, as well

as a ministerial or executive character ; each county in that State having its Board of Supervisors, who constitute a little parliament, which legislates in its capital on all matters connected with the finances, the roads and bridges, the schools, &c. of the county. Like the township offices, those of the county are, generally speaking, in the hands of the agricultural class. It is not the fate of the county politician, even when he is desirous of so doing, to confine himself to his county. Once upon that platform, his horizon expands until it embraces his State. He may be one of the few who care little for State honours and dignities himself, but his party cannot afford to have him indifferent, and he is dragged into the vortex of State politics. Here, for the first time, he finds his own class in serious competition with the other classes of the community. The lawyer and the merchant may not unfrequently be found in the ranks of the county officials, but in the scramble for the offices of the State, the farmer has generally to take his chance with them. The bulk of the legislative bodies are usually farmers, but the majority of influential and leading men in them belong to the other classes. The agricultural politician is by no means debarred from State preferment, but the loaves and fishes of the more extended arena are not so exclusively his perquisites as are those of the township and the county. Even when he confines his own personal views to his county, the instances are very rare in which he confines his political exertions to county questions. By the time he has become the perfect county politician, he is too thoroughly imbue, with the political spirit to refrain from taking his part in all the political contests of the State, whilst the more enterprising and ambitious only make the county the spring-board, from which they bound in due time into a wider and a more enticing field. Once thoroughly embarked in State politics, their next ambition is to take their part in national affairs, and to appear upon the platform of the Union.

This is the great aim and object of the aspiring politician, to attain which he makes use of all the minor stages only as so many steps in his progress. A man never becomes known to the nation as a politician, until he transcends the political bounds of his State. He may be a leading man in New York or Ohio, for instance, but unless he happens to have been long a Governor of his State, or to have largely identified his name in his own locality with some question of great national import, it is only by his *debút* at Washington that he becomes known to the rest of the confederacy. Thus it is that men, who are very great men at home, find themselves frequently utterly unknown, even in the neighbouring State, and particularly so on their first appearance in the federal capital. Such as cannot secure a footing on the federal stage, or care not for getting it, enter more disinterestedly, but in most cases quite as eagerly, into the contest as their more successful or ambitious fellows; the township, county, and state discipline having made every man not only a politician, but a warm and even violent partizan.

With so many spheres of action before him in regular gradation, and with so many calls as a political integer upon his attention, one might, at first, think that politics must be the sole business of life in America. It is really surprising, considering the amount of time which is annually devoted to politics, that the ordinary affairs of life are at all attended to.

Nobody ever thinks of accusing the American farmer of being forgetful of his plough, or the merchant of being negligent in the transaction of his business, from over-attention to the affairs of State. With the most unremitting devotion to politics, they combine the greatest industrial activity. This is very much owing to their party discipline. The greatest inroad upon time, especially upon that of the farmers, is occasioned by their personal attendance at elections; but these, numerous as they are, have been so arranged as to the period of their occurrence, as to occasion the least possible loss in this respect. The rest is managed by a system of political organization, which enables the man of business, be he farmer, merchant, or mechanic, to attend to his business without relaxing his hold upon his party, or diminishing the influence which he may conceive himself entitled to exercise over it.

The American party-man may be the follower, but he is never the blind follower of a leader. In a country which is one great industrial and political hive, and where every man is a politician, no matter what may be his station in life, it is not to be wondered at that some should be met sublimely ignorant of what they are contending for. But, taking the great mass of American politicians, their party predilections are less the result of accident than of inquiry; their party loyalty does not spring from a blind but from an intelligent allegiance. In countries where education is less universally diffused than it is in the United States, parties consist of a few leaders, and a great body of unintelligent followers. Even in our own country, how very few of the multitude really think for themselves! The American, on the other hand, is from his earliest boyhood inured to politics and disciplined in political discussion. The young blood of America exercises an immense influence over its destiny. Perhaps it would be better were this otherwise. Frequently are elections carried, in different localities, by the influence exercised upon the voters by the active exertions of young men, who have, as yet, no vote themselves. Majority is one of the conditions to possessing a vote; but a minor may, and often does, make exciting party speeches to an assembly composed of men, many of whom might individually be his grandfather. Nor is this regarded as in any degree out of the ordinary course of nature, the more elderly politicians being rather pleased than otherwise at the precocity of those who are about to supersede them ere they become their successors. The consequence of this is, that the party-man in America is almost always able to define his position, to point out the precise line of demarcation between himself and his opponents, and to sustain his own side of a question by argument, which may be fallacious, but which is nevertheless ingenious and intelligent. Enter, for instance, in the evening, an unpretending farm-house, and it is a chance if, after the labour of the day, you do not see the occupant in his homespun grey, reading his newspaper by the fireside; for both he and his family can invariably read, and he thinks that the least he can do for his party is to sustain the local party newspaper, many receiving, in addition to this, their daily metropolitan paper. In conversing with him, you will generally find, if you leave him to himself, that, as a duck takes to water, so does he very soon take to politics. The markets and a few other topics may receive a passing attention, but the grand theme is politics; and you will be surprised by the ease and readiness with which he speaks upon the most intricate national questions. For the last fifteen years, no question has occupied so large a share of the public attention as that of the "Sub-treasury," the dispute on which turned on the best mode, not only for the collection, but also for the safe keeping and disbursement of the public revenue, involving, at the same time, the whole question of a metallic and a mixed currency. With the *pros* and *cons* on this, as on all other political topics, I found the farmers, in the remotest districts, not all equally, but all tolerably conversant, each man being able to assign an intelligent reason for the side which he took and the vote which he gave. Nor are their minds biased by viewing a subject only on one side, the newspapers of one party frequently agreeing to publish speeches and dissertations opposed to their own views, provided those of the other will do the same with regard to them. Thus a county newspaper, in the Democratic interest, will publish Mr. Webster's speech in full on a particular subject, if the Whig and opposition organ will do the same with Mr. Benton's on the same subject; an arrangement by which their readers are enabled to consider, at their leisure, both sides of a question. The party-man, whose mind is thus schooled and disciplined, is seldom the man to be bought or bribed. That bribery is practised in the United States is too true; but it is on very different material, as will be immediately shown, that it successfully operates. It may be that party is more easily managed when each man thinks less for himself, and becomes more readily the mere instrument of others; and that, so constituted, it may serve all the purposes of mixed governments; but in a country like America, where the safety of the State rests with the intelligence of the masses, they

did well for their fellow-countrymen who first laid
the foundation of that universal system of education,
which enables the American of the present day to
combine in himself the apparently incompatible characters of a violent, and yet a reasoning politician.

It is not to be supposed that, when the very atmosphere is infected with it, the American ladies escape
the contagion of politics. But whilst they are quite
ready to discuss questions which have but little to do
with their own appropriate sphere, an active female
politician is a phenomenon of rare occurrence in the
United States. They freely vindicate their prerogatives of speech; but it is seldom that a Georgiana
of Devonshire is comprised in their ranks.

To appreciate the violence of party spirit in
America, it must be witnessed on the eve of an election. From the rabid manner in which the newspapers then attack each other, and all those who are
opposed to them ; from the speeches uttered at
public meetings, and the determination evinced by
both parties to achieve a victory, the inexperienced
stranger imagines that the country is certainly on the
eve of a catastrophe. It is with rather unpleasant
misgivings that he opens his eyes on the critical day of
election, during which, judging from the premonitory
symptoms, he makes up his mind that not a throat
will be left uncut—not a bone unbroken. But to
his surprise the whole evaporates in smoke, the poll
proceeding in the quietest possible manner ; and a
President of the United States, or a Governor of a
State, or some other officer, is peaceably made or
unmade, by men who can look one another very kindly
in the face, after having, but yesterday, said such
hard things of each other. The mode in which the

elections are conducted has been devised chiefly with a view to the saving of time, and the preservation of the public peace. An election is generally over in one day, no matter how many offices, federal, state, or county, have to be filled by it. Both towns and counties are divided into districts, each district having its own poll, and being so small that but a fraction of the electoral body votes in it. Being thus separated from each other, but a few hundred voters meeting at each polling place, the numbers assembled together never become formidable, and the election is over before they can unite and get up any dangerous excitement. There are no hustings at which nominations take place and speeches are delivered, so prolific of excitement and tumult in this country, during an electoral contest. The nominations are made, and the speeches are delivered elsewhere ; nothing occurs at the poll, from its opening to its close, but the depositing of votes in the ballot-boxes. Perhaps in the whole electoral history of America a more exciting time was never witnessed than that which immediately preceded the elevation of General Harrison to the presidency. Throughout the Union, upwards of two millions of votes were polled on that occasion, more than double the number ever polled in the United Kingdom, and nearly ten times the number of the whole electoral body of France under the Orleans dynasty ; and yet not a life was lost at that election, whilst scarcely a drop of blood was drawn. Fatal affrays sometimes take place, but they are rare considering how numerous are the occasions on which they might arise, and are invariably confined to the large towns, where it is not always easy to keep the dregs of the rabble in subjection.

When one gradually, by the study of American politics, brings himself into the position of an American partizan, he is not only able to distinguish the lines which separate political questions from each other, but also to appreciate the relations which the different parties respectively bear to the various points at issue. When one enters a large factory, unprepared for what he is to witness, it is not easy, amid the buzz and whirl of the machinery, to understand, in the first place, what is being done, and in the next, the mode in which it is effected. It is precisely so with the Maelstrom of American party—it is one thing to understand party questions, quite another to comprehend the relations of the different parties towards them—for parties so separate and unite, that it is difficult to distinguish permanent from occasional opponents. Generally speaking, there is but little n their names which can serve as an index for the stranger to their political principles. It is all very well to understand the points at issue, but who, having gone no further than this, can tell what it is that Democrats, Democratic Republicans, Loco-focos, Nullifiers, Seceders, Federalists, Whigs, and a variety of other parties, are driving at? Some of these appellations, it is true, are suggestive of the principles which are contended for under them, but it is not so with all the party names in the United States. Some of them are the names assumed by parties themselves, and had originally a meaning, which, if not since lost, has at all events become obscure; whilst others are mere nicknames invented for them by their opponents, as the Tories in this country have been in the habit of designating all as Radicals, who have stood out for reform and national progress. Nor does the

designation of newspapers always afford a clue to the
principles which they advocate. It is not rare to find
the " Democrat" of a particular place the foe of
democratic, and the organ of whig principles ; or a
long-established paper called the " Whig," doing
battle in its neighbourhood, in the cause of the most
undiluted Jeffersonian democracy. There is thus a
great difficulty,—from the multitude of points which
arise, of a general and local character, and the multitude of parties which contend for them, under their
different banners and designations,—in ascertaining,
after the points in dispute are mastered, who they are
precisely that are in favour of, and who against, a
particular one. The only way to solve the problem
satisfactorily, is to sift both questions and parties
carefully, distinguishing between such as are of a
general, and such as are of a purely local character.
This once done, it is no difficult matter afterwards to
scramble through the political labyrinth. Chaotic as
party in the United States at first sight appears to
be, it resolves itself into a regular system, easily
comprehended, when the spectator selects the proper
point of view.

The only satisfactory position to occupy in taking
the survey is the federal platform, from which parties,
in all their ramifose relations to each other, are to be
seen at a glance. The whole then appears to be composed of one general system, with a number of petty
systems in active revolution around it. Party observes the same subordination, in the arrangement of
its different parts, as do the political institutions of
the country. Party, in its local sense, is wholly subordinate to party in its general signification. Each
of the great parties takes root in national questions;

and although they may ramify, in a thousand directions, in permeating the masses, they all tend back
again to the same great trunk, when any national
struggle is before them. It is a mistake to believe
that the great party warfare of America is of a sectional character; party conflicts may originate in
sectional differences, but the line which separates the
combatants is seldom a geographical one. The interests of the east may not always be compatible with
those of the west, but there are no eastern and western
parties, separated from each other by the Alleganies.
The policy of the north may not always be recon-
cilable with the interests of the south; but there
are no northern and southern parties, with Mason and
Dixon's line as their point of separation. The
manufacturers of the north find some of their
staunchest supporters in the representatives of the
south; whilst the cotton-growers of the south are
powerfully supported by large numbers of all classes
of politicians in the north. Even the question of
Slavery itself does not entirely partake of the sectional
character. The stronghold of slavery is the south,
and that of abolitionism the north; but the friends
of freedom are not confined to the one, nor are the
advocates of servitude to be exclusively found in the
other. Questions, in their immediate bearing, may
be chiefly of sectional or geographical importance;
but the parties who contest them, can seldom, if ever,
be distinguished by their geographical position. It
is quite common, for instance, to find men warmly
contending with each other, on a point chiefly interesting to the south, amid the frozen wastes of Maine
on the north-east, or in the far north-west, amid the
more sunny solitudes of Illinois.

In national politics, then, we find the great and
primary source of American party. Welling from
this exhaustless reservoir, it flows forth in two mighty
streams, which become broken in their volume, and
intersect each other's channels, as soon as they tran-
scend the limited bounds of the federal territory, until,
at length, they become so divided and subdivided in
the distance as to lose their distinctiveness, except to
the `observer on the spot. But let an occasion of
periodic reaction arise, and as the veins send back
their blood by different routes to the heart, so do all
these distant streamlets return their waters into the
main channel, to concentrate once more the volume
of party into a united and compact mass, so as to act
with effect in the pending contest. Parties primarily
divide into Whigs and Democrats—in whose ranks
the whole community is comprehended. Whatever he
may be at home, in his state, in his county, or in his
township, with regard to local matters, every American belongs to one or the other of the national
parties, and is either a Whig or a Democrat.

The origin of these parties has been already alluded
to, in treating of the political aspect of the Union.
They partake of no sectional characteristic; both
being transfused throughout the entire mass of society, and each meeting the other in the face, in the
remotest sections and corners of the republic. The
great point which they originally contested, was that of
State rights and sovereignty, in opposition to a strong
and consolidated Central Government. They remain
opposed to each other, now that that question is at
rest, more from habit and tradition, than from any
permanent difference now existing between them in
views and policy. Many questions arise, on which they

accidentally take sides, and which become party questions by their ultimate identification with them. But
there are others, in taking a position on which, they
are true to their original character and hereditary predilections. The Whigs may justly be regarded as the
conservative, the Democrats as the "go a-head," party.
It is obvious, therefore, that questions which may appear desirable and highly politic to the Democrats, may
savour too much of radicalism to suit the palate of
the Whigs. By the latter the monied interest of the
Union has always been chiefly represented; and they
were impelled by instinct to the support of the National Bank, when it was first assailed by President
Jackson, and afterwards by the whole strength of the
Democratic party, when the latter successfully fought
for an independent national treasury—as they were,
indeed, to the support of all banks, when, with the
independent treasury clamour, was combined the cry
for a metallic, in substitution of a mixed currency.
And so, on the tariff question, they seek to maintain the interests of capital, in opposition to those
of labour, particularly of agricultural labour. Into
this course self-interest may drive the Whigs of
the north-east; but the conduct of the southern
Whigs on the tariff question is unaccountable, except upon the ground of their regarding the integrity
of the party as a paramount consideration to the
interests of their constituents. The Whigs too, as
a party, are more sensitive than their opponents
to public opinion, and are more disposed than the
Democrats to regulate their policy by what the
world may be likely to think of them and their
country. It is on this account that their tone towards foreign nations is more courteous and more

devoid of bluster than that usually adopted by the
Democratic party, and that they have a comparatively
strong aversion to all proceedings of a violent and un-
justifiable character, like those which superinduced
the Mexican war.   The Democrats, on the other
hand, are more reckless in their policy ; in their zeal
for ultraism in everything, taking counsel of none
but themselves, snapping their fingers at the world
beyond, whose opinions they care as little for as they
do for its feelings ; and ready at any time to exalt
their country, although it should be at the expense
of its reputation.   The Whigs decidedly represent
the " gentlemanly interest,"—the Democrats comprising in their ranks the greater portion of the
rabble, together with many of the more sturdy and
adventurous spirits of the republic.   Both parties are
excessively patriotic, by their own account, in all
they do, and unbounded in their zeal for the Constitution ; but which of them has been guilty of the
most frequent infractions of that document, it would
be difficult to say ; although I am inclined to regard
it as safer in the hands of the Whigs than in those of
their opponents—who are not always in the mood of
permitting constitutional considerations to stand between them and the furtherance of their policy.   If
the Constitution be not a dead letter, the conduct of
the present administration, in precipitating the catastrophe of the Mexican war, tried by it as a test,
has rendered them, from the President downwards,
amenable to impeachment; and yet they are sus-
tained, in all that they have done, by the whole force
of the Democratic party throughout the country.

If Whiggism and Democracy constitute the two
primary subdivisions of party in its national sense,

how comes it, it may be asked, that we hear of such
a State being Whig, or Democratic, as the case may
be? This is apt to engender confusion, if it is taken
to mean that Democracy, or Whiggism, has anything
directly to do with the peculiar politics of any State.
We hear of the different States being Whig, or
Democratic, because it is in them that all national
questions are battled for. The Americans are never
found all acting together in their electoral capacity on
any subject. The only instance in which they have
done so as a whole people, perhaps, was in devising and
adopting the Constitution. In the House of Representatives they act as a whole people by their delegates; but in no case do the people themselves, in the
exercise of their rights, directly act as one people.
Is a President of the United States to be chosen, for
instance. Each State appoints its own electoral college,
whose business it is to elect him; nor do the electors
thus chosen by any one State meet, in the perform-
ance of their duty, with the electors appointed by
another State. The whole thing, so far as the State
is concerned, is done within the limits of the State,
the electoral college of each State meeting in the
State capital, and transmitting the result of their votes
to the United States Secretary of state at Washington.
Are vacancies in the Senate of the United States to
be filled up? They are supplied by the legislatures of
the different States, who alone can appoint their
senatorial representatives. This, again, makes the
national a State question; for if the State of New
York, for example, is desirous of returning a Whig
representative to the Senate of the United States, it
must first provide itself with a domestic legislature
of Whig principles on national questions, or it loses

its opportunity.   Still further, again, are national
questions carried down into the State, in the choice
of delegates to the House of Representatives.   In
that House, as already seen, there is one member
to about every seventy thousand of the population, throughout the whole Union.   Sometimes one
county of a State, such as Monroe county, New
York, will be entitled from its population to a member of its own.   In other cases, when population is
sparse, two or three counties may be combined to
form an electoral district; but in either case the vote
is a county vote, parties in each county recording their
votes in their own county, and managing the election
by their own county organization.

Thus do national politics, in the election of a member
to the Lower House in the federal legislature, necessarily infuse themselves into the party evolutions of
each county of each State.   Nay, even further, the
township itself does not escape the contagion ; for in
voting in this case by counties, each voter records his
vote in his own township, and thus national questions
become the turning point of party, even in this, perhaps, the minutest of municipal subdivisions.   This
arrangement of confining popular action on national
subjects in all cases to State limits, is not only convenient to the people, but conducive to the maintenance of the public peace.   At the time of a general
election, the attention of the people is thereby concentrated upon many different points.   Each man
finds his centre of action in his own State, and instead of the universal excitement which prevails concentrating upon one point, which would be extremely
hazardous with a government so thoroughly popular,
its force is broken by its being turned in as many

different directions as there are States in the Union. Each State thus forms part and parcel of an elaborate breakwater, which has been reared to protect the general system of the republic from the destruction which would await it, were the accumulated wave of popular excitement permitted to sweep over it unbroken. But whilst the people have no common ground on which to fight the battles of the Union, they are constantly fighting them at home; and thus it is that the great national parties become the primary and controlling parties in each of the States. Party lines, on local points, are not always coincident with that which separates the national parties, but they are generally so. Thus the people of New York, or Pennsylvania, in squabbling amongst themselves about their banks, canals, railways, schools, &c., frequently forget that they are Whigs and Democrats, although sometimes the recollection of their being so is ever prominent. But whether forgetful for the moment or not, they readily fall back into their ranks whenever the national tocsin is sounded, or when a question of mere State import arises which involves, in the slightest degree, their respective party principles.

To pursue the subject of State party would be as profitless as it would be tedious. Its objects are as multifarious as are the wants of a continent, and its name is Legion. Besides, questions affecting any one State, which fail to interest the people of another, could scarcely be very palatable to the distant reader.

The next phase in the scale of importance, which party, nationally speaking, assumes, is that which is influenced by purely commercial considerations. But party relations having in this respect been sufficiently

considered in the chapter devoted to the commercial
policy of the Union, it is unnecessary here to dwell
further upon them, allusion being now only made to
them from their obvious connexion with the general
subject of party.   Before dismissing this part of it,
however, it may be as well to observe that, on the
great question of free trade and protection, parties in
the main preserve the general division to which attention has just been drawn.   But the Whigs, as a
party, have been longer identified with protection
than the Democrats have been with free trade, it
being only recently that the latter have inscribed
commercial freedom upon their party banners.   The
Whigs from all parts of the Union have long co-
operated in the advocacy of a high tariff, but until
lately many of the Democrats of the north and west
kept shy of the cause of free trade.   Even yet a portion of the Democratic party, especially the Democrats of Pennsylvania, abandon their ranks to join
the Whigs on commercial questions; whilst a few
straggling Whigs of the west lean, on the same
questions, towards the main body of their political
opponents.   Although, therefore, the issue between
free trade and protection has been made a party
one, sectional interests, in contesting it, are, in some
instances, too strong for party attachments.

Perhaps the most purely sectional party in the
country is that of the Nullifiers, whose views and
doctrines have been already incidentally remarked
upon.   Nullification, as a principle, is, in its advocacy, chiefly confined to the south, and only comes
to the surface in the political arena, when questions
are agitated directly affecting the sectional interests
of the Union.   Nullifiers, as Nullifiers, know no

other party distinction, whilst their opponents, throughout the whole north and west, comprise party men of all shades of opinion.

The question of Slavery gives rise to still another division in the ranks of national party ; but as I intend to treat of that subject at large in a future chapter, I shall reserve for the present what is to be said upon it in this connexion.

In concluding this branch of the examination into American party, it may not be amiss here to remark, for the sake of avoiding confusion, that "Democrats," and " Democratic Republicans," are names assumed by the Democratic party, " Loco-foco" being the nickname attached to them by their opponents ; whilst " Federalists" is a term of reproach given, for reasons already assigned, by the Democrats to their antagonists, who only recognise for themselves the style and title of " Whigs."

Of the tactics of party in America very little need be said, its strategy in most points resembling that usually resorted to in other countries with governments more or less popularised. The most curious feature about transatlantic parties is the eagerness with which they watch for questions which are likely to become popular, and the impetuous scramble which takes place for them when once discerned. In this way the Democratic party lately stole a march upon their opponents, when they appropriated the Texas and Oregon questions to themselves. It is not always that they are overscrupulous as to the means by which the party interests are subserved. This is abundantly proved by the Log Cabin agitation of 1840; when log cabins, with their songs and speeches, and their orgies on bacon and beans and hard cider, had more to do with the election of General Harrison to the presidency, than had less exceptionable means. But such devices are harmless as compared with others, which, under very equivocal names, such as " pipe laying," are sometimes resorted to. In the rural districts the electoral body may be bamboozled, but it is seldom corrupted. In the larger towns, on the other hand, corruption is frequently practised by all parties. To the position of the Irish in the commercial cities, and the political influence which they obtain, is this chiefly owing.

Notwithstanding the strength of party feeling, it is sometimes exceedingly difficult to control party in the United States. So many and so conflicting are the interests to be attended to, that it is seldom that either party finds itself without some wing or section in rebellion against its authority. The party ranks too are filled with ambitious spirits, who are impatient of subordination, and whose relations with their constituents are frequently such as to encourage them in their waywardness. Each member of the party again cherishes a feeling of independence, which often leads him to display an intractable disposition, even when he has no intention of avoiding subjection. The party leaders in America have sensitive materials with which to work, in their management of which they have to observe the utmost circumspection. But let any great danger threaten the interests of the party, let the common enemy attempt to take any decided advantage of the anarchy which may prevail in it, and all differences are forgotten in a trice; insubordination vanishes and discipline reappears, and the angry sections once more unite into one solid and compact mass, as easily swayed by its leaders as are the armies of the Czar by the generals of the empire.

Violent as are the displays of party feeling in all the political stages of the country, it is in the Federal capital that the excitement reaches its culminating point. On this account it is perhaps as well for the interests of the Republic that the heart of its political system is no stronger than it is; for were the party excitements of the capital sufficiently powerful to keep the whole body politic in a state of chronic fever, there would be but little hope of the recovery of the patient. But the political pulsations at Washington are too feeble to affect the extremities of the country. The inflammatory symptoms which may have affected the members, have partially subsided ere the heart gets into its state of periodic spasm; nor do these symptoms reappear in any intensity, until a local action reproduces them. Whilst parties are rending each other to pieces in Washington, the distant States are in a condition of comparative quiescence, but for which it would be impossible for them to attend to the ordinary concerns of life.

I shall conclude the present chapter with a succinct view of the organization of party in America. Scattered over so vast a surface, with such different relations to sustain, and so many clashing interests to reconcile, it would be impossible for any great party in the country to act with effect, unless it were thoroughly organized. How far party organization in America is complete, and likely to answer its purposes, may be gathered from the following brief sketch of it.

Party is organized with a view to the different circumstances in which it may be called upon to act. It has, therefore, its national, its state, and its county organization, to say nothing of the machinery by which its minuter evolutions are regulated. An outline of one of these will suffice to convey a correct idea of the whole. I shall therefore confine myself to a description of the organization of party in its national aspect.

The national interests of party are primarily under the superintendence and control of national party conventions. These are assemblies of delegates, representing, in their aggregate, the entire party for which they act throughout the length and breadth of the Republic. They are the creatures neither of the law nor of the constitution, being the mere offspring of party, begotten for party purposes and for these alone. They may be looked upon, in fact, as a species of party parliament, each party having in addition to its legislative also an efficient executive machinery. This latter consists of a national central committee, whose duty it is to appoint the time and place for the meeting of the convention, whenever, in their opinion, the exigencies of the party may require its convocation,—to call upon the party throughout the country to elect delegates for the same, and to prescribe their number and the mode of their election. For the better understanding of the working of this machinery, let us trace its action during an electoral campaign.

The election for President takes place about the beginning of the month of November once in every four years. The first and most important movement of each party is the selection of a candidate for the office. Let us follow the operations of one of them, and take the Democratic party as the example.

The campaign actively commences about seven months before the time of election, the first step

being taken by the Democratic national central committee, which calls, by proclamation, upon the
Democratic party to elect delegates to meet in convention on such a day and at such a place, for the
purpose of nominating the candidate, whom the party
will support in the coming contest. These delegates
are generally, in number, the same as the aggregate
of the electoral colleges, on whom the election of the
President ultimately devolves—the party in each
State sending as many delegates to the convention as
there are electors in the electoral college of the
State; by which means the representation in the convention is pretty equally distributed amongst the
States according to the ratio of their population.
The month of May is generally selected as the time,
and some central town or city, such as Harrisburg in
Pennsylvania, or Baltimore in Maryland, as the place
of meeting. In the mean time, the party choose
their delegates in the mode prescribed, who assemble
on the appointed day, at the appointed place, from
all parts of the nation. Once assembled, they remain
in deliberation until the great object of their meeting
is accomplished: that object is to determine, not who
is the fittest, but who is the most available, party candidate for the presidency. The party is represented
in all its phases in the convention; its diversified views
and wishes are brought together and compared, that
they may be, as nearly as possible, reconciled: the
strength, attitude, and tactics of the opposition are taken
into serious consideration; and finally, he is generally
selected as the candidate, not who is the most acceptable, but who happens to be the least objectionable
to all. The selection is made by ballot; sometimes
a great many ballots taking place before a final choice

is arrived at. As soon as the nomination is made, it is promulgated to the party, and, unless some section of it has extraordinary cause for discontent, the person selected receives its unanimous support, the party newspapers throughout all the States retaining the name of their candidate, in large capitals, at the head of their leading columns, until the election is determined in November.

Whilst the Democrats have been thus proceeding, the Whigs have been preserving a strictly analogous course. Their convention has been called and chosen in the same way—has met and deliberated upon the affairs of the party, and selected the most available candidate which their party ranks could supply. Sometimes, but not always, the two conventions assemble in the same place; when, generally speaking, some little time is prudently left to intervene between their meetings. Both parties being thus provided with candidates, there is, with the exception of the appointment of a committee for each candidate, to correspond, during the election, with committees in the States, an end to their national action, the control being thenceforth remanded to the sections of the parties in the different States.

Although the choice of candidates is the great, and indeed the only object of these party conventions, it is not always that they confine themselves to it. They are frequently betrayed into a discussion of various matters connected with the policy of the Union, but more directly with the general interests of the party. Such discussions usually result in a series of resolutions, which are embodied in a manifesto issued to the nation, the object of which is to excite as much enthusiasm as possible in behalf of the party, by taking a bold stand upon such points as are likely to recommend it to the populace. It was thus that in May, 1844, the Democratic convention, then assembled at Baltimore, adopted the celebrated Oregon resolutions, by which they identified the party with the Boundary question, and made it a turning point of the election, in which they subsequently triumphed. The conventions have also, latterly, evinced a disposition to assume a very troublesome and dictatorial attitude, giving the law to the party, and virtually ostracising all who may venture to deviate from their behests. Often have I heard, during the Oregon discussions in Congress, a wandering Democrat recalled to his allegiance by the terrors of the Baltimore convention. The great bulk of the party are slavishly obedient to their mandates, but some are bold enough to kick against and defy them; regarding their recent assumptions as the growth of a novel, an irresponsible, and, therefore, a dangerous power in the State.

This part of the subject naturally leads to a consideration of the tyranny of party in the United States. What has already been said with regard to the difficulty of controlling party may appear to militate against the idea of its exercising a tyrannical influence over its members. But a distinction must be drawn between the lax allegiance sometimes yielded by party men to their leaders, and the coerced fidelity which is observed to the party itself. Even with regard to the leaders, the independence of them which is sometimes assumed by the more troublesome in their ranks, is frequently more a sham than a reality. But woe to the political aspirant who is guilty of any overt act of disloyalty to the Whig or Democratic faith! His treason might as well

be branded on his brow; for from one end of the
country to the other he is denounced by a thousand
offended presses, and by tens of thousands of indignant tongues; and the whole influence of the party is
brought to bear politically to crush him. It is scarcely
within the power of repentance to expiate so grave an
offence. A man may revile those at the head of the
party as much as he pleases, and be forgiven; he may
denounce his leaders in public and in private, and go
unscathed; he may be troublesome in the ranks, but
so long as he does not forsake them, he may remain
uncashiered. But let him lift his finger against
a party movement; let him manœuvre in opposition to
a party object, or vote against a party question, and
he is at once denounced without ceremony or trial,
when his political hopes are for ever crushed, unless,
which is rarely the case, he is unreservedly adopted
by the opposite party.

It is difficult in this country to conceive the force
and influence of this unmitigated tyranny. With
us, party influences are weakened by local distribution. In America, they are concentrated into one
inflexible despotism, which every member of the
party implicitly obeys. In this respect the party-
man in America is entirely divested of his indi-
vidualism. He acts and thinks with his party; its
will is his supreme law. The mischief is that this
strict obedience is alike required through good and
through evil report. The policy of the day must be
upheld, whatever it may be. It is thus that the
flagitious war with Mexico was espoused by the
whole Democratic party, and that no Democrat who
has any favours to expect, or who would escape
annoyance, dared utter a syllable against the conduct

of the Administration. "The man who wouldn't
stand by his own Prez'dent deserves to be tabooed,"
said a Democrat to me one day, on my suggesting,
about the period of its commencement, that the war
might not be universally acceptable to the party.
This is the true spring of party action. Stand by the
President, or, in other words, stand by the party,
whatever may be the complexion of its policy. There
must be no squeamishness. The man who is not
hot, is declared to be cold. The rotten limb is immediately lopped off the tree.

It is not only the rank and file that yield to this
terrible influence—the party leaders bow to it with a
fatal submission. There are hundreds around them
who, for their own purposes, are constantly taking
the measure of their political stature, and who are
ever ready to report any questionable act, incautious
sentiment, or inapt expression, to their common
master. Nay, more, a rival is frequently got rid of
by first entrapping, and then denouncing him. This
intellectual subjugation—this utter absorption of the
individual in the party, is, perhaps, the worst achievement of American Democracy. It is felt to be a
galling tyranny by more than dare confess it so; and
establishes this curious anomaly, that in the freest
country in the world, a man may have less individual
freedom of political action or thought, than under
many of the mixed governments of Europe.

The foregoing is applicable only to the position of
individuals. When a diversity of views or interests
causes a whole section of the party to rebel, conciliation and not repression is the policy adopted.

It is by a rare chance that any of the more eminent amongst the statesmen of America are now

selected as the party candidates for the presidency. The conflict of sectional interests accounts partly for this ; for the leader who, in the main, may be eligible to the party, may be more or less committed against the peculiar views of some branch or branches of it. The slavery question is a rock on which transatlantic statesmen thus frequently split. The most eminent of all the Whigs entertains views on this question which render him objectionable to the abolitionists of the north; whilst some of the northern Whig leaders are, from their views on the same subject, equally unpopular with their party in the south. It is precisely so with the Democratic party. In addition to this, they have to contend against the envy which great talents naturally beget, and which impels little minds, from sheer malice, to oppose them. The eminent statesman who has many friends, has also many enemies in America, even in the ranks of his own party, who are ready to interpose every obstacle to his elevation. It is on this account that each party, for fear of dividing its strength, has found it necessary to select obscure candidates for the presidency. Of the compromise Presidents thus chosen, General Harrison was a specimen on the part of the Whigs ; whilst Mr. Polk is one on that of the Democrats, both of whom were recommended to their respective parties simply by their negative qualities. If their admirers were few, so were their enemies. They were selected, not because they were fit for the office ; but because they were most available as candidates. A growing feeling, however, is now discernible against these presidential make-shifts; but that it will speedily result in more worthy selections is much to be doubted.

The foregoing glance at the organization of party
in its national capacity, will serve to convey an idea
of the machinery by which it works in the different
States, and in the smaller political subdivisions of the
country. In the State, each party has its own State
central committee, which convokes, when necessary,
its own State convention, for the nomination of candidates for State offices, and the general consideration
of questions affecting the interest of the party so far
as the State is concerned. But these State conventions do not always confine themselves to questions
affecting the States in which they are respectively
held. Sometimes, indeed, they are called upon to act
in matters of national concern, as to nominate a list
of party candidates for the electoral college of each
State, by whom the voice of the State, in the election
of a President, is to be ultimately signified. But in
addition to this, they frequently volunteer discussions
on national topics, which usually end in the adoption
of sundry resolutions concerning them. But these
are not binding upon the party generally, nor are
they so, unless doggedly made so, upon the party in
the State whose representatives adopt them. They
are only thrown out as feelers, and as significant of
the wishes of those who promulgate them, but not as
imperative upon their fellow-partizans in the other
States ; nor to be adhered to by themselves, should
the general interests of the party appear on due
consideration to demand a different policy. Thus,
some months ago,* the Democratic convention of the
State of Ohio, after terminating its regular business,
passed a resolution before separating, nominating
General Cass as their candidate for the presidency.

* In 1847.

But this meant neither more nor less than that, for the time being, this military worthy appeared to the Democrats of Ohio as the most eligible candidate for the office in the Democratic camp. They were by no means committed by it to the General, leaving their final action to depend upon the nomination to be made some months afterwards by the national party convention. It is a common feature in the tactics of American party, to have these straws thrown up from different quarters, to ascertain how the wind is setting in, before fairly embarking on a presidential campaign; the different parties in the different States thus giving to their coadjutors throughout the country premonitory symptoms of their political predilections for the time being. The consequence is, that before the meeting of the national convention, the conflicting views, when they are in conflict, of the different sections of the party are all ascertained; so that that body is never taken by surprise by the introduction of questions of which no notice had been afforded it.

Parties carry the same machinery into their county organization for county purposes; their interests, in this respect, being confided to the care of county central committees and county conventions. The legitimate business of the latter, when they meet, does not extend beyond party matters of local concern, but they frequently, by their resolutions, communicate their views and sentiments to their fellow-partizans throughout the State, as the State conventions have just been shown to communicate to the party throughout the Union the peculiar views of the section of it confined to their respective States. The same organization, and with the same results, is carried down into the township, which, with the exception of the school district, is, perhaps, the minutest political subdivision known to the United States.

In addition to the regular machinery just described, by which party in America usually works, its action is sometimes thrown into extraordinary channels, when party exigencies may appear to demand a deviation from the regular course. When it is deemed desirable to excite a spirit of enthusiasm, occasional demonstrations are resorted to for that purpose, for the management of which an incidental organization of party is found necessary. Thus, instead of, or in addition to, meeting by its conventions, the party, both in the State and in the county, is sometimes summoned to meet in its primary assemblies. If either party deems it desirable to make a State demonstration in its elementary capacity, its State central committee is competent to do so, and generally does summon it; and so when an extraordinary county meeting is determined upon, the county central committee is usually the organ through which it is called together. But the younger members of either party are sometimes desirous of making a demonstration of their own, which they effect, whenever it is deemed expedient, through the instrumentality of a Young Men's (Whig or Democratic) State central committee, each county being provided with a similar agency for summoning county meetings when they are required. These aggregate meetings of party in its primary capacity, whether of the party generally, or of its younger branches, are not without their weight in determining the issue of party contests. I have seen them sometimes, when they assumed a very imposing aspect, assembled, as men

of one opinion were, from all parts of a State, in
their tens, their fifties, and even their hundreds of
thousands. In meeting, they converge from their
different counties to some central point in the State,
when such as cannot find other accommodation, en-
camp in the open field. They pass through the different towns and villages, on their way to the place
of meeting, in gay procession, with bands of music
at their head, and flaunting banners, on which party
devices are emblazoned, waving over them. Sometimes they enliven their march with a song, which
generally embodies a political pasquinade. They are
always well received and lustily cheered by their
adherents in each place through which they pass,
whilst their opponents make it a business to turn out
and laugh at them. But the whole affair passes off
very good-humouredly, each party having the opportunity of laughing, as well as of looking serious, in
its turn. To the county conventions the farmers
repair on foot, or in their heavy lumbering wagons,
several of which, from the same township, are sometimes formed into procession, with flags and music.
Those who attend from the towns generally go in
lighter vehicles. Sometimes a central town, or village, is selected as the spot for holding a county convention; at other times, it is held in the depths of
the forest; and it is curious, on these latter occasions,
to see the assembled multitude divided into groups,
some on the ground, some clustering in and around
the wagons, some on horseback, and others dangling,
as it were, from the trees, listening to their favourite
orators, who address them from a platform hastily
erected by throwing some wagons together—their
hurrahs reverberating, every now and then, through the

forest glades, whilst they are sheltered from the burning heat of the sun by the leafy canopy which overhangs them. And not unfrequently, during these meetings, do you see parties stepping aside, in twos and threes, to do a " bit of trade."

Allusion has frequently been made to the nomination of candidates, and I cannot close this chapter without briefly adverting to the difference which exists, in this respect, between party conduct in America and in England. With us, electors have generally to choose between candidates who voluntarily come forward. In America there is no volunteering one's services as a representative. Not that the post is less coveted than it is with us, but party, in each locality, reserves to itself the double right of selecting its candidate, and then electing him as its representative. This plan tends very much to the preservation of the unity of party; the individual selected, when parties are pretty equally balanced, being generally the most available candidate in his district for the time being, and receiving the unanimous support of his political coadjutors. As with us, in districts where a party is overwhelmingly strong, it can afford to quarrel with itself on any topic, and frequently does so on the selection of a candidate. But, generally speaking, the person selected is unanimously adopted by the party; the plan being first to ballot, to ascertain the different views of the party with regard to a candidate; and then to nominate, by an unanimous ballot, him who has the decided majority in the first, or subsequent ballots. None but the person so nominated has any chance of success. The mere volunteer is treated with derision, and contemptuously styled a " stump candidate." Such a phenomenon rarely manifests itself, and when it does, it meets with but little encouragement.

I have now said enough to show how prolific a subject is that of American party. In the foregoing pages it has been but cursorily treated, to meet the exigencies of a work like the present. I trust, however, that the examination has been sufficiently pursued to enable the reader to form at least a general idea of the whole subject, and to convince him that, however diversified may be its ramifications, complex its machinery, and apparently intricate its movements, party in America is a system when studied easily understood, because well organized.

CHAPTER II.

THE EAST AND THE WEST.

The Potomac above Washington.—The Chesapeake and Ohio Canal.
—Artificial Ties between the East and the West.—Their Political
and Commercial consequences to the Confederacy.—The Shade.—
An Attack and a Defeat.—The Falls of the Potomac.—South
Lowell.—The Forest at Sun-set.—Pic-nic Parties.—An American
Thunder-storm.

IT was a fine morning in the month of May, when my
friend Mr. G—— proposed a stroll along the banks
of the Potomac. Passing through Georgetown, in
ascending the stream, we found ourselves upon the
tow-path of the Great Maryland canal, designed to
unite the waters of the Ohio with those of the Chesapeake. At Georgetown, which is at the head of
tide-water, and of the navigation of the Potomac, the
river suddenly narrows, and here the canal is conveyed
across to its southern bank by means of a stupendous
aqueduct, the trunk of which is of wood, supported,
at a great height, above the stream by several abut-
ments of heavy masonry. As we proceeded along
the tow-path we had the canal on our right, and on
the opposite side of it, a wall of rock, hewn into
irregular shape in excavating its channel. Above the
line of rock rose the Maryland bank of the river, its

gentler acclivities having been rescued from the forest, but, in its abrupter parts, still shrouded in luxuriant foliage. On our left, and far below us, was the Potomac, now confined to a comparatively narrow bed; its volume swollen with recent rains, and rolling tumultuously along; sometimes lingering in dark eddying pools, covered with circular patches of foam, resembling myriads of water-lilies; then brawling over broken rocks and gurgling around stony islets, clothed in stunted shrubbery. The Virginia bank opposite was lofty and precipitous, the glorious primeval woods sweeping down, in most places, to the water's edge. There is no walk about Washington to compare to this. There is a loneliness about the scene, which is only now and then interrupted by the solitary canal boat, which glides noiselessly by; and a stillness, which is only broken by the sleepy music of the river, and the symphony of the winds among the foliage on its banks.

The sun was powerful, but, as we strolled leisurely along, a fresh breeze from the west protected us from its heat, and from the swarms of insects with which we should otherwise have been assailed. The face of the canal became wrinkled under its touch, and every leaf swung tremblingly to and fro, as if eager to be fanned by its cooling breath.

"The Potomac has played some part in your military annals," said I to my companion, as we wound round a bend of the river, which opened up to us a magnificent expanse of the two contiguous States, stretching back, in gentle undulations, to a great distance from either bank of the stream. "The operations at Harper's Ferry constitute a prominent page in your revolutionary history."

" As do the evolutions of the British squadron in the Chesapeake, in the story of the late war," replied he, with a look, which, in meaning, went much further than his words.

" You allude to the descent upon Washington," said I.

" And to the burning of the Capitol, and the destruction of the civil records of the country," added he hastily, with somewhat of bitterness in his tone.

" An unfortunate, if not an indefensible act," said I; " but one of the almost unavoidable excesses of a protracted contest. Let us hope that Oregon may never be the cause of a second visit of a similar character to the Potomac."

" Amen!" ejaculated my friend; " but such another visit, should it occur, will not be the precursor of another Bladensburg."

" Nothing," I observed, changing the conversation, " seems so much to impress the mind of the stranger with the greatness of the scale on which all the natural features of this continent are constructed, as do the extent and grandeur of its streams. Here is the Potomac, which, with its magnificent estuary, would be entitled to rank amongst the first-class streams in Europe, rising in America no higher than the third class in the scale of rivers."

" Its chief value above tide-water," observed Mr. G——, " is as a great geographical feature, not only forming a dividing line between two independent jurisdictions, but giving additional stability to the Union, by adding one to the many other links which exist to connect the eastern with the western section of the confederacy."

" It is a common thing in Europe," said I, " to speculate upon the probabilities of a speedy dissolution between the northern and southern divisions of the Union ; but I confess that, for myself, I have for some time back been of opinion that, should a disseverance ever take place, the danger is that it will be between the East and the West."

" On what do you base such an opinion ? " inquired my companion.

" On referring to the map," replied I, " it will be found that fully one-third of the members of the confederation are situated in the same great basin, having one great interest in common between them, being irrigated by the same system of navigable rivers, and all united together into one powerful belt by their common artery, the Mississippi."

" Admitting this," observed my friend, " what danger arises therefrom to the stability of the Union ?"

" Only that arising from a probable conflict of interests," replied I. " The great region drained by the Mississippi is pre-eminently agricultural, whilst much of the sea-board is manufacturing and commercial. The first-named region is being rapidly filled with an adventurous and energetic population ; and its material resources are being developed at a ratio unexampled in the annals of human progress. The revolution of a very few years will find it powerful enough to stand by itself, should it feel so inclined, and then nothing can prevent a fatal collision of interests between it and the different communities on the sea-board, but the recognition and adoption of a commercial policy, which will afford it an ample outlet for its vast and varied productions."

" But suppose it finds this outlet in the Atlantic States ? "

" Impossible," replied I. " The myriads who will yet people the great valley cannot be confined to the markets of America. Should the States on the sea-board swarm with population, their wants will suffice to absorb only a fraction of the surplus produce of the States on the Mississippi. The exigencies of the latter position will require that they have unrestricted access to the markets of the world, by unfettering, as much as possible, the trade which the world will be anxious to carry on with them. And on this they will be all the more able, by-and-by, to insist, and at all hazards too, when it is considered that the Mississippi offers them an easy, and at the same time an independent outlet to the ocean."

" Precisely so," said Mr. G——; " you have discerned the danger, but have made no account of the remedy."

" I see no remedy which can reach the case short of that which is very difficult of attainment—a final and satisfactory adjustment of great conflicting interests."

" I am free to admit," said my friend, " the necessity for such an adjustment, as an essential condition to the stability of the Union ; at the same time, I am sensible of the difficulty of fulfilling that condition, from the character, magnitude, and importance of the interests involved. The exuberant fertility of the Mississippi valley can scarcely be exaggerated, whilst the tendency of population thither cannot be repressed. An idea may thus be formed of the influence which the great agricultural section of the Union is speedily destined to assume. On the other hand,

nearly five hundred millions of dollars have already
been invested, east of the Alleganies, in manufactures.
Daily additions are being made to this huge investment; and the miner, the iron master, the woollen
manufacturer, and the cotton spinner, are taking
rapid strides in extending their operations and
enhancing their power.   Between two such interests,
should a collision arise, the results would be most
disastrous.   Political considerations would vanish in
the contest between material interests, and the frame-
work of the Confederacy might dissolve before the
shock.   These are the difficulties of the case.   An-
tagonistic as they are in many respects in their
interests, were the East and the West to be left
physically isolated from each other, the difficulties in
the way of a compromise of interests would indeed
be insurmountable.   Had the East no direct hold
upon the West, and had the West no communication
with the rest of the world but through the Mississippi, one might well despair of a permanent reconciliation.   It is in obviating the physical obstructions,
which, unremoved, would throw the current of their
interests into different directions, that the great
barrier to a permanent good understanding between
the East and the West has been broken down; it is
by rendering each more necessary to the other that
the foundation has been laid for that mutual concession, which alone can ensure future harmony and give
permanence to the Union."

   " And how have you done this ?" inquired I.

   " We have tapped the West," replied he.

   " Tapped the West !" I repeated, looking surprised
and inquiringly into his face.

   " The expression, I perceive, requires explanation,"

added my friend. " This very canal, along the banks of which we are now strolling, illustrates what I mean by tapping the West."

" How so ?" I demanded. " The Chesapeake and Ohio canal is one of those stupendous attempts at internal improvement, for which, whilst they have as yet accomplished nothing, so many of the States of the Union have unfortunately pledged their credit. What has Maryland gained by this gigantic undertaking, but a sullied reputation and a bankrupt treasury ? "

" The work is unproductive," said Mr. G——, " simply because incomplete. Only one half of its whole intended length has as yet been constructed; but were the waters of the Ohio and the Chesapeake once fairly united by it, it would speedily replenish the treasury, and restore the credit of Maryland. But waiving this, and regarding the canal as an unfinished specimen of the many other works of a similar character, which have been begun and ended, and which are now in successful operation, it still illustrates my meaning, in saying that the East has tapped the West."

" By tapping the West, then, you mean opening direct communications between the East and the West?"

" Exactly so," said he. " Had matters been left as nature arranged them, the whole traffic of the Mississippi valley would have been thrown upon the Gulf of Mexico. Two classes of considerations impelled us to attempt to obviate this ; the first having reference to the interests which the East would subserve in establishing a direct communication with the West; and the second, to the prevention of the inconvenient commercial and political alliances, to which the isolation of the West might have given rise."

" But of what value is the Potomac to you in this respect?" inquired I. " The falls and rapids, with which its channel abounds, render it unnavigable above Washington."

" The advantage is not so much in the river itself," said my friend, " as in the valley through which it flows. The great impediment to be overcome, is in the spurs and ridges of the Alleganies, which separate the waters flowing to the Atlantic from those falling into the Mississippi. We take advantage of the channels of the Atlantic streams to penetrate to the nearest navigable points of the tributaries of the Mississippi. When the streams are impracticable, nothing is left us but to improve their channels, or to avoid them by artificial navigation. Even the cataract of Niagara is avoided by a canal, after which no difficulty could be made of the rapids of the Potomac."

" When I consider," said I, " the many parallel lines of artificial communication which you have established between the East and the West, I must say that, in tapping the latter, you have tapped it liberally."

" We have taken, or are taking, advantage of all our opportunities in this respect," replied he. " Virginia is tapping the West by uniting the Ohio to the Atlantic, by means of the James River and Kanawha canal, constructed in the valley of the river. Maryland is doing the same by this Chesapeake and Ohio canal, which follows the course of the Potomac, and is doubling her hold upon the Mississippi and its tributaries by the Baltimore and Ohio railway, which debouches upon the same valley after first ascending that of the Patapsco from Baltimore. Pennsylvania has tapped the West by means of her double line of railway and canal, descending upon the Ohio after ascending the Susquehanna; and New York, which took the lead in the process, has done the same by directing the waters of Lake Erie through her great canal, along the fertile valley of the Mohawk, to the Hudson, and, consequently, to the Atlantic."

" And to these you look," observed I, "as your securities for the integrity of the republic?"

" As bonds," said he, " the existence of which renders improbable the severance of the East from the West. These four great parallel lines of inter-communication have effectually counteracted the political tendencies of the Mississippi. That bond of political union to the States of the Far West, if not actually broken, is now rendered harmless as regards the safety of the Confederacy, for it is now subsidiary to the ties which unite the great valley to the Atlantic sea-board. An element of weakness has been converted into an element of strength; for as the Mississippi binds together the whole West, so do these gigantic artificial communications inseparably connect the whole West, thus bound together, with the East, by closely identifying the interests of the two. It is no longer the policy of either section of the Union to stand alone. By-and-by the commerce of the Mississippi valley will outgrow the facilities for traffic which the Mississippi affords it. It will then require more seaports than New Orleans, and to what quarter can it look for them but to the

Atlantic? The time will come, if not already come, when its teeming population and accumulated resources will find their best and most expeditious roads to the markets of the world, through the defiles of the Alleganies. Much of its produce will continue to seek the markets of the West Indies, and of South and Central America, through the Gulf of Mexico; but its starting points for the great marts of the Old World will assuredly be Boston, New York, Philadelphia, and Baltimore. Even already the great bulk of Western produce, on its way to Europe, seeks the Atlantic instead of the Gulf. New York is now as much a seaport of Indiana and Illinois, of Iowa, Missouri, and Ohio, as is New Orleans.

"To the more northerly States of the valley, the former is now more accessible than the latter, whilst for many purposes it is preferable, such as for the shipment of grain; some species of which are so sensitive, that they run great risk of being damaged by the hot sun of New Orleans, and the protracted voyage around the peninsula of Florida. Every thing, too, which improves the position of the West, as regards the Atlantic seaports, renders the mutual dependence between the two sections of the Union, as respects their home trade, more intimate and complete. In addition to this, it strengthens more and more the sentiment of nationality, by bringing the denizens of the West and the East in constant communication with each other. They freely traverse each other's fields, and walk each other's streets, and feel equally at home, whether they are on the Wabash, the Arkansas, the Potomac, the Susquehanna, the Genesee, or the St. John's. This is what we have effected by tapping the West. We have united it to us by bonds of iron, which it cannot, and which, if it could, it would not break. By binding it to the older States by the strong tie of material interests, we have identified its political sentiment with our own. We have made the twain one by our canals, our railroads, and our electric telegraphs, by making the Atlantic more necessary to the West than the Gulf; in short," said he, " *by removing the Alleganies.*"

Our conversation here dropped, and we proceeded for some time in silence. My thoughts were busy with the singular, but yet undeveloped, destinies of this extraordinary country. To have the conflicting interests of two halves of a continent thus reconciled and harmonised by a few ditches filled with water and a few belts of iron, seemed too startling for credence. How different the relations between the Mississippi and the Hudson from those of the Danube and the Rhine! The more I pondered on his premises, the more satisfied did I become of the correctness of his conclusions. I was reconverted to the opinion that slavery alone could give a shock to the Union. No where in the world is the influence of material interests, in controlling social and political phenomena, more obviously displayed than in America. The difficulties in the way of the supremacy of this influence in Europe are infinitely greater than in the transatlantic world. But even here, where differences of race, language and religion, of historic associations and national traditions, interpose to retard the fraternization of the great European community, the strides which are being daily made in the career of material improvement cannot be resultless, but must rapidly break down the barriers which ages of discord and alienation have accumulated in the way of fusion and union ; until linked, as they soon will be at innumerable points, by railways and canals, in the bonds of one common interest, the different States of this continent will yet approximate the political condition of confederate America.

We had now walked several miles, and having reached an indentation in the river's bank completely sheltered from the sun, took advantage of the deep shade which reposed in it, to rest and refresh ourselves. A small rivulet came gurgling down the bank, sometimes leaping, in its way, over a tiny ledge of rock; at others, stealing noiselessly under the withered leaves of many autumns, which the eddying winds had deposited in the crevice; and gathering close to where we sat into a cool limpid pool, in a natural basin of stone, encrusted with small patches of pale green vegetation. From this bowl we mixed the cool draught with the contents of our flasks, and lay back to enjoy the shade. Our enjoyment, however, was but short-lived, for we were soon driven from our retreat by the persecutions of an enemy, with which, in these latitudes, it is next to impossible to cope. Swarms of insects, seeking shelter from the breeze, filled the secluded nook in which we sat. They were of various sizes, from the almost invisible gnat, to the plethoric and well-armed musquito ; whilst, every now and then, a gorgeous dragon-fly, poised like a well-directed arrow, would cleave its way through them, and whirr about our ears, innocuous but looking mischief. Our entrance seemed at first to disturb the tiny throng, but they soon rallied into legions, and attacked us on all sides, amid an unmistakeable flourish of trumpets. It was in vain that we strove to fan them off. Though

mown down in myriads, like Russian infantry, they
were undismayed by the slaughter, continuing their
assaults and accompanying them with a ceaseless hum,
which soon threw every nerve of our bodies into
a state of painful vibration.   Passive endurance was
out of the question, whilst gallantry against such numbers was but being prodigal of a virtue.   There was
nothing left for us but to retreat, which we were glad
to do; pursued, until we gained the sunshine and
the breeze, by hosts of flying lancers, to whom was
assigned the duty of following up the victory.

A walk of another hour or two brought us to the
Falls of the Potomac, about fifteen miles distant
from Washington.   Here we found a very good inn,
where we dined, and took up our quarters for the
night.   After dinner we strolled about the Fall,
which, although striking and picturesque in itself, is,
for this country, where lake, river, and cataract are
on so magnificent a scale, rather insignificant.   It
affords an almost inexhaustible, and most available
water-power; a circumstance not overlooked by the
prying eyes of American enterprise; the property in
its vicinity having been purchased by a few energetic
speculators, with a view to converting it into a new
seat of manufacturing industry.   With this intent it
is already laid out into land and water lots.   In the
hands of Virginians it might never advance beyond
this point, but stimulated by the roving enterprise of
New England, it is not improbable that South Lowell,
for so the embryo city has been called, will yet rival
the Lowell of the north.

A descending sun was gilding the tree-tops as we
directed our steps into the neighbouring forest; the
western heavens were in one blaze of light, the sun's

disc being scarcely distinguishable in the flood of
pearly lustre which he threw around his setting moments.   We strolled for some distance under a lofty
canopy of the richest foliage, supported by the stately
trunks of the primeval trees, which towered high
before their colossal proportions were broken by a
single branch.   The skirt of the forest, which had
a western aspect, was densely fringed with a most
luxuriant vegetation, underlaid with beautiful shrubs
and variegated wild flowers.   The honeysuckle and
the wild vine here and there hung in graceful festoons
between the young trees, which intertwined their
sappy branches, in their common struggle for air and
light ; the departing sunlight streaming through their
large juicy leaves, as through a medium of liquid
amber, and bringing out every vein and artery which
permeated them, as the microscope does the exquisite
anatomy of the butterfly's wing.   Myriads of insects
floated in the shade, and rendered the air tremulous
with their monotonous evening hymn ; whilst every
now and then, the tiny but lustrous humming-bird
swept across our path, to take for the day his last cup
of nectar from his favourite flowers.   In the cool of
the evening we returned to our hotel, and fatigued as
we were by the day's exertions, slept soundly, although
it was abundantly evident next morning that the
blood-thirsty musquito had profited by our uncon-
sciousness.

We returned next day to Washington by the route
which we had traversed on the previous day. We encountered but few travellers to interrupt the solitude
of our journey, with the exception of meeting every
now and then a slave, generally with a burden, but
seldom a heavy one, who accosted us as he passed

with a " Good day, Massa," bowing to us at the same time, with an air of stereotyped humility.

Large pic-nic parties frequently proceed, in summer, to the Falls, from Washington, Alexandria, and Georgetown. It is not unusual for them, on such occasions, to hire a canal packet-boat, with which they proceed comfortably to their destination. About half-way from town we met one of them, drawn by two horses at a brisk trot. It was well filled with a jocund party, for we could hear the merry laugh proceeding from the cabin, when they were yet some distance from us. Several of the young men were on deck, dressed in loose summer attire. They had withdrawn for a few minutes from the presence of their fair companions, to enjoy the luxury of a quid. They were discussing the merits of " Old Rough and Ready," their animated conversation being interrupted only by their expectorations into the canal. We observed several pretty faces peering at us through the small cabin windows, and fancied that their owners pitied our way-worn appearance, for by this time we were covered with dust and perspiration.

The breeze of the previous day had died away—the sun burnt like a fierce flame in the sky, and the air was hot and sultry. The canal blazed in our faces like a sun-lit mirror—the grass lay parched and motionless on the ground, and the leaves hung listless from the boughs. Every insect was driven into the shade, and not a bird ventured on the wing.

" We shall have a shower before night-fall," said my companion, wiping the perspiration from his forehead, and fanning himself with his broad-brimmed white beaver.

"I trust none of your thunder-storms will over-take us on our way," observed I.

"I think we are pretty safe," said he, turning round, and scanning with his eye the circuit of the western horizon. "We have now but about five miles to walk, and there is, as yet, no appearance of a cloud in the sky."

"You look to the west," I remarked: "do your thunder-storms always proceed from that quarter?"

"Invariably," replied he.

We proceeded for a mile or two further, our strength becoming rapidly exhausted under the burning merciless heat. By-and-by the dust moved a little in advance of us, and the glistening surface of the canal momentarily darkened. At the same time, a low murmuring sound stole gently through the forest on our left, as if nature had heaved a deep sigh—the leaves trembling at the same time, as if a slight shudder had passed over the woody bank. My friend looked quickly round.

"We must hurry," said he, "or we shall yet be caught."

"I see no indication of a storm," said I, casting my eye over the yet unclouded heavens.

"You would perceive such as would satisfy you," said he, quickening his pace, "but for the high bank, which now screens from us many degrees of the western sky. See," added he, as another slight puff of air disturbed the dust, which danced in little eddies at our feet, "there is an unmistakeable herald of a summer shower."

The dome of the Capitol was already in sight, and we made all haste towards the town. We had scarcely reached Georgetown ere the wind came in fitful gusts from behind us, lifting up the dust, and scattering it, as it were, in huge handfuls in the air. By-and-by a dense black curtain of clouds rose over the tree-tops on the heights to our left, and advanced with rapid yet majestic movement towards the zenith. The broad estuary of the Potomac was before us, and its usually yellow surface assumed a dark brownish hue, in reflecting the now angry heavens. The lightning at first flickered faintly in the distance, but grew brighter and more frequent as the storm gained upon the sky. By this time the low muttering of the distant thunder fell without interval upon our ears, as if the tempest were advancing to the sound of music. And now everything in nature seemed still as death—every leaf around us appeared to pant for the coming shower—the cattle stood in motionless groups in the neighbouring fields.

We had passed Georgetown, and were hurrying as fast as possible to Washington. On came the teeming clouds, swept forward by the breeze, which now set in steadily from the westward with a fury which betokened the near approach of the catastrophe. The heavens seemed now and then enveloped in a trellis-work of fire, and the thunder came in choruses from the bosom of the tempest. We had to make our way through whirlwinds of dust, but the flying sand was preferable to the coming deluge. My rooms were already in sight when the first monitory drops came down heavily, and with a sort of greasy flop, into the hot dust, speckling it with dark spots, each as large as a half-crown piece. There was no time to lose, for down they came thicker and thicker, and we took to our heels. It was as well that we did so ; for we had scarcely gained shelter ere the storm descended in all its fury. Down came the rain, literally in streams, throwing the dust up like spray, until it had fairly saturated it, which less than a minute sufficed to do. Every now and then its downward progress was stopped, and it was carried almost horizontally along, and dashed in whirling eddies against wall and window by the fierce wind. The strongest trees bent before the blast, which howled through their branches, as it stripped them of their green leaves, and tossed them wildly in the air. All this time the vivid lightning was playing about on all hands with magnificent pyrotechnic effect, not falling in single flashes, but appearing literally to rain down, the tempest seeming to expend itself in a descending deluge of fire and water. The air, too, was, as it were, full of thunder, which sometimes crackled around us like the leaping flame, which is devouring every thing within its reach, then broke overhead with a crash as if a thousand ponderous beams were giving way, and then boomed slowly off into the distance, and died, grumbling and muttering amid the watery clouds.

The storm had not continued for much more than a quarter of an hour ere the whole aspect of the town was changed. Many of the streets which before were laden with dust were now completely submerged. Pennsylvania-avenue lies low, and the streets which descend upon its northern side poured their floods upon it as into a reservoir. Boats might now have sailed where, but some minutes before, their keels would have been buried in the dust. My windows overlooked a broad street which descended into the avenue. It looked as if it had suddenly been converted into the bed of some mountain torrent; the

water dashing along in sufficient volume to carry off
several large beams which were lying at a little distance, for building purposes, on the road.

Little more than half an hour had elapsed ere the
storm began to give way. The black pall, which had
enveloped the heavens, seemed gradually to ascend
into upper air, and in doing so became broken into
fragments, which, as they slowly separated from each
other, were illuminated in their outlines by the
bright sunlight, which shone from above through
their watery fringes. Piled in masses, one upon the
other, the heavy clouds rolled away to the eastward,
their dark bosoms still gleaming with fire, and belch-
ing forth thunder. The storm thus passed away with
the majesty which had marked its approach, leaving
the sun once more in undisputed possession of the
sky. But the face of nature was greatly changed.
It no longer looked languid and sickly; all was now
cheerful and glad, and fresh-looking as the nymph
from the fountain. The frogs croaked lustily from
the neighbouring marshes, and the birds flew about
on renovated wing, and sang merrily on the boughs.
Vegetation resumed its vigour; the foliage on the
trees looked doubly green; whilst from every shrub
and plant the pendant rain-drops sparkled like so
many diamonds. The air was pure and crisp; for
the haze, which before pervaded it, seemed to have
been literally washed out, and through its clear
medium the Capitol shone, over the rich greenery
which lay beneath it, like a mass of alabaster, surmounted by a dome of ebony. But the streets were
in many places ploughed up by the torrents which
had taken temporary possession of them; and the
red clayey bank of the Potomac was torn into still

deeper gullies. Not far from my residence, on a
field of several acres in extent, flourished, before the
storm, a crop of luxuriant wheat. Having a gentle
declivity, the deluge passed over it with such effect
as to tear both wheat and soil away, exposing a
cadaverous surface of cold impassive clay. Many of
the cellars in Pennsylvania-avenue were flooded,
and much valuable property was injured, if not
destroyed.

Such is a thunder-storm in these regions. An
Englishman's experiences in his own country can
give him no idea of its terrific grandeur. They frequently make their appearance as often as twice
a week, during the burning summer months, although
not always with the severity just described: the
climate would else be intolerable. Their refreshing
effect, after some days of parching heat, may be
readily conceived. Their duration is brief, but they
are terrible whilst they last, particularly when they
occur at night, when the incessant and ubiquitous
lightning seems to keep the whole atmosphere in a
blaze. The clouds descend and appear to trail along
the surface of the ground, and earth and sky seem to
meet in conflict, whilst all the elements mingle for
the moment in one appalling jumble of confusion and
strife, the effect of the whole scene being infinitely
heightened by the loud and continuous rattling of
heaven's artillery, by which the raging tornado is
saluted in its course.

CHAPTER III.

VIRGINIA.

IT was towards the close of May, on a sunny and
brilliant morning, that, after several months' residence
in the capital, I took my departure for the South.
Having half-an-hour to spare, I strolled for the last
time around the grounds of the President's house,
which were contiguous to the hotel. In doing so, I
soon overtook an elderly man, rather slenderly made,
about the middle stature, and with a slight stoop at
the shoulders. He carried a gold-headed cane under
his arm, and with his head bent upon the ground, as
if lost in thought, went slowly along with measured
pace, seemingly forgetful of the purpose for which he

had come out, which was evidently the enjoyment of
a constitutional walk before breakfast. In passing
him, I saluted the President of the United States.
He seemed as if roused from a reverie by the momen-
tary interruption. He had need of all his thoughts,
for his dispute with England was still unsettled, and
the first blow of the Mexican war had already been
struck.

The steamboat wharf is immediately below the
great bridge, and about a mile distant from the town.
Thither I repaired in due time, the journey southward commencing with a descent of the Potomac for
forty miles by steamer. Half-a-dozen negroes, who
grinned and chattered at each other incessantly, were
busily engaged replenishing her stock of fuel from the
piles of cord-wood which encumbered the wharf; and
other preparations for departure were still going on
when I stepped on board the United States mail
steamer Powhatan.

There was some delay in starting, during which I
occupied myself in pacing the promenade deck, enjoying the bright sunshine and the fresh morning air.
There were several groups of loungers on the wharf,
who seemed to take a deep interest in all that was
going on, whilst there were others who took an interest in some that were going off. Apart from the
rest was one whose demeanour and attitude soon
attracted my attention. In leaning against a post, his
tall emaciated figure fell into a number of indescribable curves, presenting a *tout ensemble* to which nothing can compare, that I am acquainted with, either
on the earth, or in the waters under the earth. His
face was so sunburnt that it vied in brown with the
long, loose, threadbare frock-coat which, from his
reclining position, hung perpendicularly from his

shoulders. Deep furrows traversed his sallow cheek, commencing at a point near the outer corner of the eye, and diverging as they dropped, so as to attain a broad basis on the lower jaw. His eyes, which were deep set, were very small, the pupil being of a light grey, in a yellow setting. In his hand was a large clasp knife, with which he was whittling to a very fine point a piece of wood which he had sliced from the post. In this occupation he appeared absorbed; but, on closely watching him, you could see that from under his matted eyebrows he was looking at everybody and observing everything. Save in the movement of his hands, he gave little outward symptom of life; but not a movement escaped his restless glance. He was a thorough type of the genuine Yankee, concealing much curiosity, cunning, and acuteness beneath a cold impassive exterior. I watched him still occupying the same attitude for some time after we had put off, and it was not until every one else had disappeared from the wharf, that he uncoiled himself and walked moodily away.

The cause of our detention was the non-arrival of the Governor of Virginia, who it seemed was to be a fellow-passenger. His Excellency at length appeared, panting and breathless, and, on stepping aboard, was told by the captain that the next time he was late he would have to find a boat of his own.

The sail down the Potomac is interesting and beautiful. On a summer morning, when the sky is without a cloud, and the breeze is yet fresh and bracing, the broad and lively expanse of the river, stretching in some places for miles across, flashes like silver in the slanting sunlight, whilst the luxuriant verdure which clothes the long terraced slopes on either side of it, sweeps down to its very edge, until bush, tree, and waving grass, seem all afloat upon the water. Here and there, too, the bank, on either side, is indented by small tortuous bays, which straggle up into the land, until they lose themselves amid laby-rinths of greenery, and beneath arcades of the richest foliage. As the day advances, a slight haze gathers over the scene, which confuses its outline and gives it an indistinct, dreamy look. The whole way from Washington to its junction with Chesapeake Bay, the Potomac presents the tourist with a succession of pictures, which in their characteristics are purely American. You have land and water, the universal elements of landscape, but differently distributed from what we are accustomed to in Europe. The river is so lordly and spacious, and forms so great a feature in the scene, that the whole looks like a vast mirror set in a frame-work of elaborate beauty. In addition to its scenic attractions, a sail on the Poto-mac brings the traveller in contact with many spots of considerable historic interest.

Washington should always be approached from the river, for it presents from it a most imposing appear-ance. When first seen, in ascending the Potomac, the city appears to encircle, in the distance, the head of a spacious and noble bay. Whilst the eye is yet in-capable of distinguishing its scattered character, or discerning the many gaps which intervene between its different parts, the stranger is, for the moment, from the vast extent of ground which it appears to cover, cheated into the idea that it is worthy its destiny as the capital of a great nation, an illusion which speedily vanishes on a nearer approach. To the right the Capitol is seen looming up over every other object; to the left, with the bulk of the town between them, is the Executive mansion, its white mass being relieved against the dark green body of the uplands beyond, which in their amphitheatric sweep form a background to the picture; whilst still further to the left is the suburb of Georgetown, crowning its little height, and nestled amid bowers and foliage, like a very glimpse from Arcadia. This view goes far to reconcile one, after all, to Washington. I watched it from the stern of the boat, until we doubled a point on the Maryland side, which shut the scene slowly from my view.

Our first stopping-place was Alexandria, seven miles below Washington, and on the opposite side of the river; a small town much older than the capital, of which it is the seaport. It has a quaint and antique look about it, considering where it is, its origin dating far back into the colonial era of Virginia. Until 1846, it formed part and parcel of the district of Columbia; but in that year it was re-ceded, together with the whole of that part of the district which lay to the south of the Potomac, to the State of Virginia. The " ten miles square," therefore, no longer exists, the district being now confined to an irregular triangle on the Maryland side of the river.

Some distance further down, we passed Fort Washington, one of the defences of the capital, occupying a commanding position on the Maryland bank, opposite a point where the navigable channel of the river is rather narrow and tortuous. On the opposite side, in Virginia, and about fourteen miles below the city, is Mount Vernon, for some years the residence, and still the burial-place of Washington. It is a very beautiful spot; the house in which the immortal patriot closed his eventful career crowning the summit of a gentle acclivity which rises from the water, and commands within its prospect on either side a long reach of the river. No American ever passes it without doing reverence to it as a hallowed spot. When near the other side, or in the middle of the stream, it can only be distinctly seen by the aid of a glass. We passed very close to it, and the Hutcheson family being on board on a professional tour, they came on deck, and sung "Washington's Grave." The effect was good, for the melody is touching, and the majority of the audience were enthusiasts.

Our point of debarkation was the Aquia Creek, a small stream which empties itself into the Potomac on the Virginia side, about forty miles below the city. Here the river attains a colossal magnitude, which it still enhances during the remainder of its course to the ocean.

From this point, the journey to Richmond, which is about eighty miles, is performed by railway. As the line is but a single one, we had to await, before proceeding, the arrival of the up-train. It was not long ere it came cautiously up, stopping only when it got to the very end of the wharf, the passengers by it immediately taking our steamer for Washington, whilst we took their carriages for Richmond. I thought the mail agent would have been torn to pieces by my fellow-passengers from the city, in their eagerness to extract from him the latest news from the South. The Mexican war was the all-exciting topic, and they were quite disappointed at learning that the Mexicans had disappeared from the Rio Grande, and were not likely again to be heard of, for some time at least.

Amongst those who arrived by the train from Richmond, was a western farmer and his family, evidently on a summer tour.

"Father," said his son, an intelligent little boy, after looking for a few moments at the broad expanse of the river, " it's as big as the Miss'sippi."

" And as yaller too," was the reply.

" But we don't have no snags nor alligators here, my little man ; nor do we blow up two or three hundred people at a time," said a Virginian in shirt-sleeves, who was doing duty in some capacity or other, on the wharf, and who, hearing the boy's remark, was anxious that he should not go misinformed upon the points wherein the Potomac had the superiority over any and every river in the West.

" Cos you can't get up steam enough in Virginny to blow up an egg-shell," retorted the boy, discerning his informant's intention, and by no means satisfied with it ; for which he was informed by the latter, that he was " too smart by half, if he only know'd it," and that to a moral certainty, his father " must have many more like him."

About an hour after leaving the Potomac, we reached the small town of Fredericksburg, one of the seaports of Virginia, situated on the Rappahannock River. We made a short stay here, for no earthly purpose, as it appeared to me, but to enable the passengers to buy gingerbread, which was handed about in enormous triangles, and purchased by such as were already beginning to famish.

Whence comes it that the moment the stranger puts his foot in Virginia, he seems to have passed to an entirely new scene of action ? Is it prejudice, or preconceived opinion, that leads him to think that every thing around him wears a spiritless and even dilapidated aspect ? Or is it that he sees aright, through no misguiding medium, and that there is a cause for the change that so suddenly forces itself upon his observation ? It requires no anti-slavery predilections, no jaundiced eye, no European prejudices, to recognise the two states of activity and inertness between which the Potomac intervenes, like an impassable gulf. The southerner himself, born and bred in the lap of slavery, cannot fail to distinguish the distance which separates the North from the South in the career of material improvement. Be the causes for this what they may, its existence is incontestible. The change, indeed, commences still further north, on crossing the frontier of Maryland ; but bordering, as that State does, upon the free community of Pennsylvania, it has become more or less inoculated with the activity which distinguishes it. It is only when the traveller passes the Virginian border that he becomes thoroughly aware of the difference, as regards enterprise and activity, which exists between the free and the slave States. I am quite aware that the traveller by this the main route to the South, is not carried through the better portion of Virginia. I now speak not from impressions formed on the railway, but from the convictions which have attached themselves to my mind after thoroughly traversing the State. As compared with some of its neighbours, the whole State seems to be afflicted with some ineradicable blight. In the North, such is the enterprise and such the industry which prevail,—such is the restless activity which is ever manifest, and such the progress, not gradual, but precipitate, which is constantly being made, that the stranger may almost fancy that the scene on which he opens his eyes in the morning is different from that on which he closed them the preceding night. But let him pass into Virginia, and the transition is as great as is the change from the activity of Lancashire, to the languor and inertness of Bavaria. Even amongst the southern States, Virginia is preeminently torpid. In the midst of progress she is stationary—stationary even in her population, with the exception of the negro portion of it. And yet no New-Englander is so proud of his native State as the Virginian is of his. He never permits a doubt to cross his mind but that she is the first star in the federal constellation. It matters not that you direct his attention to decaying towns and backward cultivation, you cannot divorce him from his delusive but flattering conviction. In 1776 she may have been the first amongst the revolutionary colonies. The Virginian thinks of Virginia as she was then, not as she is now ; he forgets the prodigious strides which many of the sister States have taken since that period ; and in his self-complacency overlooks the fact that she is more indebted for the slight advances which she has made, to her incapacity altogether to resist the general momentum, than to the enterprise and activity of her sons. How far the blot which rests on her social and political escutcheon is answerable for this, will be afterwards considered.

Richmond, the capital of Virginia, is a small, but certainly a very pretty town, if its people would only content themselves with having it so. It is a weakness of theirs to be constantly making the largest possible drafts upon the admiration of the visitor, by extorting his assent to the fidelity of comparisons which would be amongst the very last to suggest themselves to his own mind. He is reminded, for instance, that the prospect which it commands is very

like the view obtained from the battlements of
Windsor Castle; and to those who have never been at
Windsor, or who, having been there, have never seen
Richmond, the comparison may certainly hold good;
but such as have seen both are far more indebted to
their imagination than to the reality for the resemblance.   He is also given to understand that it occupies more hills than imperial Rome ever sat upon;
and if the number of hills on which the capital
rested was an essential element of Roman greatness,
this is one way of proving Richmond superior to Rome.

But notwithstanding these excusable partialities,
Richmond is a beautiful place.   There is a high and
a low town; the former crowning the summit of an
abrupt sandy bank, which hems in the latter between
it and the northern margin of the James River, a
stream so justly celebrated in the early colonial history of the continent.   The town itself has not much
to recommend it, consisting as it does of one good
street and a number of indifferent ones.   The portion
of it between the main street and the river, in which
the wholesale business is chiefly transacted, reminds
one very much, in closeness and dinginess, of the
neighbourhood of Watling-street or Blackfriars.   It
is in its adjuncts that the beauty of Richmond is to
be sought and found; its suburbs in the upper town
being both elegant and airy, and the view obtained
from them by no means uninteresting.   The best
point, perhaps, from which to ascertain the position
of Richmond, is the portico of the Capitol, a plain,
unpretending building, which overhangs the lower
town.   It contains within its walls, however, one of
the finest, and decidely the most interesting, of the
specimens of art in America.   In its principal lobby

is a full-length marble statue of Washington; not in
the garb of the warrior, but in the plain costume of
the country gentleman, with his staff in his hand,
instead of his sword by his side. It is the most faith-
ful portrait of the incorruptible patriot of which the
country is possessed, the features being modelled
from a cast taken of him during life. Time and
again did I return to gaze at that placid face,
that mild yet intelligent expression, that serene yet
thoughtful brow. No portrait or bust that I had
ever before seen had conveyed to me an idea of
Washington which satisfied me. But there he was to
the life, just as he appeared to his cotemporaries
after the turmoil of the great contest was over, in
which he played so important and honourable a part.
I never think of Washington now without picturing
him as represented by that marble statue.

From the portico the scene is both extensive and
varied. In the immediate foreground is the town,
the greater portion of which is so directly underneath
you that it almost seems as if you could leap into it.
Before you is the James River, tumbling in snowy
masses over successive ledges of rock, its channel
being divided by several islands, which are shrouded
in foliage, and imbedded in foaming rapids. To
the south of the river, an extensive vista opens up,
spreading far to the right and left, cleared in some
places, but, generally speaking, mantled in the most
luxuriant vegetation. The scene is one over which
the stranger may well linger, particularly on a bright
summer's day, when his cheek is fanned by the cooling
breezes, which come gaily skipping from the distant
Alleganies, carrying the fragrant perfume of the
magnolia and the honeysuckle on their wings, and

his spirit is soothed by the incessant murmur of the
rapids, which, from the height at which he stands,
steals gently to his ear.

The site of Richmond was selected chiefly with a
view to the water power which is afforded it by the
rapids of the James. These commence a considerable
distance above the city, and terminate immediately in
front of it. The fall which thus gradually takes place
in the channel of the river, is altogether about eighty
feet, the formation of the banks on either side being
such as to render the great power thus afforded perfectly available. It has, as yet, been but partially
taken advantage of. Opposite the city, on the
southern bank, is the small village of Manchester,
aspiring, I suppose, to that name, from the fact of
its comprising two cotton factories, which, indeed,
with their adjuncts, form its sum total. It is approached from Richmond by means of bridges thrown
across the rapids from the mainland on either side, to
the islands; but the chief industry of the spot is
centred in the city itself, which derives its water
power from the basin of the James River, and Kanawha canal, designed to unite the Virginian sea-board
with the great valley of the West. The canal is here fed
from the upper level of the river, and as it approaches
the town, the difference of level between it and the
falling stream becomes greater and greater, until at
length a fall of eighty feet is obtained from the canal
basin to the river. Here the water may be easily
used three times over in changing its level; a little
further up it can only be used twice, and still further
up again, only once. As yet fully three-fourths of
the power thus available is unemployed. The manufactures of Richmond are various, comprising woollen

and cotton goods, tobacco factories, and some very large iron and steel works; but its chief feature in this respect is the manufacture of flour, the largest flour-mills in the United States being found here, one of which, when in full play, can turn out from 750 to 1,000 barrels of flour per day. It is from Richmond that the South American market is chiefly supplied with this necessary of life; the wheat of Virginia, when ground, being better adapted for tropical voyages than the produce of any other part of the country, including Ohio and Genesee wheat.

Richmond is also one of the first tobacco markets of the country, the produce of the State being concentrated upon it both for export and manufacture. The tobacco, after having been dried, as it now is, chiefly in the fields, is closely packed into hogsheads, in which state it is forwarded to Richmond, where such portion of it (the greater) as cannot be disposed of by private sale is stored in public warehouses, to await the auction sales, which take place within certain hours of the day. When a hogshead is to be put up, it is unhooped, and the compact mass, as yet but raw material, exposed to view. One of the inspectors on duty, then, by means of a crow-bar, forcibly separates it in three different places, from which a few leaves are taken to form the sample of the bulk, which is then sold according to its quality as thus ascertained. The staves are then put together again, the hogshead receives the purchaser's mark, and it is left in store until he chooses to take it away. The quantity of tobacco which is thus sometimes accumulated upon Richmond, is only exceeded by that which is generally to be found in bond at the London Docks.

Much of the tobacco thus disposed of is purchased
for local manufacture, Richmond containing several
large establishments for the conversion of the crude
tobacco into a form fit for chewing. Over the most
extensive of these I was kindly piloted by one of the
owners, where I witnessed all the processes which the
weed uuderwent in its passage from dry leaves to the
marketable shape of Cavendish tobacco, in which
form it was packed in small cakes, in oblong boxes,
labelled with the seductive name of " Honeydew."
In all the departments of the factory the labour was
performed by slaves, superintended by white overseers. They appeared to be very contented at their
work, although the utmost silence was observed
amongst them, except within certain hours of the
day, when they were permitted to relieve their
toil by singing, performing a succession of solos,
duets, glees, &c. &c. in a way that was truly surprising, considering that they were entirely self-
taught. Having heard them sing, I was permitted to
see them eat ; their noon-day meal consisting of corn-
bread and beef; the males and females occupying
different apartments, and each appearing to have as
much to eat as he or she could possibly enjoy. The
factory was so complete as to be provided even with
its own tailor, who was engaged, whilst I was there, in
cutting out the summer suits of the workmen, from
thick cotton cloth, tolerably well bleached, and of a
close and by no means very coarse texture.

In a street contiguous to the public warehouses, I
encountered piles of boxes filled with a very coarse
liquorice, and which were being disposed of in lots by
auction. The liquorice was purchased that it might
be mixed with a portion of the tobacco, in the process

of its manufacture, the poison being thus sweetened, to render it palatable to the uninitiated.

The neighbourhood of Richmond is rich in mineral resources. The coal strata are not only abundant, but in some places approach so near the surface as to be worked at but little cost. The largest coal company is that called the English company; the coal, when raised, being carried from its pits, by means of a private railway, to the port of Richmond, a few miles below the city, whence it is shipped to the different markets of the Union. There is also a good deal of iron in the vicinity; but either from the difficulty of mining it, or from the hold which English and Pennsylvania iron has got of the market, it is as yet but little worked.

The people of Richmond are a peculiar people. They are proud and sensitive to a degree. They are proud, in the first place, of their State, and in the next, of its capital; in addition to which, they are not a little satisfied with the moral superiorities to which they lay claim. Their code of honour is so exceedingly strict that it requires the greatest circumspection to escape its violation. An offence which elsewhere would be regarded as of homeopathic proportions, is very apt to assume in Richmond the gravity of colossal dimensions; even a coolness between parties is dangerous, as having a fatal tendency speedily to ripen into a deadly feud. Once arrived at this point, a personal encounter is inevitable, unless, to avoid it, one party or the other is induced to quit the city. It is curious enough to witness the cool and matter-of-course way in which even the ladies will speculate upon the necessities for, and the probabilities of, a hostile meeting between such and such parties, and in which, when they hear of a duel, they will tell you that they long foresaw it, and that it could not be avoided. After all, this state of things, although it may indicate less of a healthy habit than of a morbid sensibility, gives to Richmond society a chivalrous and romantic cast, which is rarely to be met with in matter-of-fact America. It is seldom, indeed, that they imitate, in their personal warfare, the savage brutalities of the south-western States; their quarrels, generally speaking, taking some time to mature, and the parties, when the day of reckoning at length comes, fighting like gentlemen instead of like tigers or hyenas.

The society of Richmond adds the warmth and fervour of the south to that frank and ready hospitality which is characteristic of American society in general. It is rarely that the stranger, in his social contact with the Americans, has to encounter the frigid influences of formalism. In Virginia, convention is, perhaps, more than anywhere else subjugated by the heart. It is astonishing how soon each party in an assembly appears in his or her real character. Entering a drawing-room at Richmond is like entering a theatre with the curtain up, when there is no ugly, green-baize screen between you, the scenery, and the performers. In no other place has it ever appeared to me that life was so little disfigured by masquerade. The thoughts are accorded a freedom of utterance, which is never abused, and dislikes and partialities come equally to the surface; the one not being smothered, the other not concealed. He must look into himself for the cause, who does not feel himself at once at home with his frank and hospitable friends. The ladies of Richmond partake of that easy grace, the causes of which, as a characteristic of Virginian society, I shall presently trace.

At an evening party, which I had the pleasure of attending, it was my good fortune to meet with Mr. W. C. Rives, for many years one of the representatives of Virginia in the Senate of the United States, and for some time American Minister at Paris. I found him to be a man of liberal views and varied information. As a politician, however, he is now regarded as somewhat *passé*, having differed with his own party without receiving any cordial welcome from the Whigs. When I met him, he was gradually yielding to the seductive influences of Mr. Abbot Lawrence, the prince of manufacturers and protectionists in America, who had recently addressed to him several letters, in favour of a high tariff, through the columns of the newspapers, with a view, if possible, to enlisting the sympathies of Virginia in favour of protection. Mr. Lawrence was, at that very time, in Richmond, which, as the chief seat of Virginian manufacture, he was striving to convert to the prohibitory doctrines of New England.

As already intimated, American society has a peculiar development in Virginia. The social system is there beset with influences which in most parts of the country are unknown, and some of which are but partially experienced in others. Not that the manifestation of society which obtains in Virginia is exclusively confined to that State, for most of its social characteristics are common to some of the adjacent States, particularly to Maryland and South Carolina. In its peculiarities therefore, in this respect, Virginia is not to be regarded as the sole exception to the general tenor of American society.

It is at once the type and the most striking specimen
of the social development peculiar to the slave-holding
States of the Atlantic sea-board; and it is only as illus-
trative of such that I have here particularly alluded
to the more distinctive features of Virginian society.

The division of property in Virginia is totally different from that which prevails in the northern and
north-western States. In the latter it is very rarely
that one meets with great accumulations of landed
property in the hands of a single individual or family.
The system of land tenures is adverse to such accumulations; as it is indeed in Virginia, so far as statu-
tory enactments are concerned; but these enactments
are controlled by other circumstances, which go far to
counteract their operation. In the north and north-
west, large landed estates are the rare exception; in
Virginia they are the rule. Both in the one case and
in the other, the same general principle may be recognised as prevailing—that no one should occupy more
land than he can cultivate; but, from the diversity of social and political institutions, this principle does not, in
the two instances, lead to the same results. Throughout the whole north and north-west, where the frame
is hardy, where the climate invites to work, where
the competition is great and the people are inured to
toil, where slavery does not exist and labour is not
considered as dishonourable, the land is divided into
small holdings, few possessing more than they can
occupy and cultivate. But in Virginia and the adjacent States the case is very different; the land
being there parcelled off into large estates, called
plantations, consisting, in many cases, of tens of
thousands of acres. In the real property system of
these States, the Revolution has, practically, wrought

but very little change. The estate of a Virginian landlord is, in some of its features, very closely assimilated to an English manor. The transatlantic proprietor has certainly none of the political or judicial prerogatives of his English prototype; but, in all other respects, he exercises the same control over his property as the lord exercises, or was wont to exercise, over the demesne lands of the manor. In the most convenient part of the estate is generally to be found the manor-house, and, with the exception of his family and his guests, all who live upon it are the vassals or slaves of the proprietor. Each estate, too, has its appropriate name, as is the case in England; but this is very different from the principle which obtains in the north, where each man's property is known as such and such a lot, in such and such a division, of such and such a township. In short, the real property system of Virginia is the closest approximation to that which, until a very recent period, was so generally prevalent in England, of any that is to be found in the United States.

The influence which this exercises upon society is great and strikingly perceptible. It is almost impossible, in civilized life, to find two states of being more in contrast with each other than those of the landed proprietors of the north and south. It is rarely that the former is not found personally occupied in the cultivation of his own lot or piece of ground. The latter is wholly unaccustomed to labour, and, not unfrequently, delegates to others the business even of superintending the affairs of his estate. These conditions will suggest to the English reader the different positions of the country gentleman and the small farmer in this country. Not only is the American farmer generally the chief labourer on his own land, but the different members of his family—his wife, his daughters, and sons, unless ambition prompt the last-mentioned to seek the towns for the purpose of engaging in mercantile or professional pursuits, take their respective and appropriate shares in the management of the farm. This daily habit of cheerful toil, if not very favourable to the growth of the amenities of life, keeps the energies from becoming dormant, begets self-reliance, and gives rise to a sturdy feeling of independence. Very different is it with the luxurious planter of the south. To him labour would be disgrace. Vegetating, as it were, upon his estate, and surrounded by hundreds of slaves ready to obey his nod, he frequently disencumbers himself even of the management of his property, which he entrusts to the care of overseers, giving himself up to recreation and amusement, and, in many cases, to study, to which he is invited by the beauteous repose and the glorious serenity of nature, which mark his enervating climate. And so with his family. Strangers to toil, and dependent for almost every comfort upon the labour of others, they have time and opportunity to cultivate that indescribable ease and grace which are typical of the more polished circles in older communities. It is thus that one much more frequently meets with the conventional lady and gentleman in the slave, than in the free States; the latter being not only more polished in manner than his northern countryman, but also presenting a higher standard of intellectual cultivation; and the former only finding her parallel, as a general rule, in the more accomplished circles of the northern cities.

Domestic slavery predominates, perhaps, to a

greater extent in Virginia than in any of the adjoining States, where it is more generally to be met with in its predial and harsher aspect.   The slaves about the household are usually divided amongst the different members of the family, as is the case in Russia ; and it is singular to witness the attachment which sometimes springs up between the master and the slave.   Frequently, too, when there are guests in the house, to each is assigned a slave or slaves, whose duty it is to wait upon him or her during the visit.

An incident in Virginia, which will be recognised as analogous to some of the habits of English, country life, is to be found in the visiting parties, which, during a portion of the year, take place throughout the State.   A planter and his family will then have their friends in the neighbourhood, and frequently some of those at a distance, under their roof for weeks together, the whole time being spent in one continued round of gaiety and amusement.   For this their mansions are well adapted, being constructed on a large and commodious scale, as compared with the rural dwellings to be found in the free and grain-growing States ; and many of them presenting to the eye large piles of irregular architecture, quite in contrast with the prim and formal style of the north, and consisting generally of a colonial nucleus, to which a variety of wings have been appended since the epoch of the Revolution.   I was startled the first time I saw quaint old turrets and projecting and multitudinous gable ends, embowered amid the foliage of the New World.   It seemed to me that such things were more in keeping when in juxtaposition with the spreading oak and the beech, than with the hickory, the black walnut and the acacia.   What I would have looked for on the Severn and the Dee, surprised me, at first, when met with on the Roanoke and the Shenandoah.

During the continuance of these visits, the guests sometimes meet each other at, and at other times not till after, breakfast. When a general excursion is proposed, they set off immediately, before the heat of the day comes on. When nothing of the kind is contemplated, a portion of the morning is spent in walking about the grounds, or in making some preliminary preparations for the amusements of the evening. About eleven o'clock they all disappear, to avoid the heat of the day; the ladies retiring to their rooms, the gentlemen, with the exception of such as go hunting or fishing, to theirs. The chambers are partially darkened, to avoid the heat and fierce glare of midday; and the burning hours are thus passed either in reading or in yielding to their somnolent influences. In the afternoon, when parties dare to face the sun, they emerge from their hiding places, and all is life again; attention being occupied by a variety of amusements till dinner-time. The evening is generally devoted to dancing, which, when the heat is too oppressive to admit of its continuance within, is sometimes transferred to the lawn; and a pretty sight it is, in the broad moonlight, and when the dew has forgotten to fall, to see a whole party thus engaged— the ringing laugh accompanying, every now and then, the evolutions of the dance; whilst hard by may be seen a dusky crowd of both sexes, jabbering and grinning in innocent mirth, and apparently, in being permitted to witness it, enjoying the scene as much as their masters, who are mixing in it.

The English reader has already, through a variety

of channels, been made familiar with the appearance presented by an American table. I can scarcely avoid, however, here briefly referring to the prominent part borne by Indian corn in southern, and particularly in Virginia, dietary. With us the term "corn" is applied preeminently to wheat—in America it is exclusively used to designate the Indian grain, which is consumed in enormous quantities by man and beast, not only in the States, but also in the Canadas and the other British provinces. The extent to which it is used over the entire continent, is only equalled by the variety of modes in which it is prepared. Whilst it is yet green in the ear, it becomes, by boiling, a delicious vegetable for the table; and when ripe, is capable, before it is ground, of being prepared for food in a great variety of ways. To describe the multifarious uses to which it is applied in the shape of flour is almost impossible; making its appearance in every form, from the crude condition of gruel and stirabout, through the stages of pancakes, to bread in twenty different shapes, and compounds of the richest and most luscious description. In Virginia, corn-bread has almost entirely banished every other species of bread from common use, and this not only with the poorest, but also with the wealthiest classes. It is customary when Virginians have guests in their houses, to put wheaten bread upon the table; but when the family is left to itself, wheaten bread may not make its appearance, at any meal, for weeks at a time. I once saw Indian flour in seven different forms of preparation upon a private breakfast-table. It is thus universally used, because it is universally preferred to wheat in any form, although the very best wheat raised in the country is the produce of Virginia. I mention these facts to remove, as far as possible, the prejudice which, from two causes, exists in this country against Indian corn. The first is, that it is looked upon as an inferior diet, to which those who use it are driven by a species of necessity; and that it is deficient in nutritious qualities. The fact that it is not only extensively used by all classes throughout America, whilst in the south its use is almost exclusive in the shape of bread, not only in the hut of the slave, but in the mansion of his master, and that those who undergo the greatest toil, in many parts of the country, seldom consume any other grain, is sufficient to demonstrate the groundlessness of this supposition. The second cause of the prejudice is the unpalatable shape in which it has generally been presented to the people of this country. In no form in which it is used in America is it ever taken cold. When wanted in the shape of bread, no more is baked than is necessary for the time being. It is never baked, as it has been here, in large quantities, and in the shape of loaves, as ordinary flour is baked into bread; nor is it mixed with any other species of flour or meal. Indian corn is always best when used by itself, with the exception of such ingredients as eggs, butter, milk, sugar, &c., which are frequently superadded in its preparation to give it additional richness and flavour. To my palate it was never so sweet as when prepared in the very simplest manner. In preparing it for their own use, the negro women generally mix it simply with water and a little salt; the dough, which is thus formed, being made up into a roll about the size and shape of a soda-water bottle, without the neck. This is enveloped in the hot ashes of a wood fire, which is the

simple process by which it is baked. When ready
it is taken to the pump, and whilst yet hot the ashes
are washed off it. When they wish to be a little
particular, they protect it, by enveloping it in leaves
before covering it with the ashes. Simple though
this preparation be, the bread produced by it is, whilst
warm, exceedingly sweet. The "hoe cake" is the
product of a similar ceremony, with the exception of
its being toasted by the fire, instead of being baked
in the ashes.

In no other part of the country, perhaps, is the
pride of ancestry so greatly cherished as in Virginia.
Indeed, I found throughout the Republic that, when
an American was positive that he had a grandfather, he
was quite as partial to his memory as grandchildren
are wont to be in more aristocratic communities. It
is not without considerable satisfaction that descent
is thus traced back to.the Colonial era, which is of
course proportionably enhanced when the Atlantic can
be crossed, and the Propositus John Stiles of the gene-
alogical diagram can be traced to some English locality. There are many Virginian families who greatly
pride themselves on their direct and demonstrable
English connexion, more demonstrable here, perhaps,
than elsewhere, because the property of Virginia has
changed hands, since the Revolution, to a less extent
than in any other State of the Union. A Virginian was
once dilating to me upon this weakness, as he termed
it, in the character of his countrymen, but about
five minutes afterwards he confidentially informed me
that he could trace a very direct family connexion
between himself and William the Conqueror. He
must have read in my look that I regarded this as
rather a strange commentary upon his previous

criticism on Virginian character, for he immediately
added, that it was his delight to curb the pride of a
maiden aunt of his, who was very fond of referring to
the circumstance, by reminding her that on the female
side they were descended from a poor Irish girl, who
had been transported, and purchased for a hogshead of
tobacco on the banks of the James.

Nature has divided the State of Virginia into three
great and distinct sections; the tide-water region,
the central valley, and the western portion of the
State. Of these, the central valley, or the Valley of
Virginia, as it is frequently called, is by far the most
eligible in every point of view. It is on it that the
Virginians concentrate their pride. Indeed they call
it Virginia. And truly, without traversing it, the
stranger can form but an inadequate conception of the
characteristics of the State, either in a moral or a
material point of view. Properly speaking, this
central portion includes all that lies between the
tide-water and the westerly districts of the State,
embracing about one moiety of it. The valley, so
called, is comprehended in this, extending in a north-
easterly and south-westerly direction, and nestling
in the very lap of the Alleganies, which, in traversing
the State, separate into two great, with several subsidiary parallel ridges, which throw out their spurs
for considerable distances in every direction. The
area of the valley thus enclosed is equal to about
one-fourth that of the State. The more easterly of
the two ridges bears the general name of the Blue
Mountains. Nothing of the kind can be more charming to the eye than their appearance on approaching
them. Their outline is but little varied, as they
loom in the distance over the surrounding country;

but when seen through the clear air, whilst you are yet a day's journey from them, they appear as if afloat in the far off sky, clothed in the softest tint of mingled blue and green, on which the eye rests with rapture, and which it finds relief, as it were, in drinking in.

At the base of this ridge, both on its eastern and western sides, lie ranges of counties, unmatched in fertility and productiveness by any others in the State. Most of the tobacco raised in the State is produced to the eastward of the mountains, where a great deal of wheat is also annually produced. Wheat is the principal product of the valley. Here, too, the estates are far from being so large as they are in other portions of the State. In fact, life in the valley is, in the main, a condition of society intermediate between that just described, and the social development of the northern and north-western States. Labour is not here altogether discreditable to the white man, and the slaves are comparatively few in number. It is only in autumn that one can fully appreciate the richness of this beautiful and salubrious region, when the golden wheat is ready for the sickle, and the tall Indian corn is bending with the weight of its product, and when the many orchards that chequer the slopes of the hills are spangled with their mellow fruit, amongst which the apple and the peach are conspicuously abundant, so much so, indeed, that the hogs are frequently permitted to satiate themselves upon them.

The whole valley abounds in mineral springs, which are annually resorted to in great numbers by invalids and fashionables. There are the White Sulphur, the Blue Sulphur, and the Red Sulphur Springs, the Warm and the Cold Springs, and a variety of others, whose names denote their characteristic quality. Some of these are for internal, others for external, application. At some, the accommodations are good; at others, rather indifferent. Many live in hotels, others in small cottages, built by themselves near the springs, upon lots given them for that purpose by the owner, on condition that when they are not occupying them, the owner of the ground shall have the use of them. Most of those who thus live, take their meals at the hotels. In the immediate neighbourhood of one of the principal springs, the ground is owned by a Mr. C——, who has parcelled off a good deal of it on the above condition, and keeps the only hotel in the place. Everything is in first-rate style, except the table, of which great complaint is frequently made; but the landlord coolly tells his guests, that they only pay him for their accommodation in the way of lodgings, and that, as he gives them their meals into the bargain, it does not become them to complain. They have no possible redress, for he will neither sell nor lease an inch of ground in the neighbourhood, for the purpose of building a rival hotel. Many families, from all parts of the Union, prefer the quiet and retirement of the springs of Virginia, to the hurry-scurry life and fashionable vortex of Saratoga.

In many repects, the sea-board, or tide-water region, differs materially from the portion of the State just described. The soil is poor and scanty; the products are less varied and less abundant; the estates are large, and the slaves upon them exceedingly numerous; and, to crown all, from July to October a great portion of it is uninhabitable by the white man.

The reader will find, on glancing at the map, that between the Atlantic and the Alleganies, the continent is divided into two great terraces, which run parallel to the mountains and the sea-board. That next the sea-board is low and flat, and extends, at some points, upwards of 150 miles into the interior, at others to a much less distance. The other rises immediately from it, is broken and undulating, and extends westward to the mountain chain. It is evident, therefore, that the rivers, in pursuing their course eastward to the Atlantic, must undergo a series of descents, or one very abrupt descent, in their channels, in leaving the one level for the other. It is thus that almost all the rivers which drain the continent into the Atlantic have, at some point or points in their course, their respective falls or rapids. At Glen's Falls, the Hudson abruptly changes its level; at Trenton, the Delaware, though not so abruptly, does the same; at Georgetown, near Washington, the Potomac, by a series of rapids, finds the tide-water level; as does the James River at Richmond. A similar formation, though not in connexion with the same system, seems to prevail in the valley of the St. Lawrence, the waters of Lake Erie plunging by the Falls of Niagara to the level of Lake Ontario, from which they seek the still lower level of the tide-water region, by the stupendous rapids of the St. Lawrence. Up the channels of these rivers the tide flows, until it is checked by the sudden change which takes place in the level of the country. Thus in the St. Lawrence, it flows up to Three Rivers, 90 miles above Quebec, and nearly 500 miles from the Gulf, although in this case it does not reach the rapids, the lowest of which is close to Montreal, 90 miles still higher up. In

the Hudson it flows upwards of 150 miles from the
ocean; in the Delaware, past Philadelphia; in the
Potomac, 140 miles from Chesapeake Bay, up to
Washington; and in the James, to Richmond, upwards
of 120 miles from its entrance into the Atlantic.
The same physical phenomenon may be traced still
further southward, through the Carolinas and Georgia.
To the north of the Potomac, the tide-water region
is as healthy, perhaps, as any other portion of the
country in corresponding latitudes; but the exhalations
of summer from the low marshy grounds of the tide-
water districts of Virginia, North and South Carolina,
and Georgia, so poison the atmosphere, that by the
month of July, every white inhabitant who can, is
fain to fly the pestilential region, until the ensuing
October. How many things frequently, without our
dreaming of it, influence largely the institutions of
society, and the moral and political condition of man!
I now approach a painful subject, in considering
which with all the calmness and impartiality at my
command, I shall endeavour to illustrate how far even
this configuration of the continent influences the
all-imporant question of Slavery.

CHAPTER IV.

SLAVERY,—IN ITS POLITICAL ASPECT.

IF there is one subject on which, more than another,
misconception prevails in this country; on which prejudice over-rides the judgment, and philanthropy
discards from its consideration every notion of practicability, it is that of slavery in the United States.
On most questions connected with America, there is
a disposition in many quarters to jump at unfavourable
conclusions; but on no subject so much as on this, is
decision so independent of previous examination into
the circumstances of the case. European prejudice
fastens eagerly upon slavery as a welcome crime to

charge upon the American republic; and philanthropy, in the headlong pursuit of its end, defeats its own purpose by stumbling over the difficulties to which it is wilfully blind. That there is a stain on the escutcheon of the Republic is palpable to all. Political antipathies chuckle at its existence, whilst benevolence is outraged because it is not instantaneously eradicated. Few understand the merits of the case, because few care to examine into them. In the general cry against American slavery there is some justice, but more of prejudice and mistaken zeal. It is treated as a cloak, which the Republic could lay aside at its pleasure, instead of as involving a question of transcendant difficulty, from being an institution which enters into the very texture and fibre of its frame.

It is with a view to present it succinctly in all its bearings, that I devote this and the succeeding chapter to the consideration of the important question of American slavery. In making the tour of the country, I could not select a better opportunity for investigating into this subject, than whilst yet a sojourner in Virginia, the chief "breeding State." Nor will the time be deemed as inaptly chosen for its full and dispassionate consideration, when it is borne in mind to how great an extent the tide is now unfortunately turning in Europe, if not in favour of slavery, at least of something very nearly approximating to it. Whilst the public mind is becoming imbued with the notion that, in the course which was pursued in regard to the West Indies, if we have not gone too far, we acted at least with rashness and precipitation, it will not refuse a dispassionate inquiry into the perplexing and ill-understood question of American slavery. In doing what lies in my power to guide this inquiry, I shall first consider the institution in its political aspect.

It may be as well to premise that I am neither the apologist of slavery in the abstract, nor the panegyrist of the phase, which, as a domestic institution, it has assumed in America. In what follows, on this subject, my sole object will be to present the question in its true light, so as to enable the reader to form his own conclusions. To such as prefer prejudging the subject, I have nothing to say; my exposition being exclusively addressed to those whose candour inclines them to form a correct estimate of a sad reality.

As a political question, it is, beyond doubt, the prime difficulty of the Confederacy—a proposition, with the truth of which none are more deeply impressed than are the Americans themselves. However they may differ in their views as to the course which should be pursued in regard to it, as an established institution, its actual presence amongst them is a fact which they universally deplore. There it is, a great and an acknowledged evil, which they must either endure, or dissipate in a mode which will not superinduce greater evils still. It hangs about the social and political system, like a great tumour upon the body, which cannot be suddenly cut away, without risking a hemorrhage which would endanger life, and which cannot be permitted to remain without incurring perils equally certain, though not so immediate. The perplexing question is, as to the remedies to be applied for its gradual extinction, and as to the time and mode of their application. Meantime the evil is on the increase, and the worst presentiments are entertained as to its issue, as regards both the political and social destinies of the Republic.

For the better understanding of the subject, the reader will excuse me for here reminding him that slavery in the United States is not an institution common to the whole Republic. In this respect the Union resolves itself into two great institutional divisions, the line of demarcation being about the 39th parallel of latitude; in other words, the Confederacy is divided into the free States of the north, and the slave-holding States of the south. The former are as free from the taint of slavery as is England herself, most of them having washed their hands of it at a much earlier period than she did. The political balance subsisting between these two sections of the Union will be more appropriately considered hereafter. All that is now necessary for a due understanding of the position of parties with respect to slavery is, that the fact of this division should be kept in view.

It is not my purpose to go into an historical account of the abolition movement in America, but simply to show the present position of parties with respect to the question of slavery. The anti- and pro-slavery parties have no necessary connexion with the great political parties of the country. Abolitionism is a creed common both to the Democrat and to the Whig, the antagonist doctrine also finding its adherents in the ranks of both parties. As a general rule, however, the abolition tenets are more extensively harboured by the Whigs in the north than by their political opponents; the name of "Abolition Whigs" being given them by the Democrat, when it suits his humour to be particularly bitter.

The anti-slavery party is divided into two sections, comprising those who are known, *par excellence*, as the Abolitionists, and those who, not ranging themselves under the abolition banners, are opposed to slavery from considerations which will be presently adverted to. There is no division to be observed in the opposite ranks. Although the pro-slavery party are, generally speaking, confined to the south, they are not without their "sympathisers" and abettors in the north. The great stronghold of the other party is, of course, the free north, although there are many who co-operate with them, even in the southern section of the Confederacy. It will thus be seen that, even on this question, which comes nearer than any other to the division of parties into geographical sections, party feeling, instead of being confined to certain parallels of latitude, is homogeneous to the Union. Taking the two parties generally, the question raised between them is one mainly, if not entirely, of a political cast. True, the section of the anti-slavery party, known as the Abolitionists proper, make their principal stand upon the morality of the question, contending that no considerations of political expediency can justify the existence of an institution, so offensive to morals and religion, for a moment longer than the time needed to erase it by the transcendant power of legislation. Their more moderate coadjutors, comprising the great bulk of the anti-slavery party, agreeing with them as to the immorality of the institution, and the desirableness of getting rid of it, differ with them as to the safety or practicability of its instantaneous abolition. Nor are all the Abolitionists men of impracticable views; although on this question of gradual or immediate emancipation, the majority of them differ from the bulk of the anti-slavery party; and it is this difference which makes the Abolitionists act politically together, independently of the rest of that party. Thus, frequently, both in local and general elections, they are found forgetting their political differences, and acting in concert—sometimes having candidates of their own. This is the only way in which this fragment of the constituency of the

country—for, after all, they are by no means numerous
—can exert a political influence; and sometimes the
balance of parties is so nice, that that influence is not
unimportant.   It was the abolitionist vote of the State
of New York that gave to Mr. Polk, instead of to Mr.
Clay, the Presidency in 1844.   The consequences of
that vote have been the Oregon dispute, and the rupture with, and spoliation of, Mexico.   The ground
assumed by the pro-slavery party is simply that of political expediency.   Even in the south there are none
bold enough openly to defend slavery on any other
pretext.   If they entertain other sentiments, they
render homage to morals and humanity by carefully
concealing them.   The views of the different parties
may be summed up thus:—The pro-slavery party,
admitting the abstract injustice of the institution, treat
it, nevertheless, as an unfortunate fact, of which they
cannot get rid, or which, at best, they can only gradually obliterate.   The bulk of the anti-slavery party,
agreeing with them in this, urge them to commence
at once, and to hasten, by all practicable means, the
work of its extinction; whilst the more zealous wing
of that party, the Abolitionists, are ready to sacrifice
every other consideration to their grand desideratum
of immediate emancipation.

Such being the state of parties, and such the general views entertained by them, it becomes important
now to consider the constitutional question involved
in the issue between them.   This has an obvious bearing upon the whole subject, in treating of slavery as
an American question; especially when it is borne in
mind that constitutional governments are, or should
be, guided in their conduct by prescribed rules of
action.   It is only through the instrumentality of a
political agency, that the institution of slavery can be

either modified or extinguished; and I shall now proceed to show what that agency is in America, and the
mode in which alone it can be put in operation.

The majority of those who indiscriminately charge
slavery as a crime upon the whole American republic,
do so under the impression that Congress has the same
transcendent power over it as the British Parliament
rightfully exercised over servitude in the West Indies. This impression argues either an ignorance or
a forgetfulness both of the constitution and functions
of Congress. There is no omnipotent legislature in
America. Congress is the creature of the Constitution, and its action, like that of the local legislatures, is circumscribed by certain specified limits;
beyond which it has no constitutional power to act.
Its legislative powers are strictly confined to those
cases in which the power of legislation has been expressly conceded to it; in all others it is impotent for
good or evil. The question, then, obviously arises,
Does slavery fall within the category of cases in which
Congress has been expressly, or even by implication,
empowered to legislate? It does not. It follows,
therefore, that Congress has no more power over
slavery in any of the American States, than has the
British Parliament. This incompetency of Congress
to meddle with the subject, implies the abdication of
all right to interfere with it, on the part of the people,
in their aggregate capacity. To this abdication, as
will immediately be seen, the weightiest considerations
contributed, and with the most favourable results.
For what the people, in their aggregate capacity,
cannot effect, the people, in that capacity, cannot be
held responsible. Whatever charge, therefore, may
be brought against those who have absolute and

undoubted power over the whole subject, it is obviously improper to visit the entire confederacy with the peculiar sins of some only of its independent component members.

As observed in a former chapter, in the distribution of powers between the general and local authorities, a line of demarcation was drawn between such matters as were purely of a domestic, and such as were of federal concern.   It suited the views of the framers of the Constitution, to comprehend slavery within the former classification,. by which it was entirely withdrawn from federal jurisdiction.   It is, then, exclusively a question of State cognizance, with which no legislation but that of each particular State can deal; Congress, for instance, having no more authority over slavery in South Carolina, than it has to dig a canal, construct a railway, or erect a bridge in the State. Under these circumstances it is obvious, that whatever blame attaches to the institution, rests solely with the States in which slavery still legally and politically exists; for as the slave States can claim no share of the credit which belongs to the free States for the example of emancipation set by them, so it is manifestly unjust to involve the free States in the turpitude of their more guilty, and, it must be confessed, their more unfortunate confederates.

This is the reason why the more energetic and populous section of the Confederacy takes no active political part in the question of emancipation.   The people of New York, as of the other northern States, abolished slavery themselves, within their respective limits, without the intervention or interference of their neighbours; and in confining themselves to the exercise of a mere moral influence over their southern brethren, they are only according them that liberty which they themselves enjoyed, and the invasion of which they would have resented. Little as this mutual independence of the different States, in relation to this subject, is appreciated here, it is so well understood in America, that even the most zealous of the Abolitionists acknowledge that it is only through local agency that they can succeed in their object. They never think of calling upon Congress to do that which it is incompetent to do, to interfere with the domestic institutions of the slave-holding States. On this all parties are agreed; but the point on which the Abolitionists are said to have erred, is as to the mode in which they have conducted their operations within the limits of the slave States.

But although all parties repudiate the idea that Congress has any power over slavery in the slave States, the issue which has been so fiercely contested between the Abolitionists and their antagonists is, as to the power of Congress over slavery in the District of Columbia. The peculiar political position of the District, and the exclusive control of Congress over it, have been previously adverted to. It is here that the Abolitionists have attacked slavery in what they consider its stronghold. Nestled as it is within the territories of two of the principal slave-holding States, Maryland and Virginia, the Abolitionists have acted upon the principle, that by getting the District free, they would inflict a most effectual blow upon the whole system of slavery. The facility of escape which would be thereby offered to the slaves in the contiguous States, would be such as it was hoped would, by-and-by, render the continuance of the institution a matter of indifference both to Virginia and Maryland; and slavery once abolished or relaxed in these States, the others would not be long in imitating their example. Lured by this tempting and not unfeasible project, the Abolitionists have long urged the abolition of slavery in the District. But it was precisely the reasoning which led them into this track, which induced the slave States, in a body, to meet them in it, and resist them. The danger to the institution of slavery, which the success of this project would have involved, was too obvious to be long undiscovered; and it has therefore been chiefly on this point that the warfare has been waged.

A double issue was immediately raised between the parties—first, as to the power of Congress to abolish slavery within the District; and next, as to the expediency of so doing, should the power be proved to exist. As to the first issue, the Abolitionists cite the 17th clause of the 8th section of the Constitution, in proof of the affirmative. The section enumerates the powers of Congress, and the clause confers upon that body authority " to exercise exclusive legislation, *in all cases whatsoever*, over the district of Columbia." The Abolitionists contend that nothing could be larger than the authority conveyed by these words, Congress being invested by them with a species of absolute dominion over the " *ten miles square ;*" and being authorized by them to exercise, in the District, any power which rightfully falls within the pale of human legislation. They then go on to say that, as the subject of slavery falls within such pale, the constitutional right of Congress to legislate, in regard to it, cannot be disputed.

Their opponents reason otherwise. They deny that Congress has the power to do anything, within the

district, that falls within the pale of human legislation. The very section, of which the clause in question is a part, contains other clauses of a restrictive
character, which are as restrictive of the powers of
Congress in the District of Columbia, as throughout
the Union generally. Thus Congress cannot create
a separate standard of weights and measures for the
district, nor can it impose upon it a law of naturaliza-
tion or bankruptcy, which is not uniform throughout
the United States. This cuts at once at the ground
taken by the Abolitionists, since it appears that there
are some things which fall within the pale of legislation, which Congress, even in the District, can only do
in a limited and restricted sense. But then, say the
Abolitionists, the powers granted within the District
are so general, that every power can be exercised
within it, but such as are specially excepted; and
they call upon the slave-holders to show that slavery
is one of the exceptional cases. And here they fairly
have their opponents in a corner, who are thereupon
obliged to shift their ground from the letter to the
spirit of the Constitution, and particularly to the
spirit of the acts of cession, whereby Maryland and
Virginia ceded to the United States their respective
portions of the district. The clause in question was
framed before it was known what spot would be ceded
to, or accepted by, the United States as the seat of
government. Had it been intended, they say, that
any such construction could, or would, be put upon
the clause, could it be supposed, for a moment, that
two of the chief slave-holding States would have
voluntarily transferred to the government *ten miles
square* on their conterminous boundaries? And even
were the clause capable of such an interpretation, it

was evidently on the understanding that nothing would be done by Congress to disturb their domestic institutions, that they ceded their respective portions of the District. To interfere with slavery within its bounds, they maintain, would violate this understanding, and peril the social institutions, not only of these two States, but also of every slave-holding State in the Union. The whole of the slave-holding communities thus make common cause with the two States more immediately concerned, maintaining, as a general principle, in addition to the foregoing line of reasoning, that, as the federal government was organized solely with a view to the better management of federal affairs, so the powers conferred upon it, with reference to the District of Columbia, which was ceded to it merely for purposes of general convenience, cannot be so construed as to vest in Congress any right, either directly, or by implication, to compromise or interfere with the domestic institutions of any State in the Union.

As to the question of the expediency of Congress exercising this power, were it proved to exist, it is one which involves so obvious a train of argument on both sides, that it is unnecessary here to enlarge upon it.

Such is a very general outline of the constitutional merits of the question. It will suffice, in addition to explaining the precise mode in which the issue between the contending parties is raised, to show how far the Americans, as an entire people, are now implicated, if at all, in the guilt of slavery. The agitation for abolition, if it is to be conducted with effect, must be conducted within the limits of the Constitution. Confining themselves to these limits, we have seen that the inhabitants of the northern States, who form the greater section of the entire community, can legally exercise no legislative control, direct or indirect, over the subject, unless, as the Abolitionists contend, Congress has the power to abolish slavery in the District of Columbia—a power which would enable the aggregate people of the Union indirectly to reach the evil. But even if the letter of the Constitution would justify their interference, it is a grave question whether, by touching the institution in the District of Columbia, they would not be beginning at the wrong end, and perilling the very object which they had in view. Such an interference would certainly lead to the rupture of the Union, on the maintenance of which, at present, rests the only hope which exists of the spread of emancipation. It is also a question whether, if Congress has, by the letter of the Constitution, the power contended for, it is not virtually precluded from the exercise of it by the whole spirit of the federal compact. It is evident then that, if the northern States have no power to interfere in a legislative capacity with slavery in the south ; or if, having the power indirectly so to do, they are prevented from so doing as well by considerations connected with the question of slavery itself, as by the whole spirit of the Constitution and of the articles of Union ; they do all, in reference to the subject, which the world has a right to expect from them, if they exert all the moral influence at their command in favour of emancipation. Whether they do so or not is the point to which those who seek to involve them in the guilt of the southern States, should in justice confine themselves.

But it may be urged, that Congress should have been invested with the whole control over the subject;

in other words, that the American people, as an entire
people, should have retained in their own hands the
power of relaxing or abolishing slavery at pleasure,
throughout the length and breadth of the Republic.
The permanent position of this question, in the
political arrangement about to be formed, was one of
the many subjects which occupied the public mind at
the time of the adoption of the Constitution; and the
presumption is certainly in favour of the proposition
that, in determining as they did, they adopted the
wisest, if not the only practicable course.   It is
indeed difficult to see, especially when we consider
that slavery, aside of moral considerations, resolves
itself into a mere question of property, how the framers
of the Constitution could have withdrawn it from the
category of matters of purely domestic concern, over
which each State was to have, within its own limits,
exclusive jurisdiction.   Having thus determined the
character of the question, it was impossible for them
to bring it within the purview of the powers dele-
gated to the general government, which arose out
of a particular necessity, and was organized for a particular object.   And, indeed, we have not to look far
to discover that there were positive and very cogent
reasons for exempting slavery, in the different States
at least, from subjection to federal authority.   None
have more reason to rejoice that this was done, than
have the friends of humanity.   But for this arrangement, who can say that slavery would yet have been
abolished in the now free States of the north?   Let
it be remembered that the power to abolish slavery
in the hands of Congress would have implied the
power of retaining it.   It might have abolished it in
Massachusetts, and retained it in New York; or it

might have perpetuated it in all or in any of the free States. Instead of being, as now, mistress of its own actions with regard to slavery within its own territories, each State in dealing with it would, under these circumstances, have been compelled to submit to the will of the whole. In the earlier days of the yet youthful Republic, the power of the South was considered as predominant. The South, too, has always regarded with jealousy and uneasiness the approach of emancipation to its borders; and what more probable than that it would have thrown every obstacle in the way of freedom in the North, had any right been accorded it to interfere. But for the independent action of each State with regard to slavery, emancipation would not now have been the law of one moiety of the Republic. And on the same action, and on that alone, does emancipation now depend in the South. It would be monstrous as well as impolitic, on the part of the Northern States, to attempt now to effect that in the South by coercion and interference, the attainment of which, amongst themselves, they owe entirely to the abstinence from all interference on the part of their neighbours. Whatever opinions, therefore, may be entertained as to the political propriety of the arrangement effected in framing the Constitution, the cause of humanity has certainly not lost by the withdrawal of the subject of slavery in the different States from the jurisdiction of Congress.

Having thus put the reader in possession of the question in its legal and constitutional form, and having glanced at the powers and incapacities of the different sections of the Union with regard to it, I shall now proceed briefly to consider how far the

North has made use of that moral influence, which it is competent for it to exert for the extinction of slavery in the South. And here let me at once express my conviction, that the intemperate zeal of the abolitionist wing of the anti-slavery party has done more to retard, than the more judicious efforts of the rest of that party have done to accelerate, emancipation. Much of that determined opposition with which the Abolitionists are met in the South, is attributable to the utter want of discretion with which, individually and as a body, they have striven for the attainment of their object. When zeal reaches a certain point, it becomes blind to every thing but its purpose, at which it dashes headlong, reckless of consequences, and deaf to remonstrance. Thus, in America, an ill-advised philanthropy, instead of un-locking, has only rivetted more firmly, the fetters of the slave. Believing that the letter of the Constitution confers upon Congress the power to abolish slavery in the District of Columbia, they have urged, and still urge that body to exercise this power, regardless of the whole spirit in which the Union was conceived. To accede to their wishes, would be to dissolve the whole political fabric, and to ruin every hope that slavery may yet be arrested on the continent. *Fiat justitia, ruat cœlum.* But who would accept a small, and after all a questionable benefit, at the cost of a certain and permanent evil ? In carrying the warfare into the slave States they have been equally unsuccessful, because equally indiscreet. Their tone, instead of being persuasive, has been dictatorial ; their language, instead of being that of conciliation, has been inflam-matory and menacing. At first, their publications were numerous, and their emissaries were active, in the slave States themselves; but when the former came to convey, and the latter to preach doctrines which were utterly incompatible with the tranquillity of the country, it is no wonder that the one was suppressed and the other silenced—that the torch was taken from the hands of those who were ready to explode the mine in which they themselves, and all concerned, would have perished together. To preach the abstract rights of man to a numerous and ignorant population in bondage, and to press upon them the right to achieve their freedom at any cost, might have been justifiable on general principles, but it was certainly not the way in which to conciliate the masters to their views—the dominant class, without whose concurrence and aid nothing effectual could be done. They should have recollected that, if the principles on which they acted were divine, the objections which they had to encounter were human. In some parts of the country, the blacks are to the whites as five is to one. Is it any wonder that, under these circumstances, the white population should have become alarmed at proceedings, which, if unchecked, must have terminated in a servile insurrection? The Abolitionists, in arousing immediate fears, instead of appealing to remote consequences, forgot to what lengths men will sometimes be driven in consulting their own safety. They themselves conjured up an immediate danger, either real or imaginary, which the planters, acting on the defensive, took the most stringent measures to dissipate. The Abolitionists were proscribed, their doctrines branded with disrepute, and slavery in the South became sterner than ever in its character, and more revolting in its aspect. As a natural consequence, moderate counsels became as distasteful as violent doctrines; and the South, assailed without allowance or discretion, became irritated at, and jealous of, every admonition of philanthropy. The fault is mainly, if not exclusively, their own, that the South is now hermetically sealed against the emissaries of abolition; and another instance has thus been added to the many, with which the history of the world is already so rife, of a good cause having been all but wrecked by the intemperance of its advocates.

In their demands, too, the Abolitionists have been as ill-advised as they have been in their mode of pushing them. Nothing but an impossibility would satisfy them. When undertaken, as it must be, by gradual steps, God knows, the path of emancipation in the South will be found difficult enough. Immediate emancipation is a chimera. Yet this is what the less considerate of the Abolitionists insist, or have insisted, upon. They forget that even in the northern States, where slavery never obtained a very extensive footing, and where its extirpation was, therefore, a comparatively easy task, the work of abolition proceeded gradually to its consummation. And if in New York, New Jersey, and Pennsylvania, a policy of gradation was deemed advisable, *à fortiori* should it be that alone on which the South should be urged or expected to embark. It is to this that the great bulk of the anti-slavery party would drive her, from political, as well as moral considerations. I cannot say that the influence, which they might exert for this purpose is as steadily applied as it should be. It is generally in connexion with political questions that it is called into active exercise; rising and subsiding with the occasion which calls it forth.

Such is the position of the question between the Americans themselves. But it is not simply with one another that they have to deal with the subject of slavery. The Republic is arraigned before the bar of humanity, and has a question to settle with the world. It cannot be denied that appearances, at least, are against it. The people, who are rather ostentatious than otherwise of their championship of social equality and political freedom, present to the world the startling anomaly, if not of being the open advocates, of being, at least, the chief abettors of slavery. Their professions seem in glaring contrast with their practice. The asylum of the free is the prison of the enslaved; the goddess of liberty is professedly worshipped, but the demon of servitude, at the same time, extensively sacrificed to. Under these circumstances the Americans should not be surprised that the current of opinion should, on this point, have set in against them from the Old World. It is quite true that there are many in this country, whose interest and pleasure it is to aggravate their political faults; but it must be confessed that there is enough on the surface to make their friends and well-wishers, especially those who have neither time nor the opportunity to acquaint themselves intimately with the whole subject, if not loud in their condemnation, at all events dumb in their defence.

But the Americans feel that, as regards the question between them and the world, their case is one not wholly devoid of justification. They hold that an impartial inquiry into the merits of the case, if it will not lead to their entire acquittal, will, at least, mitigate the severity of the accusation. In justice both to them and the question, this inquiry should not be refused.

Let us see, then, the extent to which the Americans can justify themselves before the world, and the character of their defence.

It is charged upon the free States that they have, after all, but imperfectly eradicated the stain from themselves, as a runaway slave is capable of being reclaimed in any of them by his owner. This arises from a clause of the Constitution, which is in these words:—" No person held to service and labour in one State, under the laws thereof, escaping into another, shall, in consequence of any law or regulation therein, be discharged from such service or labour, but shall be delivered up, on claim of the party to whom such service or labour may be due." It was evidently impossible for the southern States, so long as slavery retained a conspicuous place amongst their institutions, to enter, under any other conditions, into the federal compact at all. If a slave was to become free and irreclaimable the moment he entered the territory of any State which might subsequently become free, it was obvious to what an extent this would have been fraught with peril to the institutions of the South. The whole political system of America is based upon mutual concessions, and this was one, which, if it was not right in the North to make, it was at least reasonable in the South to insist upon. On the part of the North, it was one of those elements which entered into the aggregate cost to them of the Union. It had to deal differently, in this respect, with confederate States than with the rest of the world. The necessity under which the concession was made to the States of the South is obvious from the fact, that it is denied to all others; for a slave escaping into New York, for instance, from a foreign country, is as free as if he were on British ground. If it is urged that, in England, a slave escaped from her own colonies became free; it is replied, that there is a great difference between dealing with dependent Colonies and independent confederate States. Each State has the right to regulate for itself the mode in which, when a runaway slave is claimed, the point of ownership shall be decided. In New York the magistrates have power to decide; in Vermont, the question of slave or no slave is one for a jury. When a slave voluntarily accompanies his master into a free State, the ownership of the latter is protected for a given time by the laws of the State. In New York the time is nine months.

The Americans remind us, in the next place, that they are not responsible for the origin of slavery amongst them. It is on the British government that they throw the heavy charge of having first planted it in the Colonies. They do not say that, in all cases, the system was entailed upon them against the wishes, openly expressed, of the colonists themselves. In any case in which this was done, no one can deny the sole responsibility of the mother country for the origin of the institution. But in the vast majority of cases, the colonists were not unwilling parties to its introduction amongst them. In all these cases, the mother country stood only in the position of a *particeps criminis*. But the Americans contend that, in either case, whether a sole or divided responsibility rests with the British government, it ill becomes the British people to be their accusers. This looks very plausible, until it is considered with what it is that they are accused. The continuance, and not the origin, of slavery is the stain on the Republic, which elicits here the surprise of some, the regret of others, and the condemnation of all. Even were the British government exclusively respon-

sible for the origin of the evil, by no perversity of
reasoning can it be charged with its continuance.
What have the Americans done towards its removal,
during the seventy years of their independence ? A
great deal, it is true; but have they done as much as
they might have done, or as the world reasonably
expected of them ? All honour to the North for the
example which it has so nobly set to the southern section of the Republic. But in according it the merit
which is its due, it must not be forgotten that emancipation in the North was a matter of comparatively
easy attainment. In the South the difficulties in the
way are of appalling magnitude. But whilst the North
has done everything, has the South done anything ? It
is by the decision of this question that justice is to be
meted out to the South; and even those most leniently
disposed are forced to regard the decision as unfavourable to it. The difficulties in the way may be a
sufficient answer to the impracticable demands of the
abolitionists, but they are no answer to the great bulk of
the anti-slavery party, who would urge the South into
a career of gradual abolition. Besides, delay on the
part of the South in moving, warrants a doubt as to
the sincerity of its intentions; for the difficulties, which
are now great, are fast becoming insuperable. The
steps which have latterly been taken by some of the
slave States, have been rather of a retrograde than of a
progressive character; steps which nothing can justify,
not even the conduct of the more indiscreet partizans
of abolition. The States which have thus moved in
the wrong direction, have incurred a double guilt; and
it is on them and on the States which have refused
to move at all that the concentrated odium of the
world should fall.

In reply, again, to those on this side of the Atlantic,

who are really, or who only affect to be, outraged that
slavery is not instantaneously abolished in the Union,
the Americans, without justifying the inertness of
some of the slave States, simply plead the difficulties
of their position.   This is a plea to the cry for immediate abolition, which is not generally allowed that
weight with us to which it is justly entitled.   If we
say that we made a successful effort, and that they
might do the same if they were really in earnest; they
reply, that the circumstances of the two cases are altogether different.   We dealt summarily with a slight
complaint; they have to deal cautiously with an ag-
gravated disorder.   With us, slavery was a mere local
ailment, affecting some of the extremities of the empire; with them it is a fever which pervades the entire
system, which is in its blood, and is preying upon its
vitals.   When their political and social institutions
were first taken into their own hands, as an independent people, they were already stricken with this
moral leprosy, which yet adheres to them—a blasting
and a withering curse.   Such as were least impregnated
with the disease have since been cured; others are
advancing, by slow processes, towards convalescency,
whilst others have apparently resigned themselves to
the malady which may yet overpower and destroy them.
But at once to root out slavery from the southern
States is as hopeless as it would be to attempt to cure
the fevered patient in a breath.

We take a degree of credit too for what we have
done in the way of emancipation, which the Americans are not willing to accord us.   When they compare the means with the end, they hold that our
achievement was not so very wonderful after all.
What was the evil to be cured?   The servitude of a

comparatively small number of negroes in a few distant islands. What were the means of curing it?
The resources of a great and wealthy empire, to the
whole of which, the parts affected bore but a very
slender proportion. And what were the interests to
be affected? Those of a few planters, who constituted
the merest fraction of the entire population. All this
must be reversed to get at the true state of the case
in America. Instead of a remote and petty difficulty,
take a great evil existing in our very midst, as slavery
does in the United States, interweaving itself with the
political and social institutions of one half of the
Republic. Instead of remedial resources, immense and
boundless as compared with the evil to be removed,
take means, utterly inadequate to the object to be
attained; and instead of a few fractional interests to
be affected, take those, as in each of the southern
States, of the entire community. These are the points
of divergence, which show the two cases to be anything
but parallel. And if fifteen years have scarcely yet
passed since the whole philanthropy of the British
empire was able to overcome a petty interest, and to
extirpate a petty disorder; when, they ask, would it
have been equal to the task, had the result been to
affect the general interests of the country, by the sudden subversion of an institution, existing for centuries
at home—forming part and parcel of our political
scheme, and entering even into our domestic arrange-
ments—constituting, in short, one half of all our property, and having the value of the other half dependent upon its continuance? These are the circumstances in which we must conceive ourselves to be
placed, if we would fully understand the difficulties in
the way of emancipation in America. Slavery might

yet have been the law even of the northern States,
had they had one tithe of these difficulties to encounter. In these, as with us, slavery was the exception—
in the southern States it is the rule. Let those, then,
who here cry shame upon them for not immediately
liberating their slaves, bear in mind that their libera-
tion would affect the vested interests of a whole community—that it would divest most of that community
of fully one half of their property, and some, indeed,
of all; for, particularly in the low rice-growing districts on the Atlantic sea-board, alluded to in the previous chapter, when speaking of the configuration of
that part of the continent, property would be of no
value whatever, were there no slaves to cultivate it.
This does not remove or even extenuate the moral
guilt of slavery, but it accounts for the indisposition
manifested towards immediate abolition. It would be
a truly sublime spectacle to see a whole community
impoverish itself in vindication of a great principle;
but how old will be even the Christian era before such
a spectacle is exhibited? I use the word "impoverish,"
because it is an illusion to dream of compensation in
America. The number of slaves to be liberated is
already upwards of three millions, the compensation
for whom, at the same rate as that at which we compensated the planters, would exceed two hundred
millions sterling!

Some of the writers of the present day, who are
too enamoured of their own mawkish sentimentalities
to make any question the subject of patient and
practical inquiry, are constantly taunting the United
States with the inconsistency which they allege to
exist between their practice and their professions, as
contained in the Declaration of Independence. That

document proclaims that "all men are created equal,"
and, therefore, it is urged, it behoved the United
States to have swept away all the inequalities of condition which they found existing at the date of their
independence. But all that consistency demands is,
that, as fast as possible, without endangering the
general interests, they should establish a coincidence
between their practice and their professions. Are
men to be prohibited from laying down a great principle because they cannot at once carry it into effect;
or are they to be permitted to lay it down, and work
up to it with all practicable speed? I have no desire
to shelter such of the States as have acted, and are
still acting, in direct contradiction to the principles
on which they established their independence ; but
let justice be done to such as faithfully adhered to
them, and embodied them in their subsequent legislation. The principle of the Declaration is as inimical
to inequalities of condition between the members of
the white race, as it is to the continuance of a distinction, in any of the States, between the white and
black races. The property qualification, as a provi-
sion of the electoral law, was a violation of that
principle. And yet it was only from time to time
that the different States deemed it expedient to get
rid of that qualification, and to establish universal
suffrage in its stead. But who, before this was done,
ever heard the Declaration of Independence quoted
in favour of the unenfranchised white man ? Between
the white man so circumstanced, and the negro slave,
the difference is one of degree, not principle. If the
continuance, for a time, of the property qualification
was not inconsistent with that document, neither is
that of slavery for a time, when it is more inevitable than

voluntary. I admit that the Americans were bound,
by the principle of their Declaration, to remove all
civil and political disabilities pressing upon the white
man, as speedily as possible, consistently with the
interests of the country; and that they are now
bound to do the same, as fast as they safely can, with
regard to the blacks. But I deny that that principle
demands the immediate emancipation of the latter,
any more than it did the immediate enfranchisement
of those, who were previously disqualified, amongst the
former. Strange to say, many of those who taunt the
Americans with their inconsistency, as regards the
negroes, deplore the consistency with which they have
acted up to their principle, in reference to the whites.

The foregoing will suffice to convey, however imperfectly, some idea, at least, of the present bearing
and position of the whole question of slavery, both
as regards the conflict of parties respecting it in the
United States, and the merits of the issue which it
raises between the Republic and the rest of the world.
Greatly as the majority of the American people
deplore the imputations which it entails upon them,
and the scandal which it casts upon free institutions,
their anxieties are chiefly concentrated upon its
probable effect on the destinies of the Republic. It
raises a political problem, which no American can
contemplate with indifference, and in reference to
which few dare even to hazard a solution. Ever since
the formation of the Union, it has been its chief and
constant difficulty, giving rise to jealousies and dis-
quietudes, which have, more than once, perilled its
existence. Increasing, as the evil now is, both in
strength and magnitude, the future becomes more
lowering, if not more uncertain, every hour.

For many years back, aside of all other party questions, a struggle has been constantly maintained to keep up the balance of power between the free and slave States. This was comparatively easy, so long as the one interest could keep pace with the other, in the admission of new States into the Union. But when this, as it is about to do, ceases to be the case, how can the equipoise be preserved?

The Union is now composed of thirty different States, fifteen of which are free, and fifteen slave-holding. For some years back, new States have been introduced in couples, so as to preserve the established equilibrium. When Michigan was introduced as a free, Arkansas came in as a slave, State; Iowa was a free set-off to Florida, as a slave-holding acquisition; whilst Wisconsin was balanced against Texas. With the exception of the American portion of Oregon, there is now no available territory in the north, out of which free States may be created, to counterbalance the many slave States which may be carved out of the immense regions which are regarded as open for acquisition in the South. So long as both parties could play at State-making against each other, the crisis of the Slavery question was indefinitely postponed. But this game is about to cease, and the whole subject is now assuming an aspect of gravity, such as it has never before worn. Passing events are rapidly magnifying the difficulty; and the free communities are beginning seriously to consider the course which they should adopt, in the event of certain contingencies. A large accession of territory in the south-west will be a certain result of the Mexican war.* If slavery is to be extended over this

* California and New Mexico have since been annexed.

new territory, the northern States must follow one
of these courses:—they must seize the British provinces, dissolve the Union, or resign themselves to
the predominance of the slave-holding interest in the
councils of the nation. The first of these can hardly
enter seriously into their calculations; to the last
they will not submit. The question, then, seems to
lie between a dissolution of the Union, and the exemption from slavery of the newly-acquired territory.
But what will the South say to this alternative? With
a group of free States already on her northern border,
she would regard with apprehension the formation of
another such group upon her western flank. Both
parties have thus vital interests at stake; the South,
her domestic institutions; and the North, her just share
of influence in the legislation of the Union. What compromise can be effected between interests so irrecon-
cilable? The feeling in the North against the further
extension of slavery is already almost strong enough
to urge its inhabitants, if necessary, to the establishment of a free commonwealth of their own. No one
who has had the opportunity of canvassing the
opinions of the North on this point, can shut his eyes
to the fact, that it is fast reconciling itself to the
idea of such a change in its destiny. It is being
disgusted at the slow progress which is being made
towards emancipation by some of the slave States,
and the retrograde policy of others; and has long
been annoyed at its reputed partnership in the guilt
of those, over whom it has in reality no control; and
in the questionable advantages of whose guilt it has
no participation. In addition to this, the material
interests of the North are more or less implicated
in the question. It is now liable to be involved in all

the evils, expense included, of having to quell a
servile insurrection, should such break out. As
slavery extends its area, and otherwise increases its
strength, the chances of outbreaks are multiplied.
The integrity of the Union is one of the prime
objects of an American's political affections. It is a
sentiment from which no question but that of slavery
can divorce him; and that question is now fast
approaching the crisis, which, it has long been fore-
seen, will be the great test of the strength of the
constitutional fabric. If the North could see its way
through the difficulty without separation, it would
indignantly discard the idea of dissolution. It is
because they do not thus see their way, that the best
and most patriotic of its inhabitants are now beginning to regard as probable, that which they have
longed wished were impossible. How will the question terminate? Will the North yield? Will the
South yield? Will they meet each other's views,
and both yield? In such case what will be the compromise? Let him, who can, answer these questions.

It would be a singular, yet a fitting retribution, if
the war, which the present administration so unjus-
tifiably provoked with Mexico, should result in the
disintegration of the Union.

It would baffle, I trust, the most determined effort
at misinterpretation, to put a wrong construction upon
the foregoing, either as regards the object sought to
be attained by it, or the spirit in which it has been
conceived. The object has been to represent things
as they really are, to give a true picture of a veritable
case, and to divest a great question, on which the
judgment of the world should alone be exercised, of
the false colouring which ignorance and prejudice

have given it. The spirit in which this object has been pursued, is that of justice; justice to the guilty as well as to the innocent. If I have pointed out those whom censure should spare, I have also designated those on whom it should unreservedly fall. In doing this, I have adverted to the position and views of parties in regard to slavery in America; explained the legal and constitutional question with which they have to deal; pointed out those who alone have the power to interfere, and those who are interdicted from interfering; described what has already been done, and what still remains to be done; exposed the difficulties of the question, which constitute the defence of the South only against the zealots at home, and the philanthropists abroad, who would urge her to instantaneous abolition; and alluded, in conclusion, to the growing importance of the question, as one affecting the entire country, and involving the most serious political consequences to the Union. Having done so, I leave the reader to his own deductions; confident, however, that he will acknowledge the injustice of involving the whole people, for the faults of a section, in indiscriminate censure, and see that the Northern States are no more responsible for the social and political vices of the South, than the Canton of Berne is for the religious intolerance of Fribourg, or the Germanic Confederation for the vagaries of the Court of Bavaria.*

* The annexation of California and New Mexico, since the foregoing was written, will have an important bearing upon the whole question of slavery, which will be adverted to in the concluding chapter of this work.

CHAPTER V.

SLAVERY,—IN ITS SOCIAL, MORAL, AND ECONOMICAL ASPECT.

HAVING disposed of the question of Slavery in its
political aspect, I now proceed to consider it in its
social, moral, and economical bearings.

In dealing with the subject in its social and moral
phase, it may be as well, first, to advert to the actual
condition of the slaves themselves, and then glance at
the general effects of the institution upon the society
in the midst of which it exists.

As is always the case where slavery is to be found,
the slaves in the United States are divided into two

classes, domestic and predial ; and the institution partakes of its milder or more relentless features, according to the predominance of the one or the other of these
classes in a State. Taking the slave States throughout, the predial slaves vastly outnumber those who
are held to domestic bondage ; and it is this great
predominance of predial servitude that gives its general character to the institution of slavery in America.
The proportion between the two classes of slaves greatly
varies in the different States. In Georgia, Alabama,
and Mississippi, the vast majority are held to field
and out-door work ; whilst in Virginia and Kentucky,
the numbers of the two classes are more nearly
equalized. In Virginia particularly, the class of
domestic slaves is very numerous, as is also the case
in Maryland ; although in the latter, the slaves engaged in field labour bear a greater proportion to
those in merely domestic servitude than in the
former.

It is naturally to be expected that, in those States
in which the number of domestic slaves is greatest, in
proportion to the whole number held in bondage, the
system should develope itself in its mildest form. This
is preeminently so in Virginia ; and if the stranger
penetrates no further into the slave States, he is very
apt to regard slavery with less abhorrence than he
might formerly have entertained for it. The principle is equally objectionable under whatever form it
exhibits itself; but if there is anything in the practical working of the system calculated to reconcile
one in the least degree to its principle, it will be
found in the mild aspect which it has assumed in
Virginia. There is this in favour of domestic slavery,
that the master and bondman are less frequently
separated than the predial slave is from his owner.

The agricultural slave is, in innumerable instances, frequently transferred from master to master, the object of each being to extract from him as much work as possible ; whilst domestic slaves frequently remain for generations on the same property, and in subjection to the same family. Even when the out-door slave continues for life in the same ownership, it is but seldom that he comes in contact with his master, and when he does so, it is only when the master himself undertakes the duty of the overseer, to whose merciless superintendence slaves of his class are generally entrusted. The case is different, how-ever, in Virginia, where the parties frequently con-tinue for life in the relation of master and servant, and are coming constantly in personal contact with each other. A mutual attachment is thus engendered between them ; and instead of grinding oppression on the one side, and smothered hate on the other, kindly sympathies spring up, and the humanity of the master is rewarded by the love of the dependent. I have frequently witnessed the length to which this attach-ment on both sides may be carried, so as to render the tie between the parties indissoluble, the master refusing on any consideration to part with the slave, and the slave refusing, under every circumstance, to quit his master; turning a deaf ear, as the latter does, in numerous instances, to the Abolitionists, who, when they find him in a free State with his master, endeavour to seduce him from his allegiance. Slaves of this class generally live under the same roof as the family whom they serve, and amongst the different members of which they are, as already noticed, fre-quently apportioned. They are well clothed and well fed ; and the labour which they undergo is, in amount, far inferior, generally speaking, to that to which domestic servants in England are subjected. When seen only in this aspect, slavery appears to be more a theoretical than a practical infliction. If the sentiment of freedom be not dead within the slave, he has much in the unstinted store of physical comforts which surround him, to repay him for the deprivation of abstract liberty. The possession of the abstract idea is all that the free labourer of Europe has to recommend a condition, which in most cases is, in everything else, inferior to the condition of the domestic class of American bondmen.

But, unfortunately, this is not the only side which slavery has to exhibit. It appears in its true light, in its real character, in all its revolting atrocities, in the cotton-growing States. Whatever hideousness may be imparted to it by severity of toil and brutality of treatment, it there assumes without a mask. Badly housed, and not unfrequently scantily fed, the wretched slaves are driven, morning after morning, in hordes to the fields, where they labour till night-fall beneath a burning sun, and under the eyes and the lashes of superintendents, against whom they dare not, however well founded, prefer a complaint. To the unfeeling severity which characterises the servitude of these States, there are, in the conduct of many planters, very honourable exceptions. It is natural for an American, even when loud in his condemnation of the system at home, to gloss over, in his converse with mankind, its worst features, for his country's sake; but the candour of every American citizen who has travelled in the South will bear me out in the assertion, that, in the practical working of slavery in the cotton-growing districts, humanity is the exception, and brutality the rule. It is unnecessary to dwell any longer upon this, or to specify the horrors which I myself have witnessed, and which would only be counterparts to the frightful catalogue, at the recital of which the better feelings of our nature have already so often revolted.

The slaves in America have their determinate place in the social scheme; and yet it seems to savour of anomaly to speak of their social standing. They have few social, and no political, privileges, whatever consideration is attached to them, of the one kind or the other, having a reference more to the interests of their owners than of themselves. A slave is protected by law in life and limb, but more with a view to the protection of his master's property than to the secure enjoyment of his own "inalienable rights." In few of the slave States can a white man be criminally convicted, on the testimony of slaves. There may be reasons why, in a state of society like that which the South presents, objection might be taken to a slave's credibility as a witness; but no polity can justify a sweeping objection to his competency as one. One shudders to think of the number of crimes of every intensity of dye, which may, and which do, go unpunished for want of white testimony, wherewith to inculpate the guilty party. There is a necessity for making some distinction, else the lives and the reputation of the whites would, in many cases, be sworn away out of sheer revenge; but it is one of the curses of the system, that it can only prevent one evil by resorting to another; that it can only protect the whites, by the infliction of another monstrous injustice upon the blacks. Whatever may be the advantages of the political weight which the Constitution attaches to the slaves, they are not permitted to share them. It is for the benefit of the free race, one way or another, that they are noticed in that document.

And when they are so, it is not by the term "slaves," but by the periphrase, "persons held to labour or service." The framers of the Constitution were either very confident or very sentimental. Looking forward to the speedy extirpation of slavery, they would not sully the federal charter by including the word in the text of any of its paragraphs. Until all were free, they deemed it advisable to call slavery by another name. Had they been framing the Constitution to-day, instead of about the close of last century, their sentimentality might be quite as great, but their hopes would scarcely be as strong. In apportioning the representation in the Lower House of Congress amongst the different States, the extent of the population in each is taken as the basis of the apportionment. In the slave States, the extent of the population is ascertained by adding to the whole number of free persons three-fifths of all the slaves; and according to the number thus ascertained, is the extent of the representation of each slave State in Congress. It is scarcely necessary, however, to say that, although the slaves enter largely into the scheme, they have no share whatever in the reality of representation. The result is, that the free citizen in the slave States is doubly represented; in the first place, personally, like his fellow-citizen in the north, and in the next, by virtue of three-fifths of his property. But if this arrangement has its advantages it has also its drawbacks, as all direct taxes are to be apportioned on the same principle as the representation. I know of no direct tax, however, which the general Government now levies.

A state of servitude implies an incapacity to hold or to acquire property. The slave, being himself the property of his master, draws legally after him, into his master's possession, everything which might else appertain to himself. Not only can he, strictly speaking, earn nothing for himself, but he is also incapable of becoming the recipient, to his own benefit, of a pure donation. In few countries, however, where slavery exists, is the law, in this respect, rigidly carried out. It certainly, as a general rule, is not so in the United States. It is true that the master sometimes avails himself of the absolute property which he thus has in the slave, and in all that he can produce, when he himself is not in need of his labour, to let him out on hire to others, confiscating his earnings to his own uses. This is a practice which extensively prevails in the District of Columbia, particularly in Washington. The hotel at which I took up my quarters in that city, was provided with none but black servants,—all slaves, who, with some few exceptions, were on hire. They came to duty at a certain hour in the morning, many of them returning home at a particular hour at night to their respective owners. By eight o'clock at night all slaves must be housed; and any found abroad after that hour, without being able to give a proper explanation, are liable to be challenged by any one, and brought before the authorities. This curfew law is not confined to the District of Columbia. But it not unfrequently happens that, to encourage them, their owners only appropriate to themselves the earnings of a certain number of hours per day, or of days per week, leaving the remainder at their own disposal.

It is customary, too, particularly for those who employ their own slaves in handicraft operations, to give them a set daily task, and to pay them for any extra work over and above that thus apportioned to them.

Lord though he be of all his bondman's energies, the master finds this system work to his advantage, as it stimulates to the accomplishment of a thorough day's work one who would otherwise scarcely exert himself to the extent of half his powers. In one of the tobacco factories, at Richmond, I saw a tall, athletic man at work under the influence of this stimulus. He was married; had already purchased his wife's freedom, and was then labouring for the means of acquiring his own. His expertness and activity were extraordinary, sometimes earning for him, by extra work, no less than ten dollars a week. They certainly do not all make so good a use of the means which they thus and otherwise procure, strange though it may appear, their vanity being, in most cases, an overmatch for their discretion. This weakness with them exhibits itself principally in dress. Talk of a Bond-street dandy! he is nothing to a full-blown negro in Washington or Philadelphia on a holiday. There is something intensely ludicrous in his coxcombry, as, with gloved hands, flaunting frills, an enormous display of spotless linen about his sable cheeks, and with a dress of superfine broad cloth, evidently of the latest cut, he goes stalking along, switching his cane, and indifferent to the ridicule he excites—as vain as a turkey, and as gaudy as a sunflower. This passion for dress exhibits itself, if possible, with tenfold intensity amongst the females. Often have I walked, on a hot summer day, in the streets of the capital, behind a mass of faultless muslins and other "stuffs," which enter into the composition of ladies' attire, neatly arranged over a form well rounded and graceful; and on turning partly round to steal a glance at the exquisite face, which my imagination had pictured as necessarily forming part and parcel of this otherwise attractive exterior, been startled at encountering the rolling eye, flat nose, and thick protruding lips of a stalwart negress, as black as if the sun of Guinea had shone upon her but the day before. This inordinate passion for dress developes itself in the whole race, free or bond. Of course, such as are free have the greatest opportunities of gratifying it; and the mode in which it is gratified enters not a little into the *coup-d'œil* of Pennsylvania-avenue, Chestnut-street, and Broadway.

If the physical necessities of the slave are, in numerous cases, well cared for, his intellectual and moral wants are, in almost all, most culpably neglected. Servitude cannot long co-exist with intelligence; and to keep the slave from the path of freedom it is necessary to deprive him of those moral lights by which his steps might be directed into it. This is a conviction which largely influences the policy of the South, and which has, in most of the slave States, raised a legislative barrier against every effort to enlighten the mental and moral darkness of the negro. The domestic slaves may, as individuals, but certainly not as a class, present exceptions to the unrelieved stolidity and ignorance which characterise the race; for it is seldom that the education even of a household slave transcends the line of his daily duties. It is almost impossible to conceive the utter intellectual vacuity to which the predial slave is doomed; his deprivation, in many cases, extending even to those elementary religious teachings which are of such moment even to the meanest of mankind. It is not usual to find things carried to this culpable extent in the towns, where the slaves are more in the

habit of meeting each other than they are upon isolated country estates, and where fewer impediments
are successfully thrown in the way of religion and
humanity. In the towns you sometimes find them
well provided with churches, but rarely with schools;
the children being indebted to the Sunday-school
for such education as they receive, both secular and
religious, which is in general, in neither case, of a
very sterling quality. They have their own preach-
ers, and generally attach themselves to the more enthusiastic and fanatical sects. I have found them
Presbyterians, Baptists, Methodists, and Latter-Day
Saints, but never Episcopalians. A black priest in
lawn sleeves would bring scandal on the Episcopal
body. Except in times of religious excitement,
when the most disgusting scenes are enacted, and the
most frantic and blasphemous ravings are uttered in
their conventicles, under the supposed influence of the
Spirit, their worship is conducted with tolerable order
and decorum, although it is not always practicable to
suppress the smile to which the extraordinary fancies
of the preacher will give rise. In times of revival
they sometimes become roused into a state of uncon-
trollable frenzy, when they neglect their duties, and
become troublesome and unmanageable. It was in
allusion to this that a Virginian very naively once
said to me, that " it was the greatest misfortune that
could happen to them to have a nigger turn Christian."

The mind denied a proper and healthful development is apt to take refuge in deformity. Where
there is soil there is production. Weeds spring up
where a growth, useful or ornamental, is not cherished. Thus it is that the mind of the slave,

deprived by law of all proper instruction, becomes
strongly impregnated with cunning and deceit. These,
with falsehood, are the only weapons which he possesses, with which to avenge himself on his oppressor.
It is seldom, except when a mutual attachment happens to exist between them, that the master and the
slave have any confidence in each other; the one
commands, the other obeys through fear. The
moral obliquity which usually characterises the slave,
is common, to some extent, to the free negroes of the
North. Although politically free, the latter are far
from being on a footing of social equality with the
white race, towards whom they more or less demean
themselves as do the slaves towards their masters.
Although some in the free States profess to be partial
to negro servants, the great majority, sooner than
have anything to do with them, submit to the
humours and caprices of servants of their own race.

Notwithstanding the weight with which oppression bears upon them, and the cruelties to which they
are subjected, the negroes in America exhibit a light-
heartedness which is surprising. To the great bulk
of them freedom is a hopeless aspiration; the very
desire for it is systematically subdued in their breasts;
and they are happy if their physical wants are supplied, and they are not overtasked with labour.
Having no future to live for, they make the present
as merry as possible. Of singing and dancing they
are inordinately fond, propensities in which policy
dictates that they should be encouraged rather
than interfered with. The banjo, a sort of rude
guitar, is their chief instrumental accompaniment;
whilst in dancing, proficiency with them seems to
consist in making an elaborate use of the heel. Their

voices are generally good and well trained by themselves; their airs are simple and frequently touchingly
plaintive. It is amusing to witness the zest with which
on a summer-evening, after the work of the day is over,
they will thus enjoy themselves in groups—some singing, some playing on instruments, jabbering, grinning,
and frantically gesticulating at the same time, and
others dancing with an earnestness which would lead
one to the belief that they considered it the main
business of life. But all this playfulness of disposition is sometimes only a mask used to conceal a burning thirst for vengeance, which is sometimes gratified
under circumstances of the most dreadful atrocity.

Slavery, considered in connexion with the influence which it exercises upon society, developes in
America all the vicious tendencies with which it has
ever been characterised. Whether its consequences,
in this respect, are considered in an economical or a
social point of view, they are found to be equally
prejudicial.

In many particulars society in the South differs
materially from the manifestation of it which is found
in the North. In the latter, activity takes the place of
refinement; in the former, refinement takes the place
of activity. As there is no want of refinement in the
North, so there is no absolute want of activity in the
South; but the one is characteristic of northern
society, as the other is of that of the south; and in
this one particular of refinement alone is the result
of slavery on southern society in the least degree
favourable. For this one benefit it sacrifices to slavery
every other advantage. I have elsewhere shown how
the superior refinement of southern manners is directly attributable, in part, to the existence of slavery.

The activity which pervades the North is greatly to be attributed to its absence, making every man feel the necessity of self-reliance, and driving men to do that properly for themselves, which forced labour would do but sluggishly and imperfectly for them.

It is not an absolute torpor which has fallen upon the European race in the South. There is no reason why their energies should be greatly inferior to those of their northern fellow-countrymen, nor am I aware that they are; the difference is in this, that their respective energies are directed into different channels. The southerner very often prosecutes his amusements as actively as the northerner engages in sterner occupations. But the reason why the activity of the North is so much more visible than that of the South, aside of the fact that it is a more numerous community, all being employed, is, that whilst the southerner's energies are generally devoted to pursuits which leave little or no trace behind them, those of the northern citizen are applied to objects which both take and perpetuate the impress of industry.

For all truly industrial purposes, the energies of the white race in the South might be as well utterly extinguished. They have a triple reason for abstaining from labour, unknown in the rest of the Union. They have, in the first place, an enervating climate as compared with that of the northern States; in the next, they are surrounded with hordes of human beings, who are fed and clothed for the sole purpose of working for them; and in the next, which is the most powerful reason of all, labour is considered degrading and dishonourable. In the North the very opposite feeling obtains. There is no class there exempt from work; and a perfectly idle man, particularly if a young

man, gets rather into discredit than otherwise. Where
all are employed, none can consider it a degradation to be
so; and such is the eager pursuit of material well-being
in the North, that there are few who can work as
much as they would like to do. But in the South,
where there is an aristocracy of idleness, few whites have
the courage to descend to the level of labour. When
to this is added the aristocracy of race, which, when
the two races meet, really seems to have its foundation in nature itself, and when the inferior and degraded race is alone the labouring one, the descent is
still greater, being not only that from a wealthy and
an idle to an industrious class, but also to an identification with a race in every way debased, and who
are treated as if it was their highest privilege to
labour for their masters. This much at least the South
owes to slavery, that the white man, however needy,
cannot work for his bread without putting himself,
in a social point of view, on a level with the slave.

Nowhere can the unfortunate result of this be
better traced than in Virginia. Since the abolition
of the law of primogeniture, the large estates, which
were once so numerous in that State, have in many
instances gradually dwindled away, the descendants
of those who once possessed them retaining all the
pride, but without any of the means of their ancestors. Many of these, reduced to want, have preferred subsisting on the bounty of their friends to
working for a livelihood. Others, more manly and
independent, have betaken themselves to honest em-
ployments, but to seek them have quitted their native
State, and gone where, by their own industry, they
could push their own fortunes without being degraded by so doing. This is one reason why, whilst

the population of the northern and western States is
so rapidly on the increase; the white population of
Virginia has recently actually receded. But the
numbers who are being gradually driven to employ-
ment in Virginia are now so great as to necessitate an
effort to rescue labour from its present disrepute. In
this the Virginians are aided by the energetic whites,
who emigrate to their State from the north; and who,
finding a wide field for their enterprise, where the
labour of the slave is the only competition which they
encounter, disregard all local prejudices, and set the
Virginians an example which many of them are glad
to follow.

An important branch of the subject is that connected
with the moral influence of slavery. Where has this
ever been favourable? The difference between the
morals of the North and South is great, and great in
proportion as slavery in the latter partakes of its more
unmitigated features. Making every allowance for
the difference of climate, that cannot of itself explain
the phenomenon. It is only under a system, which
promotes a laxity of habits, blunts the moral perceptions, engenders leisure, and fosters pride, that could
arise those quick resentments, that morbid sensitive-
ness, that false sense of honour, that proneness to
quarrel, and that indifference to human life, which so
broadly distinguish genuine society in the South from
the Anglo-Saxon type which it has preserved in the
North. There is something unfavourable to the development of the better feelings of our nature, when
the mind becomes reconciled to a monstrous violation
of the laws of nature. A Southerner's reconciliation
to the injustice of slavery dates from his very infancy.
It is thus that, in the moral race, he does not get a

fair start with those whose perceptions are not thus early beclouded. It is singular to witness the indifference with which all parties in the South come to regard slavery, with all its accompaniments. I once heard a lady thus accost a negro boy, in one of the back streets of Washington: " I want a boy, but the Doctor asks too much for you." In other words, she had been engaged in a negociation with his then owner, for the purchase of this very boy, and spoke of the matter with as much *sang froid* as an English woman would of the purchase of a cabbage at Covent Garden.

But if slavery be thus socially, morally, and, as will be presently seen, economically, a disadvantage, why, it will be asked, do not the people of the South get rid of it? Having already adverted, in general terms, to the difficulties which stand in the way, let me here briefly allude more particularly to the nature of some of them.

I must here again remind the reader that, in the North, where slavery has been abolished, it never attained the colossal magnitude into which it has expanded in the South. When, therefore, it was found in the former to be more prejudicial than advantageous even to material progress, it was easily discarded. The same conviction as to its worse than inutility has long since dawned upon the South, but its extirpation there would now almost seem to be impossible. Even were it otherwise practicable, the magnitude of the interests to be affected by it would be an almost insuperable barrier in its way; but the chief obstacle must be elsewhere sought for. The reader may be surprised, but that obstacle is to be found in the *antipathy of race.*

It is scarcely possible for a European who has not

witnessed it, to appreciate the intensity of this feeling on the part of the white race in America. They will amalgamate with the Indians, and are frequently proud of the aboriginal blood in their veins; but merely as partners in licentiousness will they have any converse with the negroes. Under no circumstances can the negro attain in America an equal social position with the dominant race. It matters not what proportion of white blood he may have in his veins, if he bears about him any signs—and they are ineradicable for generations—of an African origin, he is kept aloof as if his touch were leprosy. Bond or free, his fate is the same. Indeed, so far from his manumission bettering his condition, in this respect it only renders it worse. So long as he is a slave, the master may, when he pleases, treat him as an equal, because he can at any moment place him again at an infinite distance. But when the two are put in a condition of political equality, the white is chary of admitting him to a social position of which it might not be so easy to divest him. Thus the privileges of the free black are more nominal than real, whilst their very possession places the dominant race in more hopeless antagonism with him than before. It is all very well for us in Europe to philosophise upon the nature of man, and to urge that man is man, whatever be the colour of his skin or the cast of his features. There are feelings which can neither be reasoned with nor overcome, and the antipathy in question is one of them. It has always existed, and is likely ever to exist in the breast of the white man, and is most active where the two races come most in contact. This forbids their ever mingling together and fusing into one mixed race; and it is because they must thus remain two separate races that emancipation is to the South surrounded with so many perils.

It may be asked, Why did not all this operate to the prevention of emancipation in the North? Simply because, although there was the same objection in kind, there was not the same in degree. In New York, for instance, the slave population was never numerous, and the free blacks scarcely now amount to two per cent. of the whole population. This great predominance of the white race removed all the fears, which might otherwise have existed, as to the evil consequences of emancipation. It did not permit the blacks to approach any nearer the whites, but it obviously made them powerless for mischief. The precepts of religion, the dictates of morality, and the interests of the State, then, all concurring to urge upon it a policy which could be adopted without hazard, the abolition of slavery was as necessary as it was easy of attainment. Very different, however, is the case with the South, in some of the States of which the negroes form sixty per cent. of the entire population. Under these circumstances, is it likely that the existence of two free, but isolated and alien races on the same territory would be compatible with the security of either? So long as they co-exist in peace in their present numbers on the continent, must they co-exist in their present relations. They cannot exist together the equals of each other. One or the other must dominate. This being so, can it be expected that the now dominant race will consent even to run the risk of exchanging places with the subject one? That they would incur this risk by emancipation is obvious. The blacks once free, would they depart? Why should they? How could they?

Whither would they go? How long would two free races thus situated, refusing to commingle in any of the relations of social life, remain in harmony on the same soil? Not long, even if the blacks had no past wrongs to avenge.

The great question then for the South is, What is to be done with the blacks in the event of manumission? It is because it cannot solve this question that it cannot decide upon emancipation. And what does it gain by delay? Only the postponement of the catastrophe, which must inevitably occur. Whether the negroes are set at liberty, or remain enchained, the war of races is an event in the certain future. The result will not be long doubtful. With their superior skill, their discipline, their knowledge, and their wealth, the European race in the Southern States alone will prove an overmatch for the African. But with the aid of the whole North, on which they reckon with confidence in such an event, the contest is not likely, come when it may, to be of long continuance. And that aid will be given, even should the ties of the Union have been previously sundered; for in nothing are the American people more determined than this, that no black community shall, for and by themselves, occupy any portion of the North American continent.

This inevitable contest will be postponed until it is precipitated by the blacks themselves. Until it is so, they will be kept in bondage, and the more numerous and powerful they become, the more tightly will their chains be drawn around them. There can be little doubt but that their ultimate fate will be that of expulsion from the continent. But what untold miseries on all sides will be the prelude to such a consummation!

This is the true position of the South. Let an Englishman fancy himself in a similar one, not self-placed, but born in it, and inextricably entangled in its meshes, if he would judge impartially in the case. Let him do this, and learn to temper the severity of his judgment with sympathy for those who, by the faults of their ancestors, have been placed in so painful, so perplexing, so frightful a position.

I have taken it for granted, in what has preceded, that slavery is disadvantageous, even in an economical point of view. At this time of day it is scarcely necessary to enter into an elaborate argument in proof of this. It may be as well, however, here just to allude to the principal points which bear upon this part of the question in America.

It was not until slavery had been for some time established in the South that it extended itself to the North at all, and its extension in that direction was more the result of example than of any necessity which was felt for it. Whilst it was yet confined to the South, the northern colonies had evinced an aptitude for improvement, which those of the South could not exhibit. Yet the European race in the South was sprung as recently and directly from the common Anglo-Saxon stock as was that in the North. To the dependence upon the forced labour of others, to which their climate, particularly in the more southern districts, to some extent invited them, is chiefly to be attributed the striking difference which manifested itself in the development of the northern and southern colonies. Before they had actual proof of the inutility and positive disadvantage of slavery, the northern colonists had experienced the benefits of self-reliance and personal activity. In naturalising slavery amongst them they brought the two systems into immediate competition; and that it was not long before the result of the experiment was decided in favour of free labour is evident from the fact, that in none of the northern colonies did slavery ever attain any footing beyond that of an exceptional institution. The superiority of free labour once demonstrated, the extension of slavery was necessarily checked. Unfortunately for the South, it witnessed the experiment only from a distance; it never actually tested for itself the respective merits of free labour and servitude. It was thus that the latter, having no competitor in the field, expanded with a rapidity which, by degrees, left the South no alternative but to let it take its course.

But it was not solely by keeping slavery within a narrow compass that the North recorded its verdict in favour of free labour. By its entire abolition they also testified to the world their conviction as to the merits of slavery. When it was at its greatest height in the North, the effect of slavery upon the free labour system which prevailed was scarcely perceptible. In tracing, therefore, from the very first, the career of the two groups of colonies, we are in fact sitting in judgment upon the conflicting pretensions of the two systems of labour. And if material progress is to be the turning point of our decision, the evidence of superiority is all on one side. The colonies of the North, although the last founded, were constantly in advance of those in the South; demonstrating by their rapid increase, both in population and wealth, the economical superiority of their prevailing system. And what may thus be said of them as colonies is also true of them as independent States.

The inertness of the South affords to this day a painful contrast to the cheerful activity of the North. The one merely subsists; the other both subsists and accumulates. If we would be eyewitnesses of that energy and enterprise which so distinguish the American character, it is in the North chiefly that we must look for it.

The sources of wealth are pretty equally distributed over the continent. The South has its full share of them as regards soil, and vegetable and mineral products. Why does it not turn them to that profit to which all these advantages are converted in the North? The plea of climate has only a partial relevancy. It may disincline, but it does not incapacitate to work. The northern immigrant into the southern States proves by his conduct the justness of this distinction. He works for himself, and what is there to prevent the southerner from doing the same? Simply, the difference in his character, superinduced by a difference in institutions. The northerner, brought up in a rugged school, becomes imbued with the ideas and ingrained with the habits of self-dependence, and carries with him the energies of his character whithersoever his adventurous disposition may lead him. The southerner, on the other hand, bred in the lap of ease and luxury, becomes impatient of enterprise, and recoils from exertion. Even the chief mining and manufacturing operations in the South are carried on by northern enterprise and capital. Tried then by the best of all tests, that of its actual results, what room is there for attributing any economical advantages to slavery? If any one entertains a doubt upon the subject, let him contrast the condition of New York and Pennsylvania with that of Maryland and Virginia; that of Ohio with that of Kentucky; that of Indiana or Illinois with that of Tennesee. Between some of these there are only imaginary boundary lines, between others only the chanel of a river intervenes. Their striking difference of condition can only be traced to their great difference in institutions; and some of them are admirably situated for making the comparison. There is very little difference as to climate, soil, or productions between Ohio and Western Virginia, which abuts upon it; or between Ohio, Indiana, and Illinois, and the State of Kentucky, which bounds them to the south, the Ohio river alone dividing them. So forcible indeed is the inference to be deduced from all this, that it has long since pressed itself upon the convictions of the South. But the curse which rests upon this section of the Union is, that what its interest, in one sense, urges it to dispense with, its interest, in another, seemingly necessitates it to retain.

In saying that the climate of the South does not incapacitate the European from working, exception must be taken as regards the low and swampy coast districts of the Carolinas, Georgia, Alabama, and Louisiana, in which, as already observed, no white person, during certain portions of the year, can safely remain. There can be no doubt that free labour, if it could be steadily applied even to these districts, would render them more profitable than they now are. But how to do this is the difficulty. The white man cannot labour there. But if the black man can as a slave, why not also as a freeman? Simply because few free blacks, having their choice of locality, would remain there. Though not so fatal to the African as to the European, there is no doubt

but that these pestilential regions are fraught with
danger and death to both. Withdraw coercion from
those by whose labour they are cultivated, and they
would become depopulated. This shows the stake
which the possessors of land in these districts have in
the continuance of slavery. To them it is a question
of property or no property, and their influence is, of
course, regardless of ultimate consequences, steadily
exerted for the perpetuation of servitude. This
has a greater effect upon the whole question of
abolition than at first appears. The slave States
being all more or less dependent upon the same
staple productions, slavery could not well be abolished in some without being abolished in all. For
some time at least, such cotton-growing States as
resorted to free labour could not compete with those
which still adhered to the system of slavery. Its
abolition, therefore, in some of the slave States,
would, as its immediate consequence, only stimu-
late its extension in others. Even were there no
other obstacles in the way, this would of itself be
almost an insuperable one, owing to the difficulty
which would be experienced in getting the whole of
the slave States to move together in the direction of
abolition.

Independently of all comparison between the free
and the slave States, some of the latter have abundant proof, in the working of the system itself, of the
utter inutility of slavery. To no State is this now
more apparent than to Virginia, which enjoys the
unenviable notoriety of being the chief slave-breeding
State. In general, slaves are now valued in Virginia
at what they are likely to bring in the market, and
this their market value is the chief object for which

they are " raised." When all the States in the Union
shall have prohibited the further importation of
slaves into their territories from any of the adjoining
States, the slaves in Virginia will be a positive burden upon the State, and regarded in the light of so
much unsaleable stock. The extension of slavery to
the newly acquired territory of Texas has enlarged
the demand for slaves and protracted their export
from this and other States. Should the regions
ceded by Mexico share the fate of Texas in this
respect, the time will be still further postponed ere
slavery becomes an intolerable burden to Virginia.
But that time will come, when those in whom she
now traffics will accumulate upon her hands and eat
up her substance.

It may be asked why, if slavery is regarded by all
parties as fraught with such danger to the Republic,
the South is so anxious to extend it? It is so, because it desires to retain its political influence in the
Union. Should the North secure a decided ascend-
ancy, the South might be ere long involved in ruin
and confusion, by a forcible attack upon her institutions. It is to prevent the possibility of this, that
she is constantly striving to extend her political
influence by extending the area of slavery. True to
the failings of our common humanity, she is in this
avoiding an immediate danger at the risk of adding
to her ultimate difficulties.

But, in addition to those of the slave States, there
are other interests, which are deeply concerned in
the merits of slavery in an economical point of view.
But little of the great staple product of the South is
converted at home into fabrics of any kind. The
raw cotton, which is the chief product of slave labour,

finds its way into the markets of the world, Old and
New England taking together about seven-tenths of
the whole. It may be urged that as the manufacturing
interest, both here, on the continent, and in America,
are deeply interested in low-priced cotton, the abolition of slavery, by raising the price of the raw material, would be greatly injurious to them. This
objection would have some weight, but for the consideration that it would equally affect the manufacturers everywhere. If the price of the raw material
rose, the remedy would be in their own hands, which
they would apply in the shape of an enhanced price
for their goods. All being equally affected, none
could undersell the other more than at present, and
the manufactures of Europe and America would
meet in neutral markets, upon the same terms as
now. The consumers would be the chief sufferers,
and it would be from diminished consumption
that the manufacturers everywhere would feel the
effect of the change. But this, were it to happen,
would not last long, as the production of cotton
would be stimulated elsewhere, to an extent which
would soon reduce prices to their former level. All
this, however, is based upon the assumption that the
application of free labour to the growth of cotton in
America would materially enhance its price. My
conviction is that this would not be so. It is certainly reasonable to suppose that that which is the
product of labour which is paid for, would be dearer
than that produced by labour which is not paid for.
But the mistake in this case is in taking it for
granted that slave labour is not paid for. Let us
compare the present process of producing cotton with
that under a system of free labour. To meet a given

demand, the South raises a given quantity of cotton.
To do this she keeps a certain number of labourers,
each of whom, on an average, does but half a man's
work.   They are cheaply fed and cheaply clothed, it
is true; but then they are fed, and clothed, and
housed during life, at their owner's expense; including the time when they are incapable from
infancy to work, and disabled from so doing by old
age.   The consideration, then, for the labour of the
slave is his " keep;" both in infancy and age, when
he cannot work, and during his maturity, when he
only gives per day half a day's work to his owner.
Then again, it is not always during maturity that
he can be kept at work, inasmuch as there is not
always work for him to do.   But he is still on his master's hands a never ceasing expense.   Now what is the
case with free labour?   It is sought for, and paid for,
only when required.   It is the employer's own fault
if he will pay a man for his work, who does not give
him in return a full day's work for his money.   Thus
the hired labourer, in consideration of his reward,
gives the work of two slaves in a given time; so that
in estimating the cost of the two kinds of labour, we
must place against his wages the keep of two slaves
from their birth to their death, and at all seasons of
the year.   By which of the two systems is it likely that
the whole cotton required could be the more cheaply
raised?   It might require more ready capital on the
part of the South to raise it by means of free labour,
but it would be found by far the cheaper process in
the end.   One hired labourer, receiving his daily
wages only whilst at work, would take the place of
every two slaves, who are now kept the whole year
round, during the whole course of their lives.   The

fears, then, connected with a permanent rise in the price of raw cotton would seem to be groundless.

In the face of all this, the continuance of slavery can only be accounted for on the grounds already adverted to. And in dismissing the whole subject let me remind the reader that the peculiar position of the Southern States is this, that they are afflicted with an evil which they fear to attempt the removal of; an evil already grown beyond their control, and increasing in magnitude every hour; an evil of which nothing but a social convulsion can rid them; which when it comes, as it assuredly will, may give rise to a political disposition of the continent as yet undreamt of.

CHAPTER VI.

FROM RICHMOND TO CHARLESTON.

THE long chain of railway commencing at Boston, and continuing, almost without interruption, southward to Richmond, crosses the James River at the latter city on its way to Carolina and Georgia. The portion of the railway which runs through Virginia, intersects the State by a line running almost due north and south, beginning at the Aquia Creek, on the Potomac, and terminating at Weldon, on the border of North Carolina. This link of the great chain is about 160 miles in length, the city of Richmond lying about midway between its extremities. From Weldon it pursues its way across the State of North Carolina to Wilmington, where it abuts upon the Atlantic, the journey from Wilmington to Charleston being performed by steamboat.

I left Richmond by the early train for Weldon. The railway is carried over the rapids of the James by means of a stupendous wooden bridge, erected at a great height above the water upon a number of lofty stone piers, the bases of which are washed by the foaming rapids. There is no balustrade or railing on either side; and it is not without some little apprehension that the traveller, as he crosses it, looks down upon the water lashed far beneath him into foam, and into which the least freak of the engine might in a moment precipitate the whole train.

The appearance of Richmond from the bridge is very imposing. Occupying the precipitous bank from which you are receding, almost every house of which the town is composed is visible from this point of sight; its upper portion looking particularly attractive, from the quantity of foliage intermingling with the dazzling white walls of its isolated mansions and villas. Behind, a dark belt of forest sweeps round the horizon; whilst in the foreground the merry river glances from rock to rock, and straggles amongst islets clothed in the richest verdure. Brief time, however, has the tourist for this charming sight, the different features of which he has scarcely recognised ere he is whisked amid dense woods and clayey excavations, which in a twinkling shut the whole from his view.

The car in which I sat was but partially filled, and it was soon whispered about me, that amongst those who occupied it was a Mormon preacher, although he could not be precisely identified.

" He'll be game, if we can only git him out," said a passenger behind me to his companion.

" If there's such a fish on board, I'll hook him," added the other; who thereupon commenced in a voice audible throughout the whole car, denouncing as a swindler and vagabond Joe Smith, the Mormon prophet. I watched for some time to see on whom this produced the expected effect, and had just come to the conclusion that no such party was on board, when I was startled by a deep groan, proceeding from a rather stalwart looking man, who sat directly on my left, and whose face was now covered by his hands. I rose almost involuntarily and took the seat opposite, which luckily was vacant. All eyes were now turned upon him who had given such unequivocal evidence of a troubled spirit, and who sat swinging himself to and fro, his face still buried in his hands, groaning as if from the innermost recesses of his soul.

"I reckon you're out of sorts," said he whose words had conjured up this extraordinary manifestation. "You'll be better, p'r'aps, of a drain," he continued, bending over him, and offering him a small flask.

"Avaunt, Satan!" he exclaimed, and then burst into an impassioned prayer, in which he called down every conceivable species of denunciation upon those who were wilfully blind, and ignored the accredited prophets of God. Luckily there were no ladies present, or there might have been a scene. As it was, there was considerable confusion, the whole affair giving great scandal to those who regarded it as bringing things solemn into contempt. But there was a general cry of "Hear him out!" which prevailing, gave him undisputed possession of the floor. In a few minutes he rose and began to speak. It was then that, for the first time, I got a full sight of his features. In vain did I look for that fire in the eye which betokens fanaticism, or that rapid and nervous change of expression which so often characterises the enthusiastic zealot. His frame was large, his face full, his whole expression stolid, his eye dull and changeless, with far more cunning than inspiration in it. He was more like one pursuing a speculation than expounding a cherished faith, having all the appearance of one who was engaged in a swindle, and knew it.

His name was Hyde, and it appeared from his own showing that he was deeply in the confidence of the great Mormon apostle Smith. He was then on a very extensive proselytising tour, which commenced with the state of Illinois. He told us that in travelling alone over the " broad prairies " of that State on his holy mission, he lay down one evening in the grass, his stockings wet with blood, and his whole frame utterly exhausted. Whilst in this state the heavens opened, and he saw—but I will not follow him upon forbidden ground. Suffice it to say, that what Stephen witnessed was nothing to the revelations made to Mr. Hyde. His mission was then confirmed, and he was commanded to go forth and convert the whole earth. He had since been engaged in that trivial task. On being asked how he had succeeded so far, he said that he had met with considerable success in some of the western parts of Canada, but that the love of this world was far too strong in the present generation to leave them accessible to the truth. A part of the Mormon doctrine is that of association and community of goods, each convert being required to dispose of his all, and repair to the New Jerusalem with the proceeds, which are to be disposed of without any of those reservations which called down such heavy vengeance on Ananias and Sapphira. This was the point at which he found most of his converts falter, their enthusiasm appearing daily to increase until the proposal was made to them to sell their property for the benefit of the common fund, when they suddenly became as refractory as the young man with great possessions mentioned in Scripture. He then proceeded to denounce the living generation as one hopelessly rooted in unbelief, and prophesied the end of the world in ten months. The events which were to happen in the intermediate time were all contained in a prophetic handbill, of which he had some hundreds in his possession, and which he informed us were for sale at two cents a-piece. This was, after all, the moral of his preaching; I followed the example of others, and bought one, on perusing which I found that the least evil that was to happen to poor humanity between that and the ensuing May was, that a very great proportion of those alive were to fare as did Herod the tetrarch, and be eaten up by worms. The managers of the society at Nauvoo,* the New Jerusalem, were about to start a newspaper, for which he was authorised to procure subscriptions, on terms of paying for one year in advance.

" Why on airth take subscriptions for a year if this here univarsal world is to come up all of a heap in ten months?" asked a Yankee, in the furthest corner of the car.

" P'r'aps he'll let it go on for the year," suggested another beside him.

" If he don't, you can get part of your money back, the day after it's all up," said another; and a general laugh arose at the awkward turn which the

* The Mormons have since been driven west of the Rocky Mountains.

matter had taken for the prophet, who now stood scowling and discomfited, without well knowing what to say. To what length the scene would have gone it is difficult to say, had it not been here put an end to by our arrival at Petersburg, after a little more than an hour's ride from Richmond.

The town of Petersburg, though far inland, is nevertheless a seaport, being situated upon the Appomattox, about twelve miles above City Point, where it falls into the James. At the junction of the two streams is in reality the harbour common to Richmond and Petersburg, few sea-going craft ascending either river above City Point. The rapids of the Appomattox afford Petersburg a water-power, of which it has to some extent availed itself by turning it to the purposes of manufacture. Our stay here was but short, and we pursued our way afterwards, with but little interruption, until our arrival at Weldon. The aspect of that portion of Virginia traversed by the line between Richmond and Weldon is very similar to that of the district through which it runs between the capital and the Potomac. It follows, for most part, south of the James, the verge of the higher level between the tide-water region and the mountains, so that the traveller is brought in continual contact with the peculiarities of both regions —now passing over the undulating surface of the chief tobacco district, where he meets every here and there with a cotton plantation, and then penetrating for short distances into the sea-coast district, covered with interminable forests of pitch pine. Near the border of North Carolina the country becomes more uneven, picturesque, and salubrious.

Our approach to the frontier unsealed the lips of a taciturn Carolinian who was seated beside me, and who now related for my edification the following story, which he thought a good one. Some time ago, on the line separating Virginia from North Carolina being re-surveyed, it was so altered at one point as to include a small portion of the former within the limits of the latter State. It so happened that, at the point where the deviation took place, there was a marked contrast, as the line originally ran between districts of country of very different degrees of salubrity, that on the Virginia side being high, undulating and salubrious, whilst that on the Caro-linian was low, swampy, and unwholesome. An old lady, a relic of the revolutionary times, who had enjoyed her widowhood for many years on a snug little property on the Virginia side of the line, in-habited a commodious house, so situated on a sloping declivity, with a southern aspect, as to command an extensive view of the dank and sedgy region which lay immediately beyond the border. Her ideas ranged but little beyond the prospect which was visible from her windows, and one of her chief incen-tives to gratitude was, that her fate had cast her in Virginia, and not in North Carolina. Great then was her horror on discovering one day, that by the swerving of the boundary line, she herself, her house, and the whole of her property, were included in the latter State. Her complaints were bitter at having been thus transferred to the unhealthy country, and she made up her mind that, for the rest of her days, there was nothing in store for her but fevers, agues, rheumatisms, and catarrhs. So impressed was she with the idea that the change had exposed her to unwholesome influences from which she had formerly been exempt, that she made up her mind, although with great reluctance, to part with her property, and retreat into Virginia, in the sanitary virtues of which she had every confidence. It is held that the apprehension of a malady sometimes superinduces it. However this may be, the old lady in question soon afterwards fell a victim to fever and ague, convinced to the last that she had been sacrificed to a geographical innovation, and that, had her property continued as formerly in Virginia, her fate would have been very different.

We stayed but a few minutes at Weldon, a small border town, on the Roanoke, and possessing no feature of interest to the stranger. We had penetrated but a short distance into North Carolina, ere we were overtaken by one of the terrific thunderstorms so common, during the hotter months, to these latitudes. The descending deluge poured with such violence, that in a few minutes the line was at several points completely under water. On entering a deep excavation, which extended for about three miles, we were almost brought to a halt by the heavy torrent which we encountered. The bed of the railway resembled that of a canal, which had broken its banks a little beyond, and the water of which was rushing to escape and pour itself with desolating effect upon the adjacent fields. The torrent into which we were thus suddenly plunged did not proceed solely from the surcharged heavens, for a small stream, which, for some distance, ran parallel to the line and close to one side of the cutting, became so swollen by the tempest as to break into the excavation, into which, at more points than one, it poured its muddy contents in miniature cataracts. So deeply was the line submerged by this double visitation, that

the axles of the wheels were covered, as the train
slowly proceeded, groping its way, and following, at a
safe distance, enormous pieces of loose timber which
were floating before it along the rails.

The violence of these storms serves to explain what
every Englishman travelling there must have noticed
as characteristic of most railways in America. In
England, excavations and embankments soon lose the
cadaverous aspect which they first assume, by covering themselves with vegetation, in the shape either of
grass or shrubbery, or by being laid out into tasteful
flower plots, as in the vicinity of many of our stations.
In America, however, they retain, for the most part,
their original unsightliness, the frequency and violence
of the summer rains preventing them from being
again covered after they are once exposed. But it is
seldom that we find nature, in her workings, deviating
from the principle of compensations. If the traveller
does not, as with us, pass rapidly over meadowy banks,
or through excavations skirted with shrubs and ever-
greens, he is not left without some atonement for the
frequency with which his eye is brought in contact
with the cold repulsive clay; for, on the embankment,
or in the cutting, he can at any time amuse himself by
observing the varied and fantastic forms into which it
has been carved and furrowed by the descending
showers. In some places the water cuts deep gashes
in it, in humble imitation of the yawning seams on
the hill-sides, which, in the highlands, mark the
courses of the mountain torrents. When this happens in an excavation, a miniature delta of soft clay
is not unfrequently deposited upon the rails; at other
points, where the volume of water acting is less and
its course more gentle, it trickles down in a multitude

of tiny and devious channels, which, by degrees, it wears deep, leaving the projecting masses of indurated clay to form themselves into an endless variety of fantastic resemblances. Some of these masses, by successive washing, become almost isolated from the bank, when, as seen from a little distance, they look like sculptured groups of the most grotesque images. At other times they resolve themselves into fac-similes of fortified towns, as they might be seen through the little end of a telescope, with their steeples, towers, and battlements. I was most interested in observing, when they stood forth in boldest relief, the resemblance which they bore to Gothic architecture in incipient ruin. There were the deep projections, the lofty galleries, the stately pillar, the tenantless niches, the pointed window, and the flying buttresses, reminding one more particularly of the choir of a fine old cathedral in the first stages of its dilapidation. Frequently have I amused myself, not only on the railway, but also on the river and the common highway, when circumstances admitted of it, by observing the singular formations in clay thus designed and executed by the summer showers.

Amongst others who joined the train at Weldon were a young couple, who sat nearly opposite me, and whom, for a time, I regarded as brother and sister. In this belief I was first shaken by observing a variety of endearments pass between them, which are not usually indicative of the affection subsisting between parties standing towards each other in the relationship alluded to. I guessed therefore, and was afterwards assured, that they were husband and wife, being then on their way to spend all that remained of the honeymoon with some friends in South

Carolina. Their united ages could not have exceeded thirty-five. I had often heard of early marriages in America, but never before had so precocious an instance fallen under my observation. To most of their fellow-travellers they were objects of considerable interest. They were both Virginians : the bridegroom being tall, thin, and pale; whilst the bride, on the other hand, was rather short and rotund, with a round face, a full eye, and a laughing expression, but as girlish in her appearance and actions as her lord was boyish in his look and demeanour. They had early saddled themselves with the most serious responsibilities of life, plunging into the position and duties of middle age before they yet saw the end of their youth; and it was not without pain that I thought of the cares that would wrinkle the brow, and the sallow lines that would furrow the cheek of the one ere he was thirty, and the premature age which, descending upon the other, would blight her comeliness ere she had emerged from twenty-five. Such is the rapidity with which age, in many cases, stamps its impress on the form, particularly of the married woman, in most of the southern States, that I have seen two sisters, the one married and the other single, look like mother and daughter, although there was not two years difference between their ages.

We had scarcely been an hour and a half from Weldon, when the train came suddenly to a halt in the midst of a thick, tangled, swampy wood, from which so dense a vapour arose that it really seemed as if the spongy ground, in which the trees, as it were, soaked their roots, were heated by subterranean fires. I involuntarily turned my eyes upwards to ascertain if another storm had anything to do with this additional detention; but the heavens, now innocent of cloud, were again swathed in the most lustrous blue. I soon afterwards discovered that the cause of the delay was a more vulgar one than I had at first imagined, for, on following the example of others and jumping out upon the line, I beheld a horse standing between the rails, about fifty yards in advance of the engine, and looking curiously at it, as if he recognised in it an old acquaintance, but was not quite sure. With one shrill tone of the whistle the illusion vanished from his mind, and turning round he cantered off, still, however, retaining his position between the rails. He had a saddle on his back, but was riderless—a circumstance which gave rise to many speculations and conjectures amongst the passengers. We followed him slowly, and on once more making nearly up with him, he again turned round, stood, and looked as intently as before, until the whistle sent him a second time cantering along the line, from which he would deviate neither to the right nor to the left, provokingly keeping his place between the rails. The whistle was at length kept constantly screeching, much to our discomfort, but to no useful purpose, for he still kept in advance of us, causing us, in following him, materially to reduce our speed. The chase had already lasted for about three miles, and might have continued for the next dozen, but that we again came to a halt, when the animal, taking a longer look than usual at the engine, as if to satisfy himself that he had made no mistake, was taken on his flank by the stoker, who suddenly emerged upon him from the wood on one side of the line, and drove him into it on the other. A traveller by railway in America gets used to such impediments, although it is not often that it is a saddled horse that is the obstacle in the way.

As soon as we had resumed our speed, every one
began to speculate upon the fate of the missing rider.
Little time, however, had we for conjecture on this
score, for, on turning an abrupt curve, the train was
not only once more pulled up, but actually sent back.
In a twinkling, two or three heads were to be seen
projecting from each window of every carriage, first
looking up and down the line, and then full at each
other, for an explanation of the cause of our retrograde movement. It was soon made plain to us; for,
on backing about three hundred yards, we came up
to the body of a man lying close to the line and
apparently lifeless. The curve in the road had prevented the engineer from seeing him in time to stop
the train until it had shot far past him, and he very
properly put back to ascertain if any injury had be-
fallen him. He was bleeding from one of his feet;
but on examination the blood was found to flow from
a wound of the most trivial description. He had
been lying on his face, with the foot in question so
far upon the rail, that the fore-wheel of the engine
had crushed the edge of his shoe, and in so doing
produced an abrasure of the skin of the little toe.
Being in a beastly state of intoxication, he was in no
condition to throw any light upon whence he had
come, whither he was going, or how he had been
placed in so perilous a position. He was conveyed
to the nearest road-side station, where he was left to
be thankful, on recovering his senses, for his double
preservation. Whilst this was going on, I was somewhat amused at the honest indignation expressed by
some of the passengers that the wretch had not been
more seriously injured, which, had he been so, they
seemed to think would have fully compensated them
for their loss of time.

There is but little to interest the traveller in the region of North Carolina, traversed by the railway from Weldon to Wilmington. The portion of the road lying between the former place and Raleigh, the capital of the State, runs through a district of unequal fertility, the average productiveness of which falls somewhat below that of the sea-coast or tide-water region to the east of it, and of the rich and exuberant valleys to the west which are embosomed amongst the ridges of the Allegany chain, the loftiest peaks of which are to be found within the limits of North Carolina. The middle region of the State partakes much of the characteristics of the corresponding tract in Virginia, of which it is, in fact, a prolongation. The soil is light and sandy, but there are numerous tracts on which cotton, tobacco, and Indian corn, as well as wheat and barley, are cultivated to advantage. Here and there the surface undulates considerably, presenting to the eye a succession of gentle slopes and moderate elevations. As might be expected, these tracts abound in pretty situations, many of which are occupied by commodious mansions, tenanted by the possessors of the circumjacent plantations. Some of these are exquisitely situated in the midst of dells clothed in the richest vegetation, and on the margin of lively and rapid streams, which become sluggish enough when they descend into the broad and gloomy belt of the tide-water region. In general, however, this part of the State is inhabited by an inferior class of proprietors, who live in tenements of a different description, and who seemingly permit themselves to be but little disturbed by the rage for material improvement which has so completely possessed the minds and influenced

the conduct of their more northern fellow-countrymen.

North Carolina, as a State, occupies no very prominent position in the Union. She is a member of
the Confederacy, and but little more; playing, socially
and politically, a part far inferior to that of her more
active and ambitious sister, in whose wake she generally follows, though with uncertain pace, in connexion with questions particularly of a commercial
bearing. In point of material development she is
immeasurably behind many of the northern States,
her co-evals in the Union, and possessing material
advantages not superior to her own. But if she has
been exempt from their ambition, she certainly does
not now participate in the misfortunes with which
not a few of them have been visited. She has little
or no public debt, her exemption from which may
argue want of spirit as well as prudence, for with
advantages like those possessed by North Carolina,
her credit might have been safely and usefully pledged
to some extent, with a view to internal improvements
on a practicable and rational scale. The insolvent
States, or those bordering upon insolvency, have erred,
not in the spirit which they have manifested, but in
the extent to which they have permitted it to carry
them. A moderate infusion of their spirit into her
would do much for North Carolina; not that she has
been absolutely supine, whilst her sister States have,
some of them, been taking strides in the direction of
prosperity, and others hurrying to temporary wreck
under its guise; for she has executed a few works,
in the shape of canals and railways, which are useful,
so far as they go, if they do not reflect much credit

upon her enterprise.   But, both in public spirit and individual energy, the North Carolinians are far behind their active and ambitious brethren of the North and West. The stranger has not to penetrate far into the State ere he discerns sufficient evidence of this.

The blight of slavery is here, if possible, even more palpable than it is in Virginia. View it whichever way you will, whether as a crime or as a calamity, this institution in the United States invariably carries with it its own retribution.   However indispensable it may be to the wealth and productiveness of some localities, it is a present curse to the land, fraught with a terrible prospective judgment, when we consider the hopelessness of its peaceful removal, and the awful catastrophes to which it will inevitably lead. Where activity and progress are the rule, all that is not advancing assumes the melancholy aspect of retrogression. North Carolina is virtually retrograding. Since 1830 her population has increased but at a very trifling ratio, which is partly to be accounted for by the numbers who annually emigrate from her, as from Virginia and other sea-board States, to the Far West.   Her foreign trade, which was never very large, has also, of late years, been rapidly on the decline, and there is now but little prospect of its ever reviving. She still holds some rank in point of wealth and political importance in the Confederation, but every year is detracting from it, and throwing her more and more into the background. She has not only lagged behind most of the original States amongst whom she figured, but has permitted many of the younger members of the Union greatly to outstrip her.   The latter proposition, however, will hold good as to other sea-board States, which find it no

easy matter to maintain their original position, seeing
that they are annually drained of men and money
seeking new fields of action, and opportunities of investment, amongst the more enterprising and rising
communities of the West.

What is known as the Gold Region in the United
States,* extending, with more or less interruption and
with diminishing richness, as far north as the St. Lawrence, manifests itself in great productiveness in the
neighbourhood of the Rappahannock, immediately
south of the Potomac.   After traversing the State of
Virginia, it extends in a south-westerly direction
across North Carolina; embracing, in its progress
further south, an angle of South Carolina, whence it
passes into Georgia and the upper portions of
Alabama.   Throughout the whole of this region gold
is found, in greater or less quantity, mixed in the
form of small particles with alluvial deposits, or of
petty lumps imbedded in quartz and slate, from
which when it is washed or separated, it is generally
found to be of the purest quality.   The tract thus
denoted extends in a north-easterly and south-
westerly direction for nearly 700 miles, its breadth
varying much, but sometimes spreading over an area
of from seventy to a hundred miles.   It runs parallel,
for the most part, with the Allegany chain, at the
very foot of which it is sometimes found to lie; whilst
at others it embraces the spurs of the chain within
its limits.   The auriferous veins which permeate it
differ much in their richness, as they do in their form
and extent; breaking, in some places, into numerous
branches, to unite again, at no great distance, into
one broad and deep belt.   North of the Potomac,

* The Gold Region in California has since been discovered.

the tract is much more abundant in its production of
several of the baser metals than in that of gold, the
greatest quantities of the latter being found south of
that river. Some of the most beautiful portions of
Virginia are comprehended within it, the region
which it traverses in North Carolina being of a less
interesting character. It is in this State, however,
that it is found to be most productive; and here, consequently, it is most worked. But the produce of
this auriferous tract has, as yet, in no place been
discovered to be sufficiently abundant to lead to
regular mining operations on an extensive scale.

The neighbourhood of Raleigh, the capital of the
State, which is about midway between Weldon and
Wilmington, is very beautiful. The land is high, and
swells, on all hands, into graceful undulations, covered with a profusion of the richest foliage. As we
sped along, the railway seemed occasionally to be lost,
for a while, amid perfumed groves and deep forest
glades, from which it would suddenly emerge upon a
series of plantations, to dive again as suddenly into
another belt of undisturbed and exuberant vegetation. The day was bright and clear; and nothing could
serve to give a more pleasing variety to our journey
than these repeated transitions from wood to clearance,
from shade to sunshine. As we wound our way amid
the stately pillars of the forest, and beneath the rich
green translucent canopy which they supported overhead, it was interesting to watch the motions of the
numerous birds, which sought shelter beneath the juicy
foliage from the midday heat. Few of them had
anything like a sweet note in their little throats;
but their gaudy plumage glistened again and again,
as, in their fluttering to and fro, they broke through

the golden bars of sunshine which had struggled
into the shade.   The air, too, was occasionally laden
with the delicious perfume of the magnolia grandi-
flora, whose deep green leaf and large swelling milk-
white flower render it one of the greatest ornaments
of the forest in these latitudes.

Raleigh is a small and unimposing-looking town
situated near a river called the Neuse.   It is a place
of no commercial importance whatever.   The chief
building in the town is the State House, in which the
local legislature assembles once a year to deliberate
upon the affairs of the State.   It is a substantial
granite building, of no very ambitious dimensions,
but with a profusion of pillars, which add much to the
lightness and elegance of its appearance.   Much as Sir
Walter Raleigh had to do with the early colonization
of the South, this is the only town in America, that
I know of, bearing his name.   This is singular in a
country where they are so fond of designating places
by the names of historic characters.   North Carolina
set a generous example to her sister States, when she
appended to her capital a name so identified with the
reality, as well as the romance, of early American
colonization.

Proceeding southward from Raleigh, the country
rapidly changes its appearance and character.   The
distinctive features of the middle district soon merge
into the monotonous and less attractive aspect of the
tide-water region.   Your way is now towards the
coast, and you do not proceed far ere the clear and
lively streams become sluggish and muddy, the surface of the country becomes flat and uninteresting,
and the forest shade, so enticing in the uplands,
deepens into interminable gloom.   As seen from an

elevated position, commanding an extensive range of it, there is nothing in nature of so melancholy an aspect as this enormous, fertile, yet pestilential, region. Extending for hundreds of miles along the coast, with an average depth of from 100 to 150, miles it spreads out in one vast, gloomy, and monotonous plain, interposing between the more elevated districts and the sea. Where it is not so marshy that the land is literally " drowned," it is generally fertile to a degree, particularly along the margin of the rivers, which are lined with plantations; from the poisonous miasmas of which the whites have to fly during the autumn months. Here and there you meet with sandy tracts, which are in some cases barren, and in most comparatively unproductive. Rice is largely cultivated throughout the more marshy portions of the region ; wheat and Indian corn being produced in abundance in its drier parts towards the Potomac, which give way to cotton as you approach the portions of it extending into the Carolinas and Georgia. The pitch-pine with which it abounds, and which attains here a large size, adds much to the sombreness of its appearance, which becomes more and more striking as you approach the more swampy districts of the coast. Between Chesapeake Bay and Albemarle Sound, its more disagreeable features culminate to a hideous point, producing, by their combination, what is so generally known as the Dismal Swamp. Through this baleful region runs a canal, nearly thirty miles in length, connecting the two arms of the sea just mentioned. Its name well indicates its character. From the soft spongy ground springs a dense and tangled underwood, overtopped by a heavy and luxuriant growth of juniper, cypress, cedar, and sometimes oak and sycamore, which stand at all angles, and are frequently seen propping each other up, so precarious is their hold of the marshy soil. During the day-time the air is moist and relaxing; at night it is laden with pestilential vapours, which war with every form of animal life but that of the venomous reptile and the bull-frog, whose discordant croak ceases not night or day. In passing through, one cannot fail to be struck with the quantity of decaying timber which he constantly sees around him; some prostrate, and melting, as it were, into the semi-liquid earth; the rest yet standing as ghastly warnings to the still vigorous trunks around them. At night this timber emits a pale phosphorescent light, which, with the fitful and cold lustre of the firefly, only serves to deepen the pervading gloom. Take it in all its characteristics, and fancy cannot picture to itself a more repulsive or desolate region. Not that nature is here without power; but her powers are applied to hideous production. There is something awful, as well as repulsive, in the scene. It is desolation in the lap of luxuriance—it is solitude in a funereal garb.

There are many other tracts along the coast, from the Potomac to the Savannah, of which the Dismal Swamp is but a specimen and a type. They differ from the tide-water region generally, in concentrating in themselves all its disagreeable features. In most parts of it their characteristics are to be met with, although in limited combination and diminished intensity. It greatly improves on approaching the lower falls of the rivers which designate the boundary between it and the middle region. This, which may be called the upper portion of the sea-coast region, and particularly in the vicinity of the streams, yields in fertility to no other portion of the country. It is generally well cleared, but with much forest still remaining undisturbed. Here, during the healthy months, residence on the larger plantations is very agreeable, especially when a large circle of friends and acquaintances, as is frequently the case, meet upon them from different and distant parts of the country. It is to the mere traveller that the region in question is wholly destitute of attractions; its flat, dull, sombre, and monotonous aspect becoming inexpressibly wearisome to him as he proceeds, mastering one reach of it only to see another spreading out, as it were, interminably before him.

Wilmington, which we reached in the evening, is a small town, built on the east bank of Cape Fear River, about twenty-five miles from the Atlantic. It is one of the chief seaports of the State, although vessels of a larger burden than 300 tons cannot approach it. There is no other sea-board State so deficient in good harbours as North Carolina. Its whole line of coast is low and sandy, the mainland being protected from the ocean by long isolated ridges of sand and gravel, separated from it by narrow and shallow straits; whilst, in other places, long and low sandy peninsulas run for many miles parallel to the coast. It is but at few points that the coast can be safely approached; and but one or two of the many inlets which separate the islands from the mainland and from each other, are practicable to vessels of large burden. Cape Hatteras, the most dangerous point in the coasting navigation of the United States, is a portion of the coast of North Carolina. At this point, the coast, which, from the southernmost part of Georgia, has been trending in a north-easterly direction, suddenly diverges more to the northward, in which line it continues, until it is again diverted to the north-east by the position of Long Island and Connecticut. Cape Hatteras thus reaches far eastward into the Atlantic, greatly influencing the direction of the Gulf stream. To double it is at all times a matter of some hazard, and most dangerous when an easterly or north-easterly wind brings a heavy sea in conflict with the stream. The shoals, too, which extend far beyond it into the sea, add greatly to its perils. No other part of the coast of the United States could tell such dismal tales of shipwreck as Cape Hatteras. Of late years it has been the scene of some of the most melancholy and heartrending disasters. Amongst these stand fatally prominent the wrecks of the steamers " Home " and " Pulaski," the former bound from New York to Charleston, and the latter from Charleston to New York. In both cases, hundreds of human beings met with an untimely fate.

Amongst the few saved from the wreck of the " Home," were a lady and gentleman, who were rescued under circumstances of a singular character. After the awful confusion of the catastrophe was over, they both found themselves, without being able to give an account of how they got there, upon a small and rudely-constructed raft, formed of a few planks and barrels. A heavy sea was running at the time, and it was with difficulty that they retained their hold of the crazy fabric, which was their only safety. For the greater part of two days and two nights were they driven about in this perilous state, being all that time without food or drink, and afraid to change their positions, lest they should lose their hold, or disturb the equilibrium of the raft. What added much to their discomfort as well as to their peril was, that the raft was so small, that they were constantly immersed in several inches of water, even when the sea was not breaking over them, as it frequently did. At length, as they were approaching the third day of their fearful trial, exhausted with cold and hunger, and almost stupified by their protracted agony, their raft was cast ashore, not far from the Cape; and, in leaving it, it was with difficulty that they escaped being lost amid the surf. They had sufficient strength left to drag themselves to the nearest habitation, where all was done to restore them that kindness and hospitality could effect. On recovering, they began to observe each other more attentively than before, when the gentleman found that his fellow-voyager was young, pretty, and accomplished; she at the same time discovering in him all that youth and spirit could do to make a man attractive in the eyes of the sex. It was but natural that, under the circumstances, they should feel a deep interest in each other; and it was not long ere they began to think, that if a marriage was ever devised in heaven, theirs had been settled and arranged there. They were soon convinced that nothing should sunder those whom Providence had so singularly thrown together. They were afterwards married, but not till the lady's period of mourning had expired; for the catastrophe which resulted in her becoming a bride, had also made her an orphan and an heiress.

Having no inducement to delay at Wilmington, I took my passage in a steamer which was to leave that evening for Charleston. She was a large and handsome-looking vessel, and, to all appearance, much more seaworthy than many of her class in America. Below the maindeck she was all cabin; one enormous saloon, superbly decorated, stretching from stem to stern. Above the main she had a promenade deck, . extending about half way forward, the ladies' cabin being between the two. She was full of passengers, many of whom were sound asleep in their berths ere the steamer left the pier. For my own part, I remained for some hours upon deck, watching the dull flat shores of the river, the faint black outline of which it was just possible to distinguish from the darkness of the night, until we glided into the open sea, which looked like a mass of liquid fire, every wave, even to the far horizon, being brilliantly decorated with a phosphorescent crest.

The wind was fresh, with a lively sea running, but, coming as it did several points from the north, so far favoured us, that by early breakfast-time next morning we were off Charleston. The coast was still low, sandy, and uninteresting, being screened, like that of North Carolina, as well as that of Georgia beyond, by long insular ridges, rising but a few feet above the level of the sea. Many of these islands, particularly off the coast of South Carolina and Georgia, produce the finest kind of American cotton, that known as the Sea Island cotton, and commanding a much higher price, both on account of its fineness and its scarcity, than that produced, in greater abundance and with less cost and labour, in the uplands of the interior. On entering the harbour we had to cross a bar, the passage of which is narrow, and can only be effected at high tide by vessels of the largest class. Many

see, or affect to see, a striking resemblance between
the situation of Charleston and that of New York.
For my own part, I saw less of that resemblance
than I did of the data on which it is sometimes
fancifully built. You enter the harbour by a narrow
channel, and so you do the magnificent bay of New
York. The city stands upon a small projecting tongue
of land running southward into the harbour, as New
York does upon Manhattan Island, somewhat similarly situated. Nay, more; this tongue of land has
the Cooper River on its eastern, and the Ashley River
on its western side; its southernmost point being
laved by the confluent waters of the two; just as New
York is flanked on one side by the arm of the Sound,
known as the East River, and on the other by the
Hudson. In addition to this, its foreign and coasting
trades are concentrated upon the eastern side of the
town, the main rendezvous for shipping being on the
Cooper River, as the chief shipping business of New
York is confined to that side of it which is washed
by the East River. Furthermore, there are islands
in the harbour, some of which are fortified, and others
not, which is likewise so in the other case; whilst its
entrance is well flanked by fortifications, as the
Narrows are defended at New York. Taking the
ground-plan of the two cities and their respective
environs, there may be many points of similarity
between them. But viewing them as the tourist
views them, there is but little about the one to remind
him of the other; unless the recollection be suggested
by contrast, instead of by resemblance. About
Charleston, everything is low, level, and uninteresting; whilst about New York all is undulating, bold,
graceful, and infinitely varied. The one is on a con-

tracted and monotonous scale; whilst the other is cast in an expansive mould, and is replete with striking and picturesque effects. Let not the Charlestonians be too fond of comparing small things with great. There are many cities inferior, both in appearance and position, to Charleston; but it can only suffer by comparison with the great emporium of the North.

CHAPTER VII.

LIKE most other American towns, Charleston is built
on a very regular plan. The narrow tongue of land
on which it stands is low and flat; the streets which
run across it from the Ashley to the Cooper being
intersected at right angles by others which lie north
and south in the direction of its length. The breadth
of the site of the capital of the south, for it is the
largest city and most important seaport lying between the Potomac and the Mississippi, is but little
more than a mile, the length to which it has extended
in a northerly direction being under two miles. It is
situated so low that portions of it have occasionally

been inundated, when a long continuance of easterly
winds have caused an unusual accumulation of water
in the bay, and rains in the interior have swollen the
rivers which flank it on either side.   The bay, which
is about six miles long, has an average width of little
more than two miles, opening upon the Atlantic
almost due east from the city.   It is not so well sheltered from easterly winds as that of Boston, to say
nothing of New York; and during the prevalence of
gales from that quarter, the entrance to it is difficult,
vessels of large burden being almost exclusively confined, on entering it, to one narrow channel across the
bar at its mouth, the greatest depth of water in this
channel not exceeding seventeen feet at high tide.   It
is well situated for defence, the harbour being guarded,
like that of New York, with defensive works both at
its entrance and on islands within it.

Charleston is a pleasing looking town, but by no
means a striking one.   Its aspect on the bay, from
the flatness of its site, is very unimposing.   It was a
hot and sultry morning when I approached; not a
breath of air was stirring, and the waters of the bay
were as calm and unruffled as a mill-pond.   Before
me lay the city baking, as it were, in the fierce sunshine.   But even then it had a cool and comfortable
look about it; for, from the lowness of its position,
it gave one the idea of being up to the knees in
water.   Like Philadelphia, it presents one front to
the harbour, which screens the rest of the city from
view; being in this respect totally unlike Boston,
New York, or Baltimore, all which show to much
greater advantage, rising as they do in graceful undulations from the water.

The interior of the city is both pretty and peculiar.

It is wanting in the grandeur and substantiality which characterise the northern towns, but it has adapted its appearance to the necessities of its position; its architecture being chiefly designed to obviate the inconveniences of its climate. A tolerably large proportion of it is built of brick, the bulk of the town however being constructed of wood. The private dwellings are almost all wooden edifices, not lofty, but elegant, being in most cases provided with light, airy and graceful verandas, extending in some instances to the roof. They are generally painted of a dazzling white, with green Venetian blinds, the verandas being sometimes adorned with vines, and at others merely painted green. In the suburbs particularly they are embowered in foliage, with which the spotless white of the walls forms a cool and pleasing contrast. Until recently, indeed, most of the streets of Charleston were provided with trees, which gratefully interposed between its inhabitants and the fierce heats of mid-day. They have been lately removed, however, from several of the principal streets, the corporation sacrificing to some crotchet of its own that which was both an ornament and a convenience to the city. With the exception of the few busy thoroughfares which it possesses, the rest of the city is more like an extended village than a large town; the appearance of any one part of it, save and excepting its profusion of verandas, very much resembling that of the lovely little interior towns so frequently met with in New England, Pennsylvania, and New York.

Charleston is by no means the healthiest of places, although many of its inhabitants would fain induce you to think so. It is superior, however, in point of

salubrity to much of the country which lies immediately behind it, its contiguity to the sea depriving
its atmosphere of much of the deleterious miasma
with which that of the interior is laden. Still it is a
place to which the stranger has to become well acclimated, ere he can sojourn in it for any length of time
with safety; and the ordeal through which he has to
pass in so acclimating himself is perilous as well as
unpleasant. Its natives and regular residents are
seldom the victims of the acute diseases which it
inflicts upon the stranger; but, judging from their
appearance, they look as if they had all once been
very ill, and were in a state of chronic convalescence.
You meet many looking prematurely old in Charleston, but few such as could properly be designated old
men. The best race of men produced by South Carolina
inhabit the upland country, sometimes called the
Ridge, about 150 miles back from the coast. They
are a taller, stronger, and in every respect a better
developed race than their fellow-countrymen on the
coast, vieing, in most cases, in health and proportions
with the sturdy farmer of Pennsylvania or Ohio.

Charleston not being the seat of government, its
principal buildings, with one or two exceptions, such
as two small arsenals, are of a local and commercial,
instead of a political and national character. The
City Hall and the Exchange, both ante-revolutionary
in the date of their erection, are about the finest
edifices of which it can boast. Although not strictly
of a public character, the hotels here, as elsewhere
in the United States, may be classed with the public
buildings, some of those in Charleston being on a
scale inferior to none elsewhere, even in Boston, New
York, or New Orleans. None of them have the

architectural pretensions of the Astor House in New York ; it is their vastness and excellent management that strike the stranger with astonishment.

Having had but little rest on board the steamer the previous night, I slept soundly in one of them the first night ashore. How far into the morning my slumbers would have carried me I know not, but at a pretty early hour I was aroused by a noise which, for the few moments elapsing between deep sleep and perfect consciousness, I took to be the ringing of the sleigh-bells in the streets of a Canadian town. I was soon undeceived; the intense heat, even at that early hour, driving all notions of winter, sleighs, and sleigh-bells, out of my head. But though in Carolina, there was still the jingling of the bells to remind me of Canada. Every bell in the house seemed to have become suddenly bewitched but my own; and anxious to know what was the matter, I soon made it join in the chorus. Even in the ringing of bells one can trace to some extent the difference between characters; and, for some time, I amused myself, watching the different manifestations of temper on the part of those who pulled them, which they indicated. Some rung gently, as if those pulling them shrunk from being troublesome; others authoritatively, as if the ringers would be obeyed at once and without another summons; and others again angrily, as if they had already been frequently pulled in vain. Very soon all became angry, some waxing into a towering passion; for although all might ring, all could not possibly be answered at once. I had brief time to notice these things ere the waiters were heard hurrying up and down stairs, and along the lengthy wooden lobbies which echoed to their footsteps. Things now appeared to be getting serious,

and jumping out of bed I opened my door just as a
troop of black fellows were hurrying past, each with a
bucket of water in his hand. I immediately inferred
that the house was on fire; and as American houses
generally, on such occasions, go off like gun-cotton, I
sprung back into my room, with a view to partly
dressing myself and making my escape. A universal
cry for " Boots," however, mingled with every variety
of imprecation on that functionary's head, from the
simple ejaculation to the elaborate prayer, soon convinced me that the case was less urgent than I had
supposed; and, on further investigation, it turned
out that the unusual hubbub had been created by
some one playing overnight the old and clumsy trick
of changing the boots before they were taken from
the bedroom doors to be cleaned, so that, on being
replaced in the morning, each guest was provided
with his neighbour's instead of his own. I had lain
down, the happy possessor of a pair of Wellingtons,
which, in the morning, I found converted into un-
sightly highlows. Other transformations as complete
and as awkward took place, the dandy finding at his
door the brogues of a clodhopper from the North-
west, who was attempting, next door, with a grin,
to squeeze his toes into his indignant neighbour's
patent leather boots. After some search my Wellingtons were discovered in another hall, standing at a
lady's door, whose shoes had been placed before that
of a Texan volunteer, on his way to Mexico and
glory. It was not the good fortune of all so readily
to recover their property, the majority of the guests
having to breakfast in slippers, during which the
unreclaimed boots and shoes were collected together
in the great hall, each man afterwards selecting, as

he best could, his own property from the heap. Until
the nature of the joke was discovered, the poor Boots
had a narrow escape of his life; and it was amusing to
witness the chuckle of the black waiters, as, on discovering the trick, they quietly returned, with their
unemptied buckets, to their respective posts.

It would be difficult to find in the United States or
elsewhere a more agreeable or hospitable people than
those of Charleston. They have neither the pre-
tension of the Bostonian, nor the frigid bearing which
the Philadelphian at first assumes, about them, being
characterised by a frankness and urbanity of manner
which at once prepossess the stranger in their favour,
whilst they put him completely at his ease. This
delightful phase of Charleston society is much to be
attributed to its constant intercourse with the interior;
South Carolina, in its social characteristics, bearing a
close resemblance to Maryland and Virginia.

The traveller, as he proceeds south from Philadelphia, finds the proportion borne by the negroes to
the whole population increasing in each successive
town which he enters. But in no place north of it
are they so numerous, compared with the whites, as
in Charleston. In 1840, they constituted a little
more than half its entire population. Charleston has
many peculiarities to remind the stranger of its latitude, but none so striking or so constantly before his
eyes, as the swarms of negroes whom he meets. They
are everywhere, in the capacity of domestic servants
within and of labourers out of doors, about the
wharves and shipping, and in the streets, toiling,
singing or whistling and grimacing. The practice of
letting them out to hire is very prevalent in Charleston, many people making comfortable incomes in this

way out of the labour of their slaves, as horse-dealers sometimes do out of that of their cattle.

In a commercial point of view, Charleston is a place of great importance. Not only is nearly the whole export trade of the State centred in it, but much of the foreign trade of North Carolina is indirectly conducted through it. The same may be said of some portion of the export trade of Georgia, being thus a serious competitor to Savannah, the chief port of entry of that State, and lying a little more than one hundred miles to the south of Charleston. It is mainly as a place of export that Charleston figures amongst the chief seaports of the Union. Cotton is, of course, its principal article of export, of which South Carolina is a larger producer than any other Atlantic State. In addition to this, as already intimated, Charleston is advantageously situated as a place of export for large sections of the contiguous States. The greatest quantity of raw cotton exported, either for home consumption or to foreign countries, from the Atlantic coast, is from the port of Charleston.

But although the great outlet for the staple produce of the southern Atlantic States, it is not equally favourably situated as a place of import. The population immediately around it is comparatively scanty, and increases but slowly, when we consider the rate at which it multiplies elsewhere in the Union; besides, not more than one-half of the entire population of the districts contiguous to it are consumers of the chief articles of import, the slaves being exclusively fed upon home-grown produce, and now almost exclusively clothed in home-made Osnaburgs—a coarse cotton fabric, manufactured to a great extent in the South, and so cheap that not only is it impossible for the foreign manufacturer to compete with it, but it also defies competition from New England, whose coarse fabrics successfully compete in the other American markets with our own.   Charleston having thus no great interior demand to supply, imports but little as compared with the amount of its exports.   The dense and more rapidly increasing populations still further west are chiefly supplied by their own ports on the Mexican Gulf, such as Mobile and New Orleans.   They are thus independent of Charleston, which is only called upon to supply South Carolina, and portions of the two adjoining States.   And even of these it has not the exclusive supply, for much of the foreign consumption, both of Georgia and the two Carolinas, is supplied from the more northern seaports.

The trade of Charleston has fluctuated very much, its exports greatly exceeding in 1801 what they were in 1842.   If it is not a receding, it has none of the appearance of an advancing town.   Its population returns, at different periods, indicate this.   It has not doubled its population since 1790, whilst other cities around it have more than quadrupled theirs.   From 1810 to 1820 it increased only from 24,711 to 24,780. In 1830 it contained 30,289 inhabitants, being a gain of nearly 6,000 during the previous decade.   In 1840, however, it had fallen off to 29,261, since which time it has again slightly increased.   In the Old World a town does well that maintains its ground, but in the New, a community which is stationary may be ranked in the category of those that are retrograde.

South Carolina, although by far the smallest State south of the Potomac, has played as conspicuous a figure in the politics of the Union as any member of

the Confederacy.   The question with which she has
all along principally identified herself, is that of the
tariff, although her name is associated with other questions of an important character, but which sprung
from the angry disputes which the tariff occasioned.
From an early period South Carolina took the lead
in the free-trade movement, which, in its progress, has
been more than once fraught with peril to the Union,
and which only achieved its ultimate triumph in 1846.
Until the recent and rapid rise of the cotton-growing
States, on the Mississippi and the Gulf of Mexico,
South Carolina was the chief producer of the great
staple article of southern export.   She was, therefore,
the chief sufferer from the series of high tariffs, designed and adopted for the protection of the domestic
manufacturer, which prevailed, with but little intermission, till 1832.   These tariffs were obviously detri-
mental to the interests of the southern States, which
had no manufactures to protect, and which could procure all that they wanted for their own consumption
much more cheaply and better from the foreign manufacturer, who was, in turn, their best customer, inasmuch as he was the chief consumer of their raw
produce.   South Carolina took up the question as one
of vital interest to her.   She found herself injuriously
affected by the protective policy in a double sense, for
not only was her foreign market curtailed by the partial prohibition at home of foreign goods manufactured from her staple produce, but it was also still
further abridged by the enhanced cost of production
which a high tariff occasioned, by not only raising the
price of many of the necessary articles of consumption
with which the planter had to provide his slaves, but
by actually taxing the cotton bagging which he im-

ported for the purpose of packing his raw cotton for
exportation.   Dreading, in addition to this, the adoption of some retaliatory policy on the part of Great
Britain, which would still further injuriously affect
her interests, and goaded almost to madness by the
blighting effects of the tariff of 1828, as visible in the
serious declension of her export trade, South Carolina
at length attacked the whole protective system, in a
manner which, in 1832, produced a political crisis
eminently dangerous to the stability of the Union.
The contest was waged hotly on both sides; the cotton-growing States denying to Congress the right to
impose taxes for any other purpose than revenue, and
the manufacturing States of the north contending that
it had full power to protect home manufactures, with
a view to building up an "American system," whereby
the United States would ultimately be constituted
into a self-subsistent nation, independent, as regarded
the necessaries of life at least, of all the world.

Whilst South Carolina insisted that the powers of
Congress to impose taxes did not extend beyond what
was actually necessary for the maintenance of the revenue, she saw no benefit to accrue from an "American system," which threatened with ruin one moiety
of the Confederacy.   It was in vain that the domestic
manufacturer promised her as good a market at home
for her produce as she enjoyed abroad.   Even if he
could fulfil his promises, they were at best but prospective, whilst she enjoyed a present advantage from
the English market, from which it was proposed, as
much as possible, to disconnect her.   This dispute,
arraying in hostility to each other the conflicting
interests of the two great sections of the Confederacy,
gave rise, in course of time, to other questions of a

still more awkward and dangerous kind, prominent
amongst which were those of Nullification and Seces-
sion. The whole matter has already been elsewhere
more fully touched upon in these pages, but I may here
again, in treating more particularly of South Carolina,
briefly allude to some points connected with it. The
dispute concerning the tariff brought under review the
powers and duties of the federal government. After
insisting that its powers in reference to taxation were
limited as above specified, South Carolina assumed
the position that, if Congress exceeded its constitutional powers, any State in the Union had
a right, *quoad* itself, to nullify its acts, in other
words, to render them of no effect by preventing
their execution within its limits. This doctrine was
resisted by the great majority of the States, the
Unionists contending that no State had the power to
judge for itself as to the unconstitutionality of any
act of Congress, that power being solely vested in the
Supreme Federal Court, and that, consequently,
it was competent for no State to resist within its
limits the execution of any act of Congress, which
the Supreme Court had not declared to be in violation
of the Constitution. Considering the limited amount
of the imports of South Carolina, she would have
gained but little by preventing the levy of the high
duties complained of within her limits, the value of
her imports affecting but little the average cost of
imported articles to the general consumer; for it is
scarcely to be supposed that the foreign importer, or
the native engaged in the import business, except in
South Carolina herself, would have run the hazard of
making Charleston his port of entry, in contravention
of the general revenue laws of the Union. But with

the rise of the doctrine of Nullification, the question came to involve a political principle, which the one party was as desirous to promote, as the other was determined to resist. Matters at length came to such a pass that an amicable adjustment of the dispute seemed out of the question, and both parties prepared for an armed collision. General Jackson was then President of the Republic, and his impetuous character and fiery temper would have hurried him at once to extremities, but that there were about him cooler heads than his own to advise him to temporise a little. This saved the Confederacy from destruction, for had a collision ensued, it is impossible to set bounds to the lamentable results which would have followed. South Carolina was fully armed for resistance, had a blow been struck by the federal government; and for weeks before the final adjustment of the dispute, her troops were being marched and drilled, in many instances, in the neighbourhood, and even in sight of the federal forces. At length, but not before the Union had been brought to the brink of dissolution, the catastrophe was averted by the Compromise Act, which provided for the gradual diminution of the duties leviable by the oppressive tariff of 1828, by biennial reductions until 1842, when the act would expire.

The Seceders, who also figured in the dispute, carried their views even further than the Nullifiers, contending for the right of a State, if it saw cause, itself being the sole judge of the urgency of the occasion, to withdraw entirely from the Union, in other words, to abrogate, *quoad* itself, the federal constitution. This was but directly advocating a principle to which Nullification, if admitted, would indirectly lead. It had in it, however, so much of the appearance of treason to the Confederacy, that it counted far fewer adherents than the rival doctrine, which stood towards it in the relation of the shadow to the substance.

Throughout the whole of this angry contest South Carolina took the lead on the free-trade side, not alone on account of the magnitude of the interests which she had involved in it, the conspicuousness of her position being greatly attributable to the character of the men whom she produced as her champions for the occasion. Amongst the many eminent Carolinians who figured during that critical period, and whose names are destined to adorn the annals of their country, Mr. Calhoun and Mr. M'Duffie stand prominently forth, unrivalled in the zeal and energy which they displayed, and the eloquence with which they advocated their cause. Some of them have since passed away, but these two yet remain, the representatives of South Carolina in the federal Senate; Mr. M'Duffie being now aged and infirm, Mr. Calhoun, on the other hand, although far advanced in life, still possessing all the perseverance and much of the vigour which characterised his early career.

On the expiration, in 1842, of the Compromise Act, the Protectionists had once more either the power or the adroitness to re-enact, to a partial extent, the tariff of 1828. This they did, in defiance of many warnings of a recurrence of the scenes of 1832. How soon similar scenes would have been presented upon the theatre of the Union it is not easy to say, had not the possibility of their recurrence for the present been prevented by the tariff-bill of 1846, which reduced the duties upon most articles of import to the revenue standard. This settlement of the question,

so much desired by the South, is all the more likely
to be permanent, not only from its having been
secured by the cooperation of the West, which seems
at length to have been fairly, though tardily, converted to free-trade views, but also from the manner
in which its results have falsified all the prognostica-
tions of the Whigs concerning it, especially in a revenue
point of view, and more than realised in this respect
the expectations even of its most sanguine promoters.

Washington was, of course, the chief focus of excitement throughout the whole of this memorable
controversy. In both Houses of Congress the discussions which it engendered were frequent, acri-
monious, and animated. On one of these occasions,
the fervid eloquence of Mr. M'Duffie, which had
always a decided effect, produced a more than usually
powerful impression. Contrasting the condition of
South Carolina previously with that in which she
found herself subsequently to the tariff of 1828, he
detailed the blighting effects of that measure upon her
trade, commerce, and prospects, in a fine *crescendo*
passage, which he adroitly wound up by quoting, as
applicable to her situation, the couplet—

> " Not a rose of the wilderness left on its stalk,
>   To tell where a garden had been."

The importance of the subject, the momentous
nature of the issues involved, the excitement of the
occasion, the earnestness of the speaker, and the ap-
positeness of the quotation, all concurred in causing
the House to depart from the decorum which it usually
observes—audible expressions of applause breaking
from many of the benches around him.

An incident shortly afterwards occurred in connexion with the same subject, which not only produced an indescribable sensation in Congress, but also sent a thrill to the remotest extremities of the Union. As the contest was prolonged, it waxed hotter and hotter, the disputants daily assuming bolder positions, and giving utterance to more menacing alternatives. At length was fulminated, not by inuendo, but in express words, the terrible threat of a dissolution of the Union. The effect upon the House was as if a tocsin had suddenly sounded overhead. The startled senators looked incredulously at each other, in the hope that their ears had deceived them; but there was no deception in the case, for there stood the speaker, pale and trembling, his eye dilated, his lip quivering, and his whole attitude betokening that he had been awe-struck at the sounds to which his own voice had given utterance. There too, on the floor, but without the body of the House, were some of the high functionaries of State, and most of the diplomatic corps resident in Washington, looking grave and solemn; and there were the public galleries thronged with agitated but motionless occupants; whilst the very reporters looked as if they doubted the evidence of their senses, and their fingers refused to chronicle the words. The idea had long been afloat in the public mind as something merely within the range of possibility; but this broaching of it in the centre of the Republic, this open threat of it in the very temple of the Confederation, seemed to place the country, at one bound, half-way between the idea and its realisation. I have the testimony of several who witnessed the scene, that it was one of the most solemn and impressive description. It is difficult for a stranger to appreciate the attachment which an American

cherishes, no matter what part of the country he inhabits, for the federal Union,—whilst no one is in a
better position than he is to understand the perils to
which, from conflicting interests, it is liable. Until
the South, on this occasion, openly held it *in terrorem*
over the North, the idea of a dissolution of the Union
was spoken of more in whispers than otherwise. The
promulgation of it in Congress seemed to transfer it at
once from the category of things possible to that of
things probable; and it is now frequently referred to
with an unconcern more apparent than real, both
within and without the walls of the legislature. But
a great obstacle is removed from between an idea and
its consummation, when it becomes a familiar subject
of thought and topic of conversation, and when the
notion of its probability is one to which those who
are chiefly interested become more or less reconciled.
The integrity of the Union is no longer that solemn
and unquestionable reality which it used to be with
the American. His present attachment to it, great
though it be, rests upon a conviction of its expediency more than of its sacredness. The spell of its
sanctity was broken, when South Carolina threatened
to demonstrate its violability. It is now deemed
neither sacrilegious to speculate upon, nor unpatriotic
to menace it. For the present, however, it runs no
serious risk of disruption from fiscal disputes. Slavery
is its evil genius, and the question which is yet destined to put its solidity to the most perilous test.

Having no particular object in prolonging my stay,
I left Charleston, after two days' sojourn in it, *en route*
for New Orleans. My first intention was to proceed
as far south as Savannah; but as that town possessed
no feature of particular attraction, and as the sea-

coast region of Georgia had little in it to distinguish it from the corresponding districts in the two Carolinas, I abandoned the idea, and took the most direct route from Charleston to the great emporium of the West. I was all the more induced to do this on ascertaining that the route on which I had decided would lead me through some of the older and better parts of the State of Georgia back from the sea-coast, and bordering upon its more recent acquisitions from the Creeks and Cherokees,—acquisitions redounding more to the advantage of this and some of the neighbouring States, than to the credit of those who bore the chief part in the systematic spoliation by which they were effected.

The first point for which I made was Columbia, the capital of South Carolina, lying a little upwards of one hundred miles in a north-westerly direction from Charleston. The two places are connected by a railway, which, on my passing over it, was composed in most places of but a single line. For more than half the whole distance this line traverses the tide-water section of the State. Travelling upon it from Charleston to Columbia was but reversing the journey from Raleigh to Wilmington. There was but little to distinguish the one route from the other, except that, in this case, I was ascending to the higher and drier regions of the country, instead of descending, as in the other, to the low and marshy districts of the coast. The inhabitants divide the land into five or six different classes of soil, distinguishing them partly by their quality, and partly by their mere position. To the traveller, however, the State divides itself into but three great sections : the low tract on the coast, the middle region, and the high and mountainous district

to the west. These have each its peculiarities, whilst
their diversity of soil and production is found to be
advantageous to the general interests. The portion
of the low ground, known as the Tide-swamp, is rarely
found convertible to any useful purpose, rice being
extensively cultivated in the marshy soils lying immediately back of it, and beyond the range of the
tide. Along some parts of the coast hemp is also
found cultivated; on this belt, rice and cotton are the
staple articles of production of the State, and consequently figure most largely in its exports. Indigo
was at one time extensively cultivated in this State,
but it has since given way for other and more profitable crops. The principal cotton plantations are to
be found along the banks of the rivers, in the low
country, where the soil is of an excellent quality and
easily cultivated. The whole of this district, however, which has, in most places, from the quantity of
dark and sombre pitch-pine with which it abounds,
the gloomy and monotonous aspect described above
as characteristic of the great tide-water region, of
which it is but a portion, is so unhealthy that, from
May till October, every one possessed of or inheriting
a European constitution, who can manage to do so,
abandons it to the negroes, with whom it seems to
agree, or who are compelled to remain and run all the
hazards to which it may subject them. The approach
to the middle region is indicated by successive ridges
of sandy hillocks, their elevation being too trifling
to entitle them to a more dignified appellation.
Amongst these ridges flow a number of small streams,
which, in their descent to the low country, afford an
excellent water power, of which several companies have
availed themselves, by establishing factories upon them,

chiefly for the manufacture of the coarse and heavy osnaburgs already alluded to, designed almost exclusively for negro consumption. What makes the water power thus afforded all the more valuable is, that it is available all the year round, for such is the nature of the district through which the streams affording it flow, that they are seldom swollen by the heaviest rains, or dried up by the most protracted heats. It is scarcely necessary to add that they are never rendered useless by being arrested by frost.

Between these sandy elevations and the mountainous district to the westward, is a broad belt of country, in the main barren and unprofitable, but with rich and fertile veins of low-lying soil here and there intersecting it. On these are produced Indian corn, some indigo, and occasionally tobacco. Wheat is also raised, but to a trifling extent, South Carolina being chiefly provided from the north with the little quantity of this grain which she consumes. The remainder of this belt, including by far the greater portion of it, is almost entirely covered with pine, and is familiarly known as the "pine barrens." The dreary reaches of pine forest with which it is clothed are now and then broken by the *savannas*, which are neither more nor less than isolated prairies on a small scale, covered with a tall, rank grass, in the main too coarse for pasturage. Along the richer veins which permeate the tract is to be found a variety of timber, amongst which are conspicuous the hickory, the live oak, and occasionally the white and red cedar. Every here and there, too, the magnolia is to be met with amongst them, ornamenting the forest with its gay but not gaudy appearance, and perfuming the air with its luscious breath. Fruits, too, of almost all

kinds, abound in the richer portions of this region, as
they do also in the warm valleys lying beyond the
mountainous ridge to the westward, to which, however, my route did not lead me ; whilst wild flowers in
profusion are to be seen exhibiting their variegated
and dazzling colours along the skirts of the forest and
the margins of the streams.

In Europe we invariably associate with the idea of
a capital a large and splendid city, the seat of wealth,
luxury, and refinement. The European who might
carry this association with him to America would
subject himself to many singular surprises, but to none
more so than that which he would encounter on entering the capital of South Carolina.   It has fallen to
the lot of but few of the large and important towns
of America to be the seats of government of their
respective States.   The federal capital itself, as
already shown, is but a small, and, in all respects
but one, an unimportant place.   The sites of the
great cities have been selected with a view to the convenience of trade and commerce ; whereas in the
choice of those of the different seats of government,
a very different kind of convenience has been con-
sulted.   Boston and New Orleans * are the only two
large towns enjoying the dignity of capital cities—a
dignity which is denied to New York, Philadelphia,
Baltimore, Charleston, Cincinnati, and St. Louis.
In fixing upon the situation of the capital the object
in most of the States has been to select it at a point
as near the geographical centre of the State as possible.
The cities last named are all either at one side or at
one of the corners of their respective States.   Boston
is also eccentrically situated, but it still retains the

* The latter has since been deprived of it.

political preeminence in Massachussetts which it has
ever enjoyed. At first, when the population of each
State was greatly scattered, and the means of communication between one point and another were of
the most wretched and impracticable description,
there was good reason for consulting the general convenience, by placing the seat of government, in which
the legislature was annually to assemble, as nearly as
possible equidistant from its extremities.   Now,
however, that the means of travelling are greatly improved, and are still rapidly improving, the same
necessity does not exist ; and it is questionable, if the
selection had to be made now, if the large towns would
be abandoned for the sake of more central positions.
There is certainly another reason for the choice,
which still retains whatever of force it originally possessed, which is, that the deliberations of a legislature
essentially popular are much more likely to be properly and unmolestedly conducted in the midst of a
small, than of a large community. Very recent
events in Harrisburg, Pennsylvania, however, show
that even in a small town the sovereignty of a State
may be subjected to the most wanton outrage. If
the State legislature were always surrounded by a
certain amount of force for its protection, that force
would undoubtedly be of more avail against a few
than against a multitude of assailants. But such is
not the case ; the American legislatures depending for
their security, first upon the municipal authorities of
the places at which they assemble, and then, should
they fail them or prove insufficient, upon the militia
of the State. If, in a large town, the number of their
assailants might be great, the force which they could
summon for their protection would be great in pro-

portion. When in Harrisburg the legislature was summarily ejected by the mob from its place of meeting, the Governor of the State had to send to Philadelphia for aid to quell the riot. Had it occurred in that city, the probability is that no extraneous assistance would have been required for its suppression. Besides, in times of commotion, and when there may be a prospect of civil disturbances, the influence of the government should be particularly felt in the community, which, by its example, is capable of effecting the greatest good or evil; and this can only be done by its presence in the midst of it.

Columbia, the seat of government in South Carolina, is situated on the banks of a river called the Congaree, a stream of petty pretensions in America, but one which would cut a very respectable figure in the geography of a European kingdom. The town contains a population scarcely so numerous as that of Horsham, and would be esteemed as a fair specimen of a parliamentary borough in England. One would think that in selecting a site for their capital, fertility in the circumjacent region would be a *sine qua non* with any people. But not so with the Carolinians, who, in order to have it in as central a position as possible, have placed it in the midst of one of the most barren districts of the State. Luckily, its limited population renders it easy of supply, for it is difficult to see how a large community could subsist on such a spot, unless they could accommodate themselves to pinecones as their chief edible. But Palmyra managed to subsist in the desert, and so may Columbia in the wilderness, which is the only appellation which can properly be bestowed upon the dreary and almost unbroken expanse of pine forest which surrounds it.

Notwithstanding all its disadvantages in point of position, Columbia is, on the whole, rather an interesting little town. There is about it an air of neatness and elegance which betokens it to be the residence of a superior class of people—many of the planters whose estates are in the neighbourhood making it the place of their abode; as well as the governor, the chief functionaries of state subordinate to him, and some of the judges. There is little or nothing connected with the government buildings worthy of attention, their dimensions being very limited, and their style of a simple and altogether unambitious description. The streets, as in the majority of the southern towns of more recent origin, are long, straight, and broad, and are lined, for the most part, with trees, prominent amongst which is to be found the gay and flaunting "Pride of India." Here, in this small, quiet, and unimposing-looking town, are conducted the affairs of a sovereign State, at a cost of under 50,000*l.*, including not only the salaries of all its functionaries political, judicial, and municipal, but also the payment of the members of the legislature during their attendance at its annual sitting. South Carolina, however, is not so fortunate as to be free of debt like her northern namesake. Her absolute obligations exceed three millions of dollars, to which is to be added a contingent debt of about two millions, making her present total debt exceed five millions of dollars. On her absolute debt she now pays about 170,000 dollars a year by way of interest, or about 40,000*l.*, nearly as much as is required to defray the annual expense of the government of the State. She is not without something to show, however, as a set-off to the liabilities which she has incurred.

Her public works are more numerous than extensive, and are proportionate to her existing wants. By means of some of these, a communication by boats has been opened between the capital and the sea-board.

From Columbia I proceeded by railway towards Augusta. For the first half of the way the country was very uninteresting, being comparatively flat and sandy, and covered, for the most part, with the interminable pitch-pine. Indeed the pine barrens extend, with but little interruption, almost the entire way between the two places, the distance between them being from eighty to ninety miles. Here and there are some long stretches of marshy ground, over which the railway is carried, not by embankments, but upon piles, which impart to it a dangerous and shaky appearance. I was not surprised at the anxiety which almost every passenger manifested to get over these portions of the line without accident, especially when I learnt that there was danger in being detained upon them after night-fall. It was not simply, therefore, by the dread of a break-neck accident that they were animated, their fears being divided between such a possibility and any contingency which might expose them to the nocturnal miasmas of the marshes.

Whilst passing over one of these flimsy and aerial-looking viaducts, I left the carriage in which I was seated for the platform outside. In doing so, I perceived that I was followed by a little wiry-looking man of about forty years of age, who had evidently, before my making the movement, been regarding me for some time with the most marked attention. He was dressed in a pair of coarse grey trousers, a yellow waistcoat, and a superfine blue swallow-tailed coat, profusely bespangled with large and well-burnished brass buttons. His face, which had a sickly pallor about it, was strongly lined, and marked with a mingled expression of shrewdness and cunning, which gave it some fascination, at the same time that it bordered on the repulsive. He was becoming prematurely grey, his hair sticking out from his head as strong and crispy as catgut. I instinctively shrunk from him as he approached me, for I saw a large capital note of interrogation in each of his little and restless light blue eyes. Desirous of not being interrupted, I pulled out a note-book, with which I feigned to be engaged. Either the pretence was apparent to him, or, having made up his mind to address me, he was not going to be balked by a trifle. So approaching me still nearer, he put a finishing pressure upon the tobacco which was between his teeth, and the remaining juice of which he vehemently squirted over the platform of the succeeding carriage. Having done this he bent his head forward, opened his mouth wide, and the reeking quid fell at my feet. I turned half aside in disgust, and was meditating a retreat into the carriage, when—

"Good day, stranger," broke upon my ear, and intimated that I was too late.

"Good day," I replied, glancing at him at the same time; but he was not looking at me, for his eye was so vacantly intent upon the wilderness before us, that, for the moment, I doubted his having addressed me at all.

"How d'ye do?" said he again, after a few seconds' pause, nodding his head, and looking me for a moment full in the face, after which his eye again rivetted itself upon the forest.

" As well as a stranger could expect to be under such a sun in these stewing latitudes," I rejoined, at the same time wiping the perspiration, which was flowing very freely, from my face.

" You don't chew, p'r'aps?" added he, offering me his tobacco-box; on declining which he quietly replenished from its contents the void which the ejection of the last quid had left between his jaws.

" P'r'aps you snuff?" he continued.

I made a negative motion.

" Smoke?" he added.

" Occasionally," I replied.

" I don't—it's a dirty habit," said he, at the same time ejecting a quantity of poisoned saliva, a portion of which falling upon the iron railing which surrounded the platform, he rubbed off with his finger, which he afterwards wiped upon his trousers.

" In no way can the use of tobacco be regarded as a very cleanly habit," I remarked, looking at the stain which the operation had left upon the garment in question. But if he heard, he affected not to hear me, for after a brief pause, changing the subject—

" May be you'll be no Scotchman, I'm thinkin'," said he.

" May be you're mistaken if you think so," replied I.

" I opined as much from your tarting wrapper," he added, alluding to a small shepherd tartan plaid which I carried with me for night travelling.

" It has something of a Scottish look about it," I remarked drily.

" Then," said he, " I was right in my position."

" I did not say you were wrong," rejoined I.

" Stranger," added he, " had I been wrong, you'd 'a said so."

I looked again at my note-book, in the hope that

he would take the hint. But I was mistaken, for, after a brief silence, he continued—

" I'm fond of Scotchmen," looking at the same time hard at me, to see what effect was produced by the announcement of so astounding a piece of patronage.

" Indeed," I remarked, as unconcernedly as possible; at which he seemed somewhat annoyed, for he looked as if he expected me to grasp his hand.

" I'm a Scotchman myself," he added, fixing his eye upon me again.

I was sorry to hear it, but looked unmoved, simply replying by the monosyllabic ejaculation, " Ah."

" Not exactly a Scotchman," he continued, correcting himself; " for I was born in this country, and so were my father and grandfather before me."

" Then you have a longer line of American ancestors than most of your fellow-countrymen can boast of," I observed.

" We don't vally these things in this country," said he in reply ; " it's what's above ground, not what's under, that we think on. Been long in this country, stranger?"

" Some months."

" How much longer be you going to stay?" he added.

" That's more than I can tell," replied I, " the length of my stay depending on a variety of circumstances."

" You couldn't mention them?" he inquired coolly, expectorating over his right shoulder, to the imminent danger of another passenger who had just emerged from the carriage, and who, by a jerk of his body, missed the filthy projectile.

" If I were disposed to do so," said I, rather amused

at his impudence, "we should be at Augusta long before I could detail them all."

" I'm going further on," added he, as if to intimate that he would give me an opportunity of finishing my story on quitting Augusta.

" But I am not; and we are now but a few miles from it," I observed.

" May be you're on government business?" said he, endeavouring to extort by piecemeal that of which he was denied an ample narration.

" May be I'm not," was all the satisfaction he had.

" I don't think you're in the commercial line," he continued, unabashed; " and you don't look as if you was travelling for pleasure neither."

" It's very singular," was my reply.

" How long d'ye think you'll stay in this free country? " he asked, baffled in his cross-examination as to my object and pursuits.

" Until I'm tired of it," said I.

" When will that be ? " he inquired.

" Perhaps not till I'm homesick," I replied.

" That'll be very soon," said he; " for most Europeans get homesick mightily soon after comin' here."

" You give but a poor account of your country," I observed.

" You're mistaken, stranger," he remarked, " I don't mean homesick."

" You said homesick," rejoined I.

" But I meant, sick of home," he added, in a tone of great emphasis; " for they can't be long in the midst of our free institootions without a gettin' dead sick of their tyrannical governments."

" It depends a good deal upon their turn of mind, and a little upon their strength of stomach," I remarked ; for at that moment the tobacco-juice was oozing rapidly from either corner of his mouth. He did not comprehend the allusion, and I judged it as well to leave him in the dark.

I must do him the justice to say that, having exhibited himself in the best possible manner as an interrogator, he became gratuitously communicative, informing me that his name was Mackenzie, that he was descended from one of the Highland colonists who had been transplanted to Georgia more than a century ago; that his great grandfather had worn a kilt in the colony (the mountaineers preserved their dress and manners for a number of years after their arrival); that a maiden aunt of his had died, on her passage out from Scotland some years since—a great misfortune to herself, he admitted, but a blessing to him, as she left him a considerable sum of money, which enabled him to begin the world afresh, after having compounded a second time with his creditors ; that he had married, on prosperity returning to him, and that in four years he had had five children. He was of course much interested in his own narrative, and as there was nothing in the landscape to deserve attention, I listened and was amused. He soon, however, took a more enlarged range, and detailed to me with great volubility his views as to the superior and illimitable capacities of the Celtic race. It was his profound belief too, that what the Celts were to the rest of mankind, the Mackenzies were to the Celts. By some curious philological process which I could not at all comprehend, he deduced all the Presidents of the Union, either directly or indirectly, from the clan. Madison was clearly a Mackenzie, as he proved by the analogy subsisting between the two names, perceptible after dropping several letters and putting others in their places. Nay more, he proceeded to show that most of the great men of other countries and climes, if not exactly Mackenzies, appertained to the race of superior intelligences which culminated in that clan. I asked him in what light in this respect he regarded Confucius and the Apostle Paul; to which he replied, that he was not sure as to their being Highlanders, but was certain that they were not Anglo-Saxons. With one reflection he was exceedingly gratified, viz. that as St. Paul had the gift of tongues, he must have spoken Gaelic—a fact which I ventured to question, on the ground of there being no proof of there having been any Highlanders at the time to preach to in Jerusalem.

"There's no proof that there were not," he observed, "but there is of their having been settlers in the East at the time of the Patriarchs. We find," he continued, "that Abraham himself had dealings with them."

"I was aware," I replied, "that the Grants had been discovered in Genesis, but beyond this I have never heard of any text which bears you out in your assertion."

"Did not Abraham purchase the field of Machpelah, or rather Macphelah, as it should have been rendered?" he asked, in a tone which betokened his belief that he had caught me.

"Truly," said I, "but that was not a person's name, but that of the field."

"Are you not aware," he asked, "that, even to this day, properties amongst the Highlanders take the name of their chiefs, and chiefs that of their properties? There is Maclean of Maclean, for instance."

" You mean, then," observed I, " that he purchased the field of Mac Phelah of that ilk ?"

"Certainly," he replied, "and the Mac Phails of the present day are the descendants of the Mac Phelahs of old."

He had great respect for the mechanical abilities of the Anglo-Saxons, but in his opinion they owed all their greatness to their having been guided by the Celtic mind. They had done little that the " niggers " couldn't achieve if they were closely watched and kept at it; the chief difference, he thought, between the two being, that the one race was naturally industrious, and the other lazy.

One of the most marked peculiarities of his mind was the hatred which he cherished to the British government. He could not say that it had ever done him any individual mischief, but he seemed to deem it necessary, as an American and a republican, to hate all tyrannies in general, and that of Great Britain in particular. He had not the slightest conception of the existence of anything like political or conventional freedom in England. He could not believe that an Englishman could walk the streets or the fields, or proceed with his daily business, with as little molestation and with as much security as an American, and with even more security than many of them, as far as regarded his protection by the laws. From his idea of the British government, he could not dissociate the " red coats," who came in for the very quintessence of his hatred, and whom he regarded as the ubiquitous oppressors of the people all over the island. I endeavoured, but in vain, to modify his opinion in this respect. He would not be convinced, and was amazed that, as a subject of the British crown, I could not

see the system of espionage and military tyranny to
which, in common with the rest of my countrymen,
I was subjected. I afterwards found this violence
of feeling characteristic of the Scotchmen and their
immediate descendants in America, the genius of
the race being such as apparently to lead them to
extremes in the opinions which they espouse with
regard to politics, morals, or religion.

" Is that Augusta? " I inquired, as a tall and rather
handsome spire at length made its appearance in
advance of us."

" I reckon as how it is," he replied, such being his
manner of elaborating a simple affirmative.

In a few minutes afterwards we were on the banks
of the Savannah, which here separates Georgia from
South Carolina. Our halting-place was a small and
very unpretending-looking village called Hamburgh,
which in reality served as a suburb to Augusta, on the
opposite side of the river. After a few minutes' stay
here, we crossed the river to Augusta, where I took
leave of the singular being who had alternately annoyed
and amused me for the last half hour of the journey.

The Savannah, opposite Augusta, is about two-
thirds the width of the Thames at Waterloo-bridge.
It is a muddy-looking stream, with a current of from
three to four miles an hour. For most of the way
down to the city of Savannah, which is about twenty
miles from its mouth, its banks are covered with
wood, broken by numerous clearances in the neighbourhood of Augusta, on which Indian corn is raised
with ease and in great abundance. The depth of the
river suffices for a steamboat communication between
Augusta and Savannah, the former being thus directly
connected with the two great southern Atlantic sea-

ports, its junction with Charleston being effected by
the South Carolina railway, from which the line to
Columbia diverges as a branch. Augusta is situated
on a bluff, a considerable height above the river, and
when viewed from the Carolina side of the stream
presents a pretty if not an imposing appearance. It
is but a small town, its population scarcely amounting
to 8,000, and fully one-half of this number being
negroes, nearly all of whom are slaves. The principal
streets, which run parallel to the river, are of a prodigious width, being surpassed in this respect by
nothing which I met with in the United States, with
the single exception of Pennsylvania-avenue in
Washington. Like most other American towns, particularly in the South, its streets are ornamented with
rows of trees, the " Pride of India " figuring amongst
them, as it usually does in street scenery south of the
Potomac. The plan of the town is faultlessly regular,
and the streets occupied by private dwellings are
very neat, and some of them elegant in their appearance. The principal building of which it boasts is
the Court House, a large and handsome brick edifice,
surmounted by a lofty and rather awkward-looking
cupola. Behind it is the Medical-college, ornamented
in front with a Greek portico, and surmounted by a
miniature dome. On the whole, Augusta is a place
which leaves an impression rather favourable than
otherwise on the mind of the traveller.

Considering its inland position, it is a place of no
little trade. It is the point on which the planters
west of it annually concentrate their produce for sale,
and whence they procure their supplies, its position
rendering it, as it were, but an advanced post of
Charleston and Savannah.

A little behind the town are some gentle heights, which are besprinkled with neat little villas, the resort, in summer time, of many of the wealthier citizens, who retire to them with their families for the hotter months on account of their greater ɔol-ness and salubrity.

I left next day for Milledgeville, the capił of Georgia, between which place and Augusta the country resembled in its essential features the district intervening between the latter place and Columbia, with the exception that we more frequently came upon small isolated fertile tracts in the midst of the gloomy pine forests through which still lay our course. The pitch-pine, which here attains its great-est perfection, is a source of considerable wealth to Georgia, not only in supplying the Union with resin-ous matter for its consumption, but as affording the very best material for spars, masts, &c., for the navy both national and commercial. The live oak, which is also here met with, is likewise in great demand for ship-building purposes, but it flourishes much better in the lower districts nearer the coast.

Of Milledgeville but very little can be said. Its site, which is on the banks of the Oconee river, is not ill chosen, either as regards convenience or prospect; but the town itself, the greater part of which resembles a straggling village, is devoid of interest, whilst the accommodation which it affords to the traveller is not of the best description. I entered it without having formed any great expectations of it, and left it, as soon as I could, with the impression that it was one of the most undesirable places I had yet visited in America.

CHAPTER VIII.

It was late at night when I left Milledgeville.
Here, for the first time on my way from Boston to
New Orleans, I had to betake myself to a stage coach,
the previous part of the journey, extending over
upwards of 1,200 miles, having been entirely performed by railway and steamer.*   In England, after a
long railway ride, the prospect of a stage coach
journey is the reverse of disagreeable.   With a good
road, a highly cultivated and picturesque country,
and a well appointed coach, nothing can be more
delightful in the way of travelling than an outside
seat on one of those old but now almost traditional

* The railways have since been extended westward.

vehicles. It is a pity that the utilitarianism of the age could not have left us some of the poetry of travelling. The railways have swallowed up the stage coaches, and now bid fair to devour one another.

The sooner the coach is entirely driven out of the field in America the better, for neither in itself nor in its accompaniments is it poetical or convenient. Before entering it I had the curiosity to examine that which was to convey me from Milledgeville to Macon, about thirty miles off, which I was but partly enabled to do by the glimmering light of a tin lantern, which had the peculiarity of never being precisely where it was wanted. The coach was a huge bulky concern, built more with a view to strength than elegance of shape. It was not long ere I had reason to appreciate the policy of this. The night being dry, though dark, I mounted one of the hind wheels, as the first step of my progress to an outside seat, a manœuvre by which I first became acquainted with the fact that there were no outside seats upon it, an American stage being like a canal boat, all hold. This is a regulation which is more the result of necessity than choice; the condition of the roads rendering it essential that the centre of gravity should be kept as low as possible, an object which is attained by stowing all the passengers inside. In the summer time, as the coach holds nine, and as ten or eleven are sometimes packed into it, it may easily be imagined that the condition of the traveller is anything but an enviable one; for when, gasping, he opens the window for air, he gets such a quantity of dust into mouth, nose, ears, and eyes, that he is fain to shut it again with all speed. In winter they are more comfortable, as the passengers keep each

other warm ; but then the state of the roads is such
that they are in constant apprehension of being upset
into the mud, or upon the hard frozen ground,
according to the temperature ; an apprehension which,
in a journey of any length, is seldom falsified. On
examining into the state of the springs, I found that
the vehicle rested upon two broad and strong belts of
leather, each of which was securely attached, at
either end, to a species of spring which rose to the
height of about two feet from the axletree. Ordinary metal springs would have been as useless for the
support of a machine destined for such service, as a
horse trained to good roads would have been for
drawing it.

It was provided internally with three seats, one at
either end and one in the middle, extending across
from window to window. The back of the middle
seat consisted of a broad leather belt, which could be
unhooked at one end for the convenience of passengers making for, or making from, the back seat. I
had not seen them get in, and was therefore surprised,
on stepping in myself, to find every seat occupied,
but one next the window in the middle of the coach.
No one spoke, and as it was almost pitch dark, I
could tell neither the size, the age, the sex, nor the
complexion of my fellow-travellers.

After a great deal of apparently unnecessary delay
we at length moved off, the lumbering vehicle, in
passing through the streets of the town, rolling
smoothly enough, but heaving and plunging like a
vessel in a troubled sea as soon as we got into the
open country road.

" We'll have a heavy ride of it," said a gruff voice
on my left, for the first time breaking the silence
which prevailed. " The rain have been sweet here

for a day or two, and made mush and milk of the roads."

"You're forgetting that they're sandy, and that they'll be rather hard than otherwise after the showers," said the passenger immediately beyond him in a shrill falsetto tone.

"Sandy here b'aint sandy there," replied the other, who afterwards turned out to be "Judge Fish," (a county judge and not necessarily a lawyer,) from one of the "river counties" of New York, his companion being an attorney and Commissioner of Deeds from Long Island; "there are bits of the salt marsh up here, young man, where the roads will be petick'lar pretty, I reckon."

He had scarcely spoken ere the coach gave a tremendous lurch to one side, and for a moment or two remained poised upon the two lower wheels; but by all inclining as much as we could to windward, we got it restored to a more secure position. It was not without a violent struggle, accompanied by a continued torrent of ejaculations from the driver, that our horses managed to drag us from the hole into which the near wheels had slipped.

"Hope the next 'll be no worse," said the judge; whose observations, in connexion with the incident, made most of us feel as if an additional premium upon a life policy would be considered no great hardship by us.

"Best to look out for squalls in time," he continued, at the same time extending a hand on each side and grasping with one of them the looped leather strap, which, hanging from the side of the coach close to my shoulder, seemed placed there more for my convenience than for his.

"I have no objection to your holding the strap for

security," said I, " but I have a great deal to your arm rubbing against my face."

" Sorry to onconvenience you," replied the judge, " but I'm holdin' on in the same way to the other side."

" That may put the balance of advantages in your favour, but not in mine," said I, getting somewhat irritated, and not without reason, at the position in which he had placed himself.

" Some people are mighty petick'lar about trifles," he observed, as quitting his hold he passed his arm behind me and grasped the strap as before. " I'll do anything reasonable to oblige," he continued, " but self-preservation is the first law of nature, and I'm always punctual in my observance of it."

After a few minutes' pause he added, " Besides, I'm doin' you both a service," alluding to the passenger on his other side; " for if the coach tumbles to this side (mine), you'll be only half as much squeezed as you would be but for the opposite strap, whilst that on your side will serve this here gen'leman as good a turn, should we lurch into the muck on his side."

There was some comfort in this, and I held my peace.

" I'll tell you what it is," he resumed, " I have travelled a few, that's a fack, and I have found that there's nothing like the middle seat in these coaches; for if you upset you have only one passenger to fall on you, when you fall softly on another. One of you folks at the end may escape, but if we get a tumble, the other is sure to ha' two of us on the top of him. That mightn't be so comfortable, might it?"

I did not answer, but was positive that it would not.

" But only let me hold on by the upper side as

we're agoin' over," he said still continuing, " and the lowermost one will have some chance of getting his bones whole to Macon. I'm fourteen stun' weight, and would make a mighty pretty squash comin' down on any of you."

Although his precautions were dictated by the purest selfishness, I had reason to see that I was somewhat interested in them, for I shuddered at the bare prospect of an upset, with the judge and the commissioner both on the top of me.

On we went, sometimes rolling smoothly for a few yards, and then plunging and rising again as if, instead of being on *terra firma*, we were afloat and encountering a short cross sea. At length, with a jerk which nearly shook the vehicle to pieces and dislocated every bone in our bodies, we stuck fast in a hole full of mud and water.

" I'm blow'd if we ha'n't run agin' a sawyer," said the judge, fancying himself for a moment on the Mississippi.

" Passengers must walk a bit here," roared the driver from the roof, " for we're aground and can't get out of it no how else."

" Walkin's a recreation," said the judge; " let's spill out and have a little of the diversion."

We did spill out, but it was only by dint of a good leap that we cleared the hole, into which the fore-wheels had sunk up to the axletree. As it was, we were up to the ankles in mud, a circumstance which, added to the darkness of the night, made walking in that particular instance anything but a recreation. There was one lady on the back seat who remained in; but what surprised me was, that those on the front seat did not follow us out. On expressing my surprise at this to the judge, he simply observed that it was easier said than done; a remark the drift of which I did not comprehend, nor did I think it worth while to ask for an explanation.

We were about to proceed a little in advance, when the driver requested us to remain where we were, as we "might be needed." I was wondering what we could be needed for, unless it was to get in again, when the judge, after watching for a moment or two the ineffectual struggles of the horses to rescue the coach from its position, observed—"It's no use, we must have the rail." He thereupon detached one of the lamps from the vehicle, and proceeded to the side of the road to look for the article in question; but there being no fence on either hand, it was not until we had penetrated for some distance into the forest that we found a piece of timber that would answer the purpose of a stout lever. Returning with this, it was applied to the sunken wheels, by which means, after some further desperate struggles on the part of the cattle, the vehicle was raised to the natural level of the road.

"Can't get in yet," said the driver to me as I was about to resume my place; "the road's shockin' bad for the next half mile; so walk's the word."

There was no gainsaying this, so with the judge, the commissioner, and two fellow-passengers from the back seat, I set out in advance of the coach. Before doing so, however, the driver informed us that it would be advisable for us not to part from the pole, as we might frequently require it before we resumed our seats, and the absence of fences making it doubtful if we could always procure an implement so well suited to our purpose. It was, therefore, agreed

that we should take it turn about, and on the sug-
gestion of the judge we cast lots who should first
bear the burden. The lot fell upon me; so off we
started, my fellow-travellers leading, and I following
them, with an immense log on my shoulder, as well
as I could. It was so dark, that it was of no avail
to pick our steps; so on we went, keeping as near the
side as possible, generally ankle-deep in mud, and
sometimes still deeper. The coach came lumbering
after us at a snail's pace, the lonely woods reverberating to the noisy eloquence which the driver was
unremittingly expending upon his cattle. I was
about transferring the pole to the commissioner, to
whom fate had next assigned it, when a cry of dis-
tress from the above-named functionary brought us
all back to the coach again. The pole had once more
to be applied before it was extricated from its difficulties. We took nearly three-quarters of an hour
to get over the half-mile in question, when we found
ourselves once more upon a sandy, and consequently
a firmer part of the road. On getting in again, the
judge, who had become jocular with our difficulties,
advised us to wipe our feet before entering.

" I told you as how it would eventuate," said he,
as soon as we were all reseated; " it wasn't with my
eyes shut that I passed through these diggin's afore."

" I reckon not," said the commissioner, rendering
tardy homage to his companion's superior topogra-
phical knowledge.

The road, although it fulfilled none of the conditions to a good one, was now for some miles much
better than that which we had passed over. It was still
rough, but we were not every now and then brought
to a halt in the midst of quagmires as before. The

jolting of the vehicle, whenever the horses for a few paces ventured upon a trot, was terrific, throwing us about in every way, against each other, and sometimes against the roof. One of these jolts sent me upwards with such force as to knock my hat over my eyes. As I was extricating myself from my dilemma, the judge remarked that a hat was rather an "onpleasant convenience" to travel with in a stage; a proposition which I had neither reason nor inclination to dispute. I immediately put mine in the straps above me, but the next jolt nearly sending my head through the crown of it, I was fain, for the rest of the road, to carry it on my knee.

By this time the judge and the commissioner had waxed very hot on politics, the latter being a Whig, and the former a Democrat of the purest water. So long as they confined themselves to topics of a general interest I listened, and was both interested and amused; but as soon as they descended to matters peculiarly appertaining to their own State, my attention flagged, and I soon fell into that listless state in which one hears everything without comprehending anything.

I had observed that ever since our re-entering the coach, the passenger directly opposite me, one of the three who, as I supposed, occupied the front seat, with their backs to the horses, paid particular attention to the position of my boots; for, not having got out himself in the time of our difficulty, he was not disposed to go shares in the mud with which our extremities were bedaubed on re-entering. Finding him, at length, very sensitive to the slightest touch from me, I proposed, for our mutual accommodation, a settlement of legs such as would serve until our

arrival at Macon. This was at once assented to, not
by the man opposite me, but by the man in the middle
of the seat. I was puzzled to know how a limb of
his could become involved with mine, as I was also to
ascertain how my fellow-passenger opposite had disposed of his. The arrangement proposed, however,
took place to our mutual satisfaction, but my surprise was not lessened when, on addressing a com-
mon-place remark, apropos to our situation, to him
opposite me, the response came again from the man
in the middle, whose voice was not altogether unfa-
miliar to me, although I could not then recall to
mind whose it was, or where I had heard it before.

At length day began slowly to dawn behind us, and
as the grey light gradually invested objects with a
more distinct outline, I could better understand the
character of the road over which we were dragged and
jolted, at the rate of about four miles an hour. It
was artistic enough in the manner in which it had
been engineered, but its long straight vistas were
wearisome to the eye. It was about sixty feet in
breadth, and in those places where it was least sandy
it appeared to have been recently ploughed. Indeed,
as I afterwards ascertained, the roads both in Canada
and the United States become sometimes so bad and
impracticable, that they are decidedly improved by
the operation of ploughing. On seeing it in daylight,
my wonder was not that we had been delayed and
inconvenienced on the way, but that we managed to
make any progress whatever along this great southern
highway. It is but just, however, to say, that its
then wretched condition was greatly attributable to the
previous wet weather; for I afterwards found that
during a long succession of dry weather, these crude

American roads were delightful to travel over, after a gentle summer shower had fallen to keep down the dust.

The approach of day also solved the mystery which hung over the occupants of the opposite seat. Through the dim twilight I could at first discern but one head between the three, and the increasing light soon convinced me that it was the head of Mr. ——, one of the Senatorial representatives of the State of Alabama. The riddle was now explained. There was but one passenger opposite instead of three. Mr. —— was not a body with three heads, but he was a head with three bodies, or with one which was tantamount to three, for he almost entirely filled the seat. In the Senate, as already noticed, his seat was more like a form than a chair, which it purported to be; and he was familiarly known as the man of greatest weight in that body. As soon as I was sure of his identity, I accosted him, as I had frequently had the pleasure of enjoying his society at Washington. He was one of the bulkiest men I ever beheld; but his enormous physical proportions did not hamper his mind, which was cool and clear. He was a true southerner in politics, being an ardent free-trader, and a staunch follower of Mr. Calhoun. I had often wondered how he could exist under the hot suns of Alabama, but he had a preference for the State, and said he enjoyed life in it as well as anywhere else. The wretched state of the road, and our night experiences of it, soon very naturally turned our conversation upon the subject of railways; and from what I then gathered from him in reference thereto, as well as from my own previous observations, I shall now, with the reader's permission, give a brief sketch of the rise, development and extent of the railway system in America.

The stranger meets with nothing in the New World more calculated to excite his astonishment than the rapidity and extent with and to which all the improvements of this ingenious and progressive age are there applied to the various purposes of social life. Our cousins beyond the Atlantic are no dreamers, they are in haste to be practical; whatever is both new and useful they at once adopt, adapting it, in its application, to their own circumstances and necessities. Nor is theirs an imitation which springs from servility; it begins in generous emulation, and not unfrequently ends in successful rivalry.

It was not to be expected that a railway could be long in successful operation in this country before it was extensively imitated in the United States. If the advantages of such a system of communication were obvious as regarded this country, they were much more so as regarded America, considering not only the distances by which its more important points were separated from each other, but also the inferior nature of their means of intercommunication, when so situated with reference to each other that steamboats could not ply between them. Before the introduction of railways into America, canals formed the only decent means of communication between such points as lay neither upon the coast, the lakes, nor on the margin of great rivers. On these canals the maximum rate of speed seldom exceeded four miles an hour; so that if long journeys could be performed by their means without broken bones, or a serious wear and tear of the system, they could only be accomplished at great expense, and with a great loss of time. All this contributed to make distances as much the curse of the United States as they are said to be of Russia; and it is no wonder that our enterprising kinsfolk eagerly availed themselves of a discovery, the adaptation of which to their wants was as practicable as it was obvious, inasmuch as in travelling it would not only greatly diminish expense, but save much time, by almost annihilating space. In addition to this, the Americans have ever been a people peculiarly addicted to locomotion; so that, whilst the introduction of railways was a welcome event, everything conspired to accelerate their multiplication in the United States.

The extent to which the railway system has already developed itself there is truly surprising; whilst the schemes which are as yet only projected, are on a scale of vastness utterly bewildering to those who are unacquainted with the nature, the capacities, and the wants of the country. But it is not my intention to trouble the reader with any detail as to the projected schemes, my sole object being here to give him, as it were, a picture of the system as already completed and in operation.

The railways of America as already completed divide themselves into three great systems, corresponding with the great natural features of the country. The first, and most northerly of these systems, is that which permeates the valley of the St. Lawrence; the next, that which follows the course of the great sea-coast region, lying between the Atlantic and the Alleganies; and the third being collateral to that last named, and diverging from it principally through the defiles of the Alleganies to the valley of the Mississippi. The most northerly branch

of the system, first named, is that leading from Portland, on the coast of Maine, to Montreal, the capital
of Canada. The moiety of this line falls within the
limits of Canada, but I class it amongst American
railways belonging to the St. Lawrence system,
although one of its termini may be in a different
jurisdiction. We have then, a considerable distance
to the south of this, the great line leading from Boston to Buffalo, a distance of nearly 550 miles. It is
true, that the greater portion of this line is within
the territory of New England, and the valley of the
Mohawk immediately to the west of it; that portion of it alone which lies beyond the small lakes
which divide eastern from western New York, being
strictly within the basin of the St. Lawrence. But
from Boston to Buffalo is one great system of railway
communication, which will yet receive its chief development in that basin, being yet destined to expand
into lengthened and numerous ramifications on both
sides of the great lakes, in Canada, as well as in the
United States. The portion of it lying without the
basin, and particularly that extending from Albany
on the Hudson, to Boston, a distance of 200 miles,
derives its chief importance from its connexion with
the lines already constructed in the remote interior,
and will yet owe its chief value to the ramified
development which these lines will yet receive
throughout the vast and fertile districts bordering
upon the great lakes. The Portland and Montreal
railway, after crossing the northern section of the
State of Maine, enters Canada and the valley of the
St. Lawrence near the " Eastern Townships," after
passing through which, it pursues its way to Montreal, along the low flat grounds by which, above

Quebec, the river is chiefly skirted on its southern side. It leads the traveller from the coast at once into the heart of Canada, and will be of great service to the province during the winter season, when all other means of readily communicating with the open sea are interrupted by the frost. The greatest drawback to this line will be found in the rather dangerous character of the broken and deeply-indented coast of Maine. Portland is one of the best harbours which it affords, but in making it it is necessary to have a perfect knowledge of the coast, and to use the greatest circumspection. Once at Montreal the traveller can easily and rapidly gain the upper portion of the province by steamer, which will convey him, flanking the rapids by means of short canals, the whole way to Kingston, at the foot of Lake Ontario, from which point a water communication with the entire west opens before him. There can be no doubt but that at no very distant day Montreal and Kingston will be connected by railway, as will also Kingston and Toronto, when a short line from the last-mentioned place to Lake Huron will complete the chain, pursuing the north bank of the river above Montreal, from the ocean to the Far West. Its entire length will be about 900 miles. The line from Boston, pursuing a parallel course more to the south, crosses the Hudson River at Albany, the capital of New York, at which point Montreal is several hundred miles almost due north of it; and proceeding from Albany westward, along the valley of the Mohawk, enters western New York, after crossing Lake Cayuga by a stupendous wooden bridge, from which point it runs for upwards of 150 miles still further westward, until it abuts on Lake Erie at the

town of Buffalo. This highway to the West is independent of Canada, passing Lake Ontario altogether,
which it leaves considerably to the north of it, and
terminating on the American bank of Lake Erie. To
almost the whole of Canada West, however, it is a
better means of approach than the other route, for
at Rome, in the centre of New York, a branch line
diverges to Oswego, whence the traveller can be conveyed by steam to any of the Canadian ports on Lake
Ontario. From the city of Rochester also, through
which the railway passes, he can proceed by the Lake
either to Toronto or Hamilton, from which places
Rochester is about equidistant; or he may leave
the main line at Lockport, and proceed by a branch
to Lewiston, from which, about seven miles below
the Falls, he can cross the Niagara River, a link of
the St. Lawrence, into Canada, at Queenston. If
again his destination be some point still further
west in the province, he need not leave the railway
until he arrives at Buffalo, from which he can be
easily ferried across. If he is bound for the extreme
west of the province, he may be conveyed by steamer
from Buffalo to Detroit, the capital of Michigan,
between which and the extremity of Canada in this
direction, the narrow channel of the St. Clair, another
link of the St. Lawrence, alone intervenes. This line,
therefore, is as convenient as an approach from the
coast to Canada West, as it is to the north-western
States of the Union; the point at which the traveller bound for Canada leaves it depending upon
the part of the province which he has selected as his
destination.

Before this great system, thus developing itself, as
we have seen, on both sides of the basin of the

St. Lawrence, with the great lakes for the most part between, is perfected, a trunk line, with branches running southward, will have to be constructed along the southern shore of Lake Erie, extending through the north-western corner of Pennsylvania, and the northern part of Ohio, to the State of Michigan. Across the neck of the peninsula forming this State a line is now in process of formation, which will connect the upper portion of Lake Erie with the lower end of Lake Michigan. From St. Joseph's, the terminus of this line on the latter lake, the traveller can proceed by steamer to Chicago in Illinois, or Milwanki in Wisconsin. The line to be constructed between Buffalo and Michigan will, with its branches, serve more as a convenience to the great and fertile district lying between these two points, and to the south of Lake Erie, than as a link in the more direct chain of communication between the coast and the Far West. The direct line between the two extremities of the system will pass from Amherstburg, almost opposite Detroit, to Hamilton, at the head of Lake Ontario, across the peninsula of Western Canada. From Hamilton passengers will be conveyed by steamer to Rochester, where they will join the portion of the line running through New York. This will avoid the tedious navigation of the whole length of Lake Erie, or the serious detour by railway from Detroit to Buffalo.

Such is the railway system in the basin of the St. Lawrence, as it is, and as it is to be. Much of it has been already completed, but it is yet in the infancy of its development. The main line, extending from Boston westward, has numerous branches in its course, both through Massachussetts and New York, which in this general view of the system are not worth particularising. Portland and Boston are not its only outlets on the coast; for, from Albany, New York is as easily attainable, in summer, by the Hudson, as Boston is by railway. In winter, however, the river is useless; and if New York would retain its share of the winter traffic of the West, it must construct a railway along the left bank of the river.

A great State railway, extending for about 400 miles through the southern counties of the State, is already partly completed, which will put New York in direct railway communication with the Far West. This line is designed to connect the Hudson, a short distance above the city, with Lake Erie at Dunkirk, some distance above Buffalo; but it is obvious that, although it may secure the city at all times of the year a portion of the traffic of the extreme west, this line will be of no avail to it as regards Canada, and the greater and better portion of western New York. The New York and Erie railroad was undertaken more with a view to satisfy the southern counties of the State, the people of which grumbled at being so entirely eclipsed by the northern counties, which monopolized the Erie canal as well as the railways, than from a sense of its utility. The importance of this system, even in its present state of partial completion, is obvious, when we consider the vast region to which it affords an outlet; and its value when perfected, as it yet undoubtedly will be, may be appreciated by reflecting that, commencing in the Far West, and proceeding by two great and parallel branches along the two sides of the vast basin which it will permeate, with the volume of Lake Erie and that of Lake Ontario between them, which branches will have their tributary lines diverging from them in all directions, it will concentrate with facility upon the coast at Portland, Boston, and New York, the trade and traffic of the two Canadas, of the State of New York, of a great portion of Pennsylvania, of the northern half of Ohio, of the whole of Michigan, of considerable sections of Indiana and Illinois, and of nearly the whole of Wisconsin.

The line from Boston westward, as already completed, leads from that city by the towns of Springfield and Pittsfield, and through the highlands of New England, a distance of two hundred miles, to Greenbush, opposite Albany on the Hudson. The river is crossed by steam ferry-boat; after which the railway, recommencing at Albany and passing through the city of Schenectady, conveys the passenger a distance of ninety miles to the city of Utica. From this point the line is prolonged by continuous links, in the hands of several companies, through the towns of Rome, Syracuse, Auburn, Geneva, and Canandaigua, to the city of Rochester, a distance of 140 miles. From Rochester other companies prolong it for a further distance of ninety miles, through Batavia and Lockport, and by the Falls of Niagara, to Buffalo, the whole length of the trunk line being thus upwards of 500 miles.

In about forty hours after he lands at Boston the traveller may, by this line, find himself at the Falls of Niagara; so that in the months of May, June, and July, when short passages of the Atlantic are made, a party proceeding from Liverpool might be upon Table Rock, in full view of the cataract, on the fifteenth or sixteenth day after their departure. Such are the triumphs of railways and steam!

Boston may be also regarded as the starting point

of the coast system of railways. As already shown,
this city is united to New York by three distinct lines
of railway communication. Two of these terminate
on the coast, one at Stonington, and the other at
Alleyn's Point on the River Thames, a little above
New London; the remainder of the journey being
performed up the Sound by steamer. The third line
is more circuitous as a railway communication, being
that by the Long Island railway ; the only interruption to which as an unbroken line, is in the ferry
between Alleyn's Point and the island. Brooklyn,
the New York terminus of the line, situated on the
western extremity of the island, is in reality, although
a city with a corporation of its own, one of the
suburbs of New York, with which it is in communication at several points by means of steam ferry-
boats starting every five minutes from either side.
In addition to these, a new and more direct line has
recently been projected, which, passing chiefly through
the States of Massachusetts and Connecticut, will
unite the two cities without the intervention of any
steamers or ferry-boats whatever.

The next link in the chain of the coast system is
that uniting New York to Philadelphia. If the
former, which is already a triple, promises ere long
to be a quadruple one, this is at least a double link
in the chain. From Jersey city, on the opposite side
of the Hudson, and within ten minutes' reach of New
York by steam ferry-boat, the New York and Philadelphia line extends, passing by Newark, New Bruns-
wick, Princeton, Trenton, and New Burlington, all
in the State of New Jersey, to the small town of
Camden, on the eastern bank of the Delaware, and
directly opposite Philadelphia. This line, the whole

of which is within the limits of New Jersey, and for the right of way of which the company pays to the State treasury so much a head for every passenger conveyed by it, is that exclusively used during the winter season, when the Delaware is impassable from ice. During summer, however, passengers generally proceed from a little beyond Trenton to Philadelphia by the river, the steamer which conveys them sailing at a rate equal to average railway speed. There is another line of railway which extends from Amboy to Camden, the former being a seaport of New Jersey on Raritan Bay, and approachable from New York, from which it is from thirty to forty miles distant, by the devious and romantic passage known as Staten Island Sound. This route, however, is more used for goods, than for passenger traffic.

The next link in the chain is that leading from Philadelphia to Baltimore. The line connecting these two cities, and passing, in its course, through the State of Delaware, is unbroken, except at the Susque-hannah, the estuary of which is both too broad and too deep to bridge, passengers and goods being conveyed across by steam. Starting from the Delaware, this line crosses successively the Schuylkill near Phila-delphia, the Brandywine near Wilmington (Delaware), the Susquehannah by ferry at Havre-de-Grace, and the Gunpowder Creek, by a long wooden viaduct between the last-named place and Baltimore. During the winter season, it is the only line of communication between Philadelphia and Baltimore. There is a summer route, however, generally selected by passen-gers during that season, and which, like some of those already adverted to, combines steamboat with railway travelling. Proceeding by this route, the traveller first descends the Delaware for about 40 or 50 miles, from Philadelphia to Newcastle, in the State of Delaware. From Newcastle he is then conveyed to Frenchtown, by a railway sixteen miles in length, over the narrow isthmus which here separates the estuary of the Delaware from Chesapeake bay. From Frenchtown, which is at the head of the bay, he proceeds the rest of the way to Baltimore by steamer. This is the more pleasant journey of the two in summer, but the quicker route is, of course, that which leads directly by railway; one train per day generally running from and to both cities, for the accommodation of such as wish to proceed by it.

In the short line extending from Baltimore to Washington we have the next link in the chain, and it is at the latter place that we encounter the first serious break in the long and continuous line of railway communication from Boston. Proceeding southward from Washington, the traveller descends the Potomac for forty miles, to the Aquia Creek, on the Virginia shore, where the line of railway, snapped, as it were, at the capital, recommences. From this point, in a direction almost due north and south, it traverses the State of Virginia, through Fredericksburg, Richmond and Petersburg, entering the State of North Carolina at Weldon, through which, passing by Raleigh, it pursues almost the same course to Wilmington. Here, having first diverged from the coast towards the interior at New York, and having pursued a course more or less parallel to it for about 600 miles, it abuts upon the Atlantic. At first sight, this would appear to terminate the railway system under consideration. But not so, for the sea-coast region, in which it developes itself, and the principal

points of which it is designed to connect, flanking the
Alleganies, whose long and varied chain subsides into
the rich alluvial flats of Alabama, extends westward
by the Gulf of Mexico to the delta of the Mississippi. From Wilmington to Charleston there is
another serious break in the line of railway following
the course of this region, the passage between these
two points being made along the coast for about
130 miles by steamer. At Charleston, however, the
traveller finds himself once more on the rail, the
South Carolina railway, from that city to Augusta,
being the next link in the system. Here Georgia
contributes her contingent to this long and important
chain of communication, the line of railway proceeding from Augusta to Milledgeville, and being, by
this time, prolonged still further to the westward.
The central railway in Georgia connects Macon
with Savannah on the coast, but it is to be regarded
more as an important branch than as a con-
stituent link of the direct and main line. From
Macon to New Orleans the communication by railway is not yet complete, but a very few years will
suffice to make it so. This will terminate the railway
system in question, unless it is afterwards found
expedient to push it still westward across the Sabine,
and along the Texan coast to Galverton and Hous-
ton, and across the Nueces to Matamoras; after
which, having crossed the Rio Grande, there is no
reason why it should not yet be continued southward
to Vera Cruz. But waiving speculation as to what
may be done, and confining attention simply to what
has been effected, we find, with two exceptions, one
at Washington and the other at Wilmington, an unbroken line of railway communication, extending from

Boston in New England to beyond Macon in Georgia, a distance of upwards of 1,200 miles. Deducting the part of the journey made on the Potomac, and that effected by steam between Wilmington and Charleston, we have, between the two points, nearly 1,100 miles of railway communication. When the scheme is completed to New Orleans, the length of line which it will embrace, independently of branches, will exceed 1,600 miles.

The object of this great railway system is a double one—to unite together the chief commercial and industrial communities of the sea-board, and to facilitate the intercourse between the North and the South. Considering the character and resources of the extensive region which it thus belts together, embracing, as it does, within its limits the whole of the original States of the Union, it is not to be wondered at that its tributary branches are both numerous and important. To specify these, however, in detail, would interfere with the general view which alone is here taken of the railway system in America.

The third and last scheme of railways which attracts attention is that which is, as it were, collateral to the coast system, diverging westward from that system at different points, penetrating the defiles of the Alleganies, and extending to the valley of the Mississippi. The most northerly manifestation of this system is to be found in the Pennsylvania railways ; uniting, by means of successive links, the Delaware with the Ohio. With Philadelphia as their starting point, Pittsburg may be regarded as their terminus west of the mountains, that city being situated at the confluence of the Monongahela and Allegany, which there unite and form the Ohio. The Baltimore and Ohio railway constitutes the next branch of this scheme.   This line, commencing at Baltimore, ascends, for some distance, the valley of the Patapsco, which it leaves for that of the Potomac, a little below Harper's ferry, where it crosses the latter river into Virginia, and whence it proceeds westward to Cumberland, which is about 180 miles distant from Baltimore.   Here, for the present, it terminates, the design being to carry it on until it reaches the Ohio, a considerable distance below Pittsburg.   This line is destined to be one of transcendent importance in the communication between the East and the West.   The parallel branch of the system, extending through Pennsylvania, has about it more of a local importance than this has, the Pennsylvania branch being interfered with as a medium of direct communication between the two great sections of the country, by the system of railways already considered as partly developed in New York.   But the Baltimore and Ohio railway, situated further to the South, has more of a general than a local importance, being yet destined to be the great highway for passengers between the great valley to the west and the Atlantic States to the east of the mountains, and south of the Hudson.

Of this system these are the only two great branches as yet fully or partly completed.   That others will soon be added to them is obvious, considering both the necessities which will arise for their construction, and the conveniences which the country affords, in many points, for their comparatively inexpensive erection.   There can be but little doubt, for instance, but that a great line of railway, ascending the valley of the James from Richmond, will yet proceed westward through Virginia to the Ohio.   A

great oblique line, to unite the valley with the coast
at Charleston, is already in contemplation, a company
existing for the purpose of carrying it into effect.
This line, which, when complete, will be 718 miles
in length, will commence at Cincinnati, on the Ohio,
aud proceeding by Louisville, the capital of Kentucky, will descend through Tennessee to Augusta in
Georgia, where it will join the South Carolina
railway, which has already been purchased by the
company as the last link of their intended chain
from Cincinnati to Charleston.

If, in this rapid sketch of the railway system in
America, no mention has been made of any scheme
more particularly identified with the valley of the
Mississippi, it has been because no such scheme has
as yet been developed. Here and there short and
comparatively unimportant lines may be found within
the limits of the valley ; whilst portions of those
forming, or to form the system last considered have
penetrated, or will yet penetrate more or less into
it ; but no great scheme, having an exclusive reference to the valley itself, has as yet been contemplated,
far less carried into effect. Population is still too
widely scattered there to justify the expense of constructing such lines of communication between its
more important points, situated as they are at such
enormous distances from each other; whilst the numerous navigable rivers with which the region abounds
in every direction, amply minister to its existing
necessities in the way of traffic and locomotion.
Besides, for the present, the intercourse of the inhabitants of the valley is more with the sea-board than
with one another, rendering lines connecting the
East with the West more important to them now than

a network of railways could be in the valley itself.
When the necessity for them there shall arise, there
will not be wanting capital for their construction,
whilst the nature of the country will be found to be
such as to throw every possible facility in the way of
their completion. Whenever a railway scheme shall
be developed in the great valley, the railways penetrating the mountains, and connecting the sea-board
with the far interior, will constitute a central system,
uniting, as it were, by indestructible ligaments, the
railway systems of the Atlantic and the Western
States.

Such is the foundation of the system of railways
which this country is yet destined to possess. It
will be seen that the outline of the picture is not yet
complete, far less the filling up. The dimensions
which it will yet attain will only be limited by the
requirements of the people. What these requirements will be when all the resources of the country
are called into play, and when it teems with a population proverbially addicted to locomotion, and but ill
provided with other means of intercommunication by
land, it is not easy to foresee.

The number of miles of railway already constructed in the United States exceeds 5,700. Of this
aggregate, nearly 2,000 miles are within the limits of
New England and New York alone. In Massachussetts itself there are no less than 783 miles of railway,
whilst there are completed and in actual operation in
New York 758 miles of road. Of the New York
and Erie railway, traversing the southern counties of
that State, but a small portion is as yet finished.
When it is completed throughout its entire length,
which will be about 450 miles, the number of miles

of railway in operation in New York will exceed
1,100. So much for what is done. As to what
remains to be effected, charters of incorporation
and rights of way have already been conceded for
nearly 4,000 miles more ; so that when the roads for
the construction of which companies are already formed
are completed, there will be upwards of 9,000 miles
of railway in the United States.

The population of the United States has just been
spoken of as but ill provided with other means of
personal intercommunication by land. In England,
and throughout a great part of Europe, in addition
to the railway, there is the well-constructed and convenient highway, over which it is not only easy but
pleasant to glide. In the United States the latter is
almost unknown. The great national road, a macadamized highway, leading from Baltimore westward,
and at one time designed to penetrate to St. Louis—
a design now abandoned on account of the alleged
want of constitutional power on the part of Congress to accomplish such an undertaking—is the only
specimen, on anything like a large scale, of a good
and convenient highway in the Union. Generally
speaking, the roads leading in different directions
from the larger towns are macadamized for a few
miles out ; whilst between Albany and Troy there is
an excellent road of this description, of about seven
miles in length. But, with these exceptions, the
American roads are yet comparatively in a state of
nature ; each man, particularly in the north, being
compelled by law to keep them as practicable as possible where they lead through his own property, the
plough being the only effective remedy for them
when, from neglect or from the nature of the soil,

they become periodically reduced to a state of utter impracticability. For a few months in summer they are pleasant and feasible enough, but in spring and during the " Fall," as the autumn of the year is universally called, they are only to be attempted in cases of sheer necessity. The same may be said of them in winter, when they are denuded of snow, and frozen as hard as granite, with their surface as rough as that of a shelled walnut. The railways and canals came too soon for the sake of the common highways in America. In addition to the enormous expense of properly improving them, there is now their comparative inutility, at least so far as great distances between important points are concerned, the railways or navigable rivers having, in such cases, monopolized the traffic. It will be long, therefore, ere America exhibits to the eye that pleasing feature of material civilization, a network of good common highways. The American may plead, and not without reason, that material civilization is, in all its features, the offspring of necessity, and that such roads will appear in America as soon as the want for them becomes urgent. The necessity will not arise until the population greatly increases in density, when railways and steamers can only accommodate a portion of the intercourse of civilized life. But, in the meantime, they find their railways and great rivers adequate to the meeting of their necessities; the common roads, bad as they are, being sufficient for the shorter traffic, particularly if the time for taking them be properly chosen.

In estimating what our transatlantic kindred have done in the way of railways, we must not overlook the facilities which, in more ways than one, America affords for their construction. In the first place, nothing could be better adapted for such undertakings than the surface of the country. It has been my lot to travel for thousands of miles upon railways in America, and, with the exception of one or two of the Pennsylvania lines, I do not recollect encountering a tunnel upon any of them. Whether they follow the course of streams, or traverse the surface of the vast plains with which the country in almost every direction abounds, but little difficulty is experienced in finding a practicable and an inexpensive route for them. The coast system of railways is particularly favoured in this respect, there being but few natural obstacles of any magnitude to overcome, for the whole way between Boston and New Orleans. Indeed, from Philadelphia to Wilmington, a distance of about 500 miles, it is seldom that the line is found much above or below the surface. There is some heavy cutting in the neighbourhood of the Susquehannah, as there is also, but rarely, between Richmond and Wilmington. Nor should I forget to mention a short but heavy cutting through rock, a little beyond Jersey city, on the way from New York to Philadelphia. These, with the great rivers, some of which are ferried, and others spanned by stupendous bridges, and the marshes in Georgia and South Carolina, which are crossed in some places by embankments, and in others by expensive but ricketty looking wooden viaducts, constituted the chief natural obstacles in the way; but considering its ramifications, and the length of route embraced by the system, they are but few and far between. Some of the greatest impediments of this kind were encountered in the construction of what now constitutes the outlet, through New Eng-

land, of the system in the basin of the St. Lawrence;
the western railway, extending from Boston to
Albany, having been carried through the mountainous district intervening between Springfield and
Pittsfield. In penetrating this highland district, the
line follows the course of the Pontousac, a lively
mountain stream, which it crosses upwards of twenty
times. There is also a good deal of cutting and
embankment in western New York, the surface of
which is generally undulating and picturesque; whilst,
in the neighbourhood of "Little Falls," on the Mohawk, there is likewise some rock cutting on a heavy
scale. Taking them as a whole, the Pennsylvania
railways have had to encounter the greatest natural
obstacles to their construction. There are heavy
tunnels not far from Philadelphia, whilst, in the
more westerly portions of the State, the road is carried over the mountains by inclined planes constructed
on a stupendous scale. The Baltimore and Ohio
railway, which crosses, about nine miles from Baltimore, the line leading from that city to Washington,
just as the latter is about to enter upon a stone viaduct, which carries it over the Patapsco, and is decidedly the finest thing of the kind in the Union, has
little difficulty to encounter in ascending the river
just named, which it crosses several times, the greatest cutting required for it being in the neighbourhood of Harper's ferry, where it penetrates the portion
of the Alleganies known as the Blue Ridge. Such
being the case with the railways east of the mountains,
the valley of the Mississippi is already, as it were, levelled
by the hand of nature herself for the railway system
which will yet develope itself there. I may mention
here, in illustration of the facilities which, in this

respect, America affords for the construction of great
public works like those now considered, that, in the
line of the Erie Canal, uniting the Hudson with
Lake Erie, there are two levels, each upwards of
seventy miles long, without a single lock,

In estimating the facilities which exist for the construction of railways in America, the comparative cheapness of land is an element not to be overlooked. In the
Old World the purchase of the land required constitutes one of the heaviest items of expenditure, whilst
the litigiousness of proprietors has, in numerous
instances, added enormously to its amount. Taking
into consideration the aggregate length of American
railways, the proportion running through forests as
yet unreduced, or passing over irreclaimable wastes, is
very great. With us, in the construction of a line,
timber figures as an item of expense by no means insignificant. Frequently for miles the timber which is
employed in constructing one in America, is that
which is cleared away to make room for it in the
forest. Indeed, in the construction of any line it is
seldom that the Americans have to look far, or to
pay much for timber. Its abundance and cheapness
frequently lead to a solidity in the formation of the
line which it would not otherwise possess ; for on
many of the American railways, the transverse are
underlaid by longitudinal sleepers. In their construction, too, there is a great saving in connexion
with iron, only some of them having solid iron rails,
such as are to be found universally in Europe. The
rest have the rail constructed of wood, the inner edge
of which is shod by an iron "ribbon," as it is called,
about three inches wide and from half to three-quarters of an inch thick. This is laid down in bars

about twelve feet long upon the wood, to which it is securely nailed by large iron spikes at the distance of about every two feet. Sometimes these spikes get loose, and if they do so near the end of a bar, it is not unfrequently found elevated a little above the level of the line, when it is designated a "snake's head." Instances have been known in which these snakes' heads have stuck up so high, that slipping up on the wheel they have perforated the flooring of a carriage, and in a twinkling impaled a passenger against the roof.

Nor should it be forgotten that most of the American railways are as yet composed of but single lines. The cuttings and embankments, however, have in most instances been prepared with a view to double lines at some future period.

These things considered, it is not to be wondered at that there should be a great disparity between the cost of American and that of European, particularly English, railways. Notwithstanding this, one is hardly prepared for the difference which really exists. Whilst the average cost per mile in England has been about 30,000l., that in America has scarcely reached 5,000l.

There can be no more convincing proof of the success of railways than that afforded by their dividends. Tried by this test, it cannot be said that American railways have not answered the ends of their promoters, at least if the results of railway speculation in Massachussetts can be taken as a fair specimen of their results throughout the Union. The dividends of the Massachussetts railways in 1846 varied from 10 to 5 per cent., most of them being 8, and few lower than 7. The average dividend was 7½ per cent.

This is no bad return for a secure investment, even in a country where 6, 7, and 8 per cent. are to be found as the legal rates of interest. Whether in making these dividends the directors of railways in New England have, or have not, abstracted from their capital, is more than I can say; but when the above average dividend was declared in Massachussetts, no suspicion that they did so appeared to disturb the equanimity of the shareholders. As a set-off to this, however, it is to be borne in mind that American railways are by no means so durable as English lines. They will, consequently, have not only to be more frequently repaired, but also more frequently entirely removed than with us. It were needless to dwell upon the effect which this consideration must of necessity have upon them as permanent investments.

If their durability as compared with that of English railways were to depend upon their completeness and strength of construction as compared with those of English railways, they would not seem to be much superior in point of profit to most English lines at the present day. But the durability of a railway depends much upon the wear and tear to which it is subjected; and if American are more flimsy in their construction than English lines, they are not so perpetually worked as English lines are. Between the most populous and important communities it is seldom that more than two trains a-day either way are run. The combined populations of New York and Philadelphia would exceed 600,000, and yet two trains a-day, from and to either city, are found to be quite sufficient in a country where personal locomotion is carried to such an extent as it is in America.

But these two trains carry with them their hundreds of passengers ; as many being conveyed by them, perhaps, as by eight or ten trains in the course of a day between London and Birmingham. By this means the line escapes a great deal of wear and tear, much in the way of expense is saved in a hundred different ways to a company, and all the reasonable wants of the communities at either end of the line are complied with.

With very few exceptions the American railways, as with us, are all in the hands of private companies. Their management, on the whole, is exceedingly good, the chief defect being in the want of a sufficient police superintendence along the lines. Were this defect supplied, fewer obstructions would be encountered by the trains than now, chiefly from the trespassing of cattle upon them. But this is a feature in railway management which is in some cases rendered almost impossible in America, on account both of the length of the lines and the wildness of the districts which they traverse. They will necessarily be more guarded as the country becomes more opened up, as population becomes more dense, and as the traffic upon them increases.

The peculiar construction of the railway carriages, or " cars," as they are invariably called in the United States, has been already adverted to in an early chapter. A carriage built to carry sixty passengers generally rests upon two axletrees, each of which divides at the extremities into two, so that the carriage is in reality borne upon eight wheels. Four of these are in front, the two on each side being close together, and four behind similarly arranged. This leaves a long space between the two sets of wheels,

which, although eight in number, rest the carriage
but upon two points, as if there were only four.
The double wheels terminating each axletree, the
one wheel following close upon the other, seem to
impart great safety to the train in motion; for if one
wheel were inclined from any cause to deviate from
the rail, the hold which the other immediately behind it has of the line tends to keep it in its place,
unless the disturbing cause be sufficiently great to
throw the carriage at once from the rail. The one
wheel thus acts as a corrective upon the other, to an
extent to which it could not act were it much further
removed from it. In whatever way they operate,
there must be something conducive to safety in the
mode in which the wheels forming each of the two
sets on which the carriage rests are closely grouped
together; for not only has the carriage a clumsy, an
unwieldy and unsteady look to the eye, but it has
very often to encounter, at a pretty high rate of
speed, curves which in this country would be considered dangerous, and which would in their abrupt-
ness be positively contrary to law. I have seen one
of these carriages drawn by horse power out of Philadelphia, whipped at a trot, with its full comple-
ment of passengers, along the rectangular streets of
the town, there being no apparent diminution of
speed on turning the corners. But it is on the Baltimore and Ohio railway that their safety is put to
the severest test, for in ascending, or descending, the
valleys of the Patapsco and the Potomac, the trains
are dragged at full speed along curves which in this
country would be considered impracticable. It really
requires one to be somewhat accustomed to these
abrupt turnings, ere he can pass them with cool

nerves or an easy mind. I have often wondered at
the indifference with which the Americans themselves passed one of these cranky curves, when the
carriages would be swinging to and fro at a rate
which threatened to jerk all the heads which they
carried from their respective shoulders. They are
enabled to make these sudden turns with safety, by
the wheels in front being made movable like the
fore-wheels of a common carriage. When this line
was first put in operation, some of the carriages were
so constructed that at night they could be fitted up
with small berths at the sides, after the fashion of a
canal boat, on which passengers by the night trains
might repose till morning.

In regard to luggage an excellent system prevails
in America, which might be adopted with much
advantage in this country. Every one who has
attended a large private party, or a public dinner, or
resorted to any public place of amusement in this
country, knows the mode in which his hat, coat, and
umbrella are taken charge of, and in which he is
enabled to secure them without difficulty when
wanted again. The same system of management is
applied to luggage on American railways. To each
parcel is strapped a brass ticket, having a certain
number impressed upon it, the counterpart of which,
with the same number on it, is delivered to the
owner. Sometimes several small parcels are strapped
together, so that a single ticket serves for them.
Each ticket held by a passenger is a receipt for a
parcel of luggage, consisting of one or more articles
as the case may be. At the end of the journey the
number attached to each parcel is called out as it is
taken out of the van, and it is delivered to him, and

to him alone, who can produce the counterpart of the ticket attached to it. This system answers admirably, the little loss of time that it may occasion being more than compensated for by the safety with which luggage is conveyed from point to point through its means.

There are no distinctions of class on American railways, all the carriages being first-class, or second-class carriages, just as the traveller may please to view them. To have different classes travelling on the road would appear in this country an invidious distinction; and yet it is singular that they never carry that feeling into the regulation of their steamers, most of which have deck, as well as cabin, passengers. To say that all shall travel alike upon a railway, or on board a steamer, is but to prevent one man from spending more money on his comfort than another, if he chooses and can afford to do so, and to prevent another from economizing his means, however strongly he may be inclined to do so. It would be as reasonable to insist upon hotels being all of the same grade, and equally expensive or equally cheap. And yet, mark the difference between the Astor House and a third or fourth-rate hotel in New York; a difference of which no sane man would think of complaining. If they differ in price, so do they also differ in comfort; enabling the traveller to gauge his comfort by his means. Why proscribe this principle upon a railway? Why compel the man whose notions of comfort would be satisfied with the accommodation which the company could afford him for three dollars between New York and Philadelphia, for instance, to pay four; or the man who has five to give the company, and is willing to give it, for extra comforts, to

limit his expenditure to four? The Americans view
our class system in a false light.   It may have had
its abuse on railways in this country; but it rests
upon no more invidious principle than that which
distinguishes between the inside and the outside of a
coach, the cabin and the steerage of a steamer, and
the first-rate and the inferior hotel, or even between
different rooms in one and the same hotel.   So long
as all are rendered, at least, comfortable, there is
nothing invidious in enabling a traveller to regulate
his expenditure in travelling, as well as in other
instances, by his means.

The rate of travelling on American railways is
much less than in this country.   The journey from
New York to Philadelphia usually consumes five
hours, although the distance is only ninety miles. The
average speed is from fifteen to eighteen miles. Fares
are also considerably lower than with us, but it
does not follow that railway travelling is, on the
whole, cheaper. For short distances it undoubtedly is; but when long journeys are made, a comparatively long time is consumed in making them,
giving opportunities for, and indeed necessitating,
some expenditure by the way. The traveller by
first-class in England pays more for his transfer from
London to Liverpool than the traveller in America
does for being conveyed for a similar distance; but
then the former, accomplishing the distance in from
five to six hours, has simply his fare to pay; whereas
the latter, taking about twelve hours to accomplish
it, has generally to procure two meals on the way at
least. On the whole, I found but little difference between the expense, in actual cash outlay, of railway
travelling in the one country and that in the other; to

say nothing of the saving of time caused by the
superior speed at which English railways are traversed. There is but little difference, in point of
amount, between our second-class fares and American fares, whilst our third-class passengers travel
much more cheaply than passengers do on any of the
transatlantic railways.

In describing the incidents of a journey from New
York to Philadelphia, I have already noticed the
chief peculiarities which attend railway management
and railway travelling during the winter months in
America.

It may not be an inappropriate supplement to
what has been here said upon railways, if I add a few
words descriptive of the progress made by the Electric
Telegraph in America.

If the circumstances of the United States rendered
the introduction of railways a matter of peculiar
advantage to them, they were so situated as to render
preeminently serviceable to them the application of
the electric telegraph to the annihilation of time and
space. In this country, limited as it is in its extent,
and with the means of communication so complete,
even independently of railways, correspondence between point and point has long been accomplished
with comparative rapidity. Our railway system,
which preceded the telegraph, of course rendered the
means of correspondence all the more rapid and complete. Whilst, therefore, the limited surface of this
country failed to afford the telegraph those opportunities for a full display of its wonderful powers which
it possesses when extended over a vast area, the
effects which it produced at its introduction, although
startling, were not so marvellous to us as to our American friends; simply because they were not in such

contrast here as they were there to the results of
the preexisting means of intercommunication. Railways must of course have greatly expedited correspondence in America; but still so much remained to
be done towards their completion as a system when the
telegraph was introduced, that its effects were judged
of more by comparison with the old system than with
that by which railways were superseding it. Thus
estimated they seemed like magic, and quite as marvellous as Fortunatus's cap or Aladdin's lamp. There
were many points of the Union so distant from, and
inaccessible to, others, notwithstanding all that the
railways had done, that they could sooner have com-
municated with Europe than with one another.
To bring these into close and instant communication
with each other by means of an agent which recognised no obstacle in the mountain or the plain, the
river, the morass, or the forest, was a triumph to
the powers and capabilities of this wonderful invention which could only await them in a country situated like the United States. This triumph has been
accorded to the electric telegraph in America, embracing as it now does there, in its numerous ramifications, nearly half a continent.

To whomsoever may belong the merit of its original application, certain it is that the electric telegraph, as it is developed in America, is greatly
indebted, both for its introduction and its success, to
the enterprise and perseverance of Professor Morse.
Whilst some of the more scientific minds on both
sides of the Atlantic were doubting as to the applica-
bility or practical utility of the invention, he never
ceased from pressing the subject upon the attention
of Congress; until at length, and when only half convinced by his earnestness and demonstrations, the

federal legislature consented to make the experiment; and with that view appropriated a sum of money for the construction of a telegraph forty miles in length, between Washington and Baltimore. This may be considered as the parent telegraph of the transatlantic world, from which a system has since sprung, which, from its extent and achievements, is well calculated to fill both native and foreigner with astonishment.

The number of miles of telegraph already constructed exceeds 5,000. The telegraph is frequently though not always seen in the same line with the railway; sometimes pursuing a shorter road from point to point, through a wild, broken and uncultivated country, which would be impracticable to the railway; and at others connecting places together between which there is as yet no line of railway whatever. A continuous line of telegraph already extends along the Atlantic coast, from Portland in Maine to Richmond in Virginia, a distance of 760 miles; taking Boston, New York, Philadelphia, Baltimore and Washington in its way. This enormous line is now in progress of completion to New Orleans, a distance of 1,400 miles; so that the whole line when completed from Portland to New Orleans will be upwards of 2,100 miles in length. Another line, which will be upwards of 800 miles in length, is in process of construction in the Mississippi valley, from New Orleans to Louisville in Kentucky, which will also be united by the same means with Cincinnati on the other side of the Ohio; from which point the line will extend again westward to St. Louis on the Mississippi, a little below its junction with the Missouri. From St. Louis another line is being constructed to Chicago on Lake Michigan, a distance of 400 miles; which again will be united to Buffalo, at the foot of Lake Erie, by another series of lines, amounting in all to 800 miles and upwards in length.   A line already extends from Buffalo to Albany ; passing through Rochester, Auburn, Syracuse, Utica and Schenectady, on the way; as does also one from Albany to Boston ; the distance from Buffalo to Boston exceeding 500 miles.   This makes an unbroken circuit of the existing States Union; the aggregate length of line being upwards of 4,000 miles.

Within this, as a mere framework to the picture, other results, almost equally astonishing, are being produced.   From Philadelphia a line extends to Harrisburg, the capital of Pennsylvania, from which point it proceeds by Pittsburg, in the western part of the State, to Columbus, the capital of Ohio; from which it still further proceeds to Cincinnati, where it joins the great line in the Mississippi valley, extending between New Orleans and Chicago.   The entire length of this line is about 630 miles.   From Cincinnati, again, another line is to proceed to Sandusky, on Lake Erie, a distance of about 230 miles, where it will connect with the great east and west line extending from Chicago to Boston.   New York and Albany are of course thus connected ; and a line, upwards of 500 miles in length, is designed to proceed along the course of the New York and Erie railway ; which, as already observed, unites that city with Lake Erie, at Dunkirk, a little above Buffalo.   There are numberless minor lines completed, or in progress, to which it is not necessary here to advert, more than enough having already been said to show the extent to which this wonderful invention either has been, or is about to be, applied to the purposes of social life in

America. Nor is the sketch thus given, either in whole or in part, a hypothetical one. The whole of the lines mentioned are either completed or in progress; and, with few exceptions, all of them will probably be in operation ere this issues from the press. There are a few lines extraneous to the Union, but deserving of notice here, as they are all part and parcel of the same system. One of these extends into Canada from Buffalo, proceeding to Toronto, whence it goes forward to Montreal. Another line runs from Albany northward, along the line of Lake Champlain, and through Burlington, the capital of Vermont, to Montreal; thus completing a direct telegraphic communication between the capital of Canada and New York, the great emporium of the continent. From Montreal a line will shortly be constructed to Quebec; which, again, it is in contemplation similarly to unite with Halifax; between which place and Portland (Maine) another line is in process of erection. This will complete another circle, the greater portion of whose vast circumference will be comprehended within the limits of the British provinces.

According to the American Almanac for 1848, which is an authority which may be relied upon, the number of miles of telegraph in operation in 1847 was 2,311; the number of miles nearly completed, 2,586; whilst the number projected, and which would probably be in operation by the close of 1848, is 3,815; making a total of 8,712 miles! The electric, has succeeded to the iron, age.

The effect which this invention, as thus developed, has produced, and that which it is still likely to produce on many of the operations of society, are almost

past comprehension. As an instance of the change
already effected, let me adduce one fact. On landing
in Boston late in January, 1846, I hastened, with all
speed, to Washington. Travelling with the mail, I
did not arrive at the capital until the third day after
landing. In other words, the greater part of three
days was consumed in conveying the European intelligence from Boston to the capital. It was a time of
feverish excitement, the Oregon dispute being then
at its height, and the news just arrived being the
first from Europe after the promulgation of the President's warlike message. All parties were, therefore,
anxious to know, with as little delay as possible, the
effect which it had produced; but, notwithstanding
their anxiety, the government and legislature had to
wait for nearly three days after the arrival of the
steamer before they were relieved from it. I left
Washington about five months afterwards, and great
indeed was the change which, in the mean time, had
taken place. The telegraph had been completed to
Boston, and the result was, that the chief features of
the European news were sometimes known in Washington before the steamer was even in port at Boston!
On Cape Ann, to the north-east of Boston, there is a
telegraphic station. When in sight of this, the steamer,
by ordinary signals, conveyed the heads of her news
to Cape Ann. From this point it was transmitted to
Boston, whence, by one pulsation, extending over
500 miles of wire, it was forwarded without delay to
Washington, where it was received and circulated
ere the steamer was in harbour! Being one day
loitering in the Telegraph Office at Washington, I
asked one of the clerks, from mere curiosity, to
inquire what the weather was at Boston. He did so,

and in a few minutes the answer received was, " Very hot, but a thunder-storm in the north-west." In these few minutes the question and reply had together travelled upwards of 1,000 miles !

These are but mere specimens of what has already been done, and shadows forecast of what is yet in the future. Already, and before the system is complete, it enabled most of the important points of the Union to be in possession of the result of the late presidential contest a few days after the election. Formerly it took as many weeks to learn it. The time will come, too, and that ere many years are sped, when the sensitive wires will extend in all directions, acting, in regard to the body politic, like the nerves in the human system ; when the frame-work of nature will, as it were, become sentient, so that no important intelligence can transpire at any one point of the country without its being simultaneously transferred through all its parts ; and when the news from the Old World will have scarcely landed on the coast, ere it is known from Maine to Louisiana, from New York to Wisconsin ; ere it is promulgated and commented upon in all the Atlantic States, and through the length and breadth of the valley of the Mississippi ! And, more than this, the time will yet come when the news from Europe will pass, almost in a twinkling, from New York to San Francisco ; and that from Asia, from San Francisco to New York. The two extremities of the Old World will thus, one day, hold converse with each other by means of the American wires ! What would our forefathers have said to this?

CHAPTER IX.

FROM MACON TO MOBILE AND NEW ORLEANS.

I was still engaged conversing and reflecting upon the
topics which form the subject-matter of the foregoing chapter; when, at length, after a protracted and
wearisome journey, we arrived at Macon. For the
last half of the way the road seemed to lead through
a clayey tract, well wooded, but not over fertile; the
clay, which was of a reddish hue, being so heavy and
tenacious as sometimes to threaten to hold fast the
lumbering vehicle, as the unwary bird is secured by
the birdlime.

Macon is a pleasant little town, occupying an advantageous position at the head of the navigation of
the Ocmulgee river, a tributary of the Alatamaha,
which is the most southerly of the rivers flowing
through the body of the continent, which empty

themselves into the Atlantic. Near its mouth is the
port of Darien, which largely shares with Savannah
the export trade of Georgia. The plan of Macon is
the counterpart of that of most of the southern
towns, being open, airy, and scrupulously regular ;
and the streets being wide and shaded, as usual, with
an abundance of trees. Its population cannot much
exceed 5,000; but it is entirely the growth of the
last twenty years. But this is by no means equal to
the specimens which the North affords of the rapidity
with which even large communities are conjured into
existence, it being no uncommon sight in that section
of the Union to find a spot which, twenty years previously, was covered by the forest, the site of a thriving
and wealthy town of 20,000 souls.

As Mr. —— was to stay for a few days at Macon,
I parted with him next morning on leaving for
Columbus. The seat which he had occupied on the
preceding night was now in possession of three travellers who joined us here, the rest of the passengers
being the same, and similarly situated as on the day
before. On my extreme left sat, as formerly, the
commissioner, with the judge between us. The temper of this latter functionary was by no means improved by a night's rest, for he seemed to have a
lively recollection of the persecution with which he
had been visited overnight by the musquitos, whose
number was legion, and whose size was " onaccount-
able." They appeared to him to have met for the
purpose of making a night of it at his expense ; and
he described them as setting at him with knife and
fork, and as having eaten his beef and drank his
claret to their hearts' content. He was convinced
that he must have been " sweet eatin'," for he " didn't
get no sleep."

As we receded from Macon, the surface of the country began to improve a little, but not the condition of the roads. An additional quantity of rain had fallen during the night, with which the heavy clay was so churned up, that sometimes it was a marvel to me how we made any progress at all. On, however, we went at a painfully slow rate, sometimes stuck fast for a minute or two, then released by the horses, after they had been accorded a little breathing time ; sometimes kept dancing between seat and roof, and at others reeling for minutes at a time from side to side. One of the frightful jolts which we every now and then experienced, caused me to receive a severe blow in the cheek from the side of the coach, which left its ugly mark upon me for some days afterwards. We were so often threatened with an upset, that I at last came almost to wish for one, that, on this score at least, we might be relieved from our anxiety. It was not long ere I was gratified. Giving a tremendous lurch to the side at which I was seated, the coach seemed for a moment to poise itself upon the two side wheels, as if deliberating whether to lie down at once or restore itself to its equilibrium. I looked at the judge, and shuddered at the idea of the "fourteen stun';" so, pressing towards the left, I called upon the rest to lean to the weather side. This they did but too effectually, for, on the coach righting, the opposite wheels plunged into another hole, or " rut," with such violence as to carry over the whole concern. It went gently enough, and I felt an inward satisfaction, as we were falling, that my weight was to come on the judge. I regretted it afterwards, on account of the rather severe contusions which together we occasioned to the commissioner.

For a moment after the vehicle was fairly on its side there was neither motion nor sound within, every one seeming to be collecting his thoughts, and assuring himself precisely where and how he was. At length, the lady in the back seat found courage to scream, which seemed to bring it to the recollection of the rest that there was something to be done as well for themselves as for others. There was accordingly a general movement of arms and legs ; at least, of as many as were in a position to move ; an operation which, unless checked, might have led to rather serious results, as heads and heels were in awkward juxtaposition. At one time, the iron nails in the shoe of one of those who, but a little before, had been occupying the front seat, gleamed ominously before my eyes, causing me to remove my head without delay as far as I could from the awkward apparition.

"Lie still all 'cept them as are at the top," said the judge, in a muffled voice, as if he were speaking with his arm in his mouth, " and let the topmost git out at oncet, so that the rest can foller."

As I had the good luck to be one of the upper stratum, I prepared at once to follow this injunction. In doing so, my first care was to ascertain how a release could be effected. On looking upwards, I observed a square hole directly above me, which resembled the hatchway of a ship as seen from the hold ; but which, after a little scrutiny, I discovered to be neither more nor less than the window of the coach. In the first moments of such a *bouleversement* one cannot at once collect his thoughts ; and I can now recall a variety of fancies which passed rapidly through my brain, before the window, at which I had been seated, and which was now in the position of a skylight, was recognised by me. The illusion, whilst it lasted, was heightened by my observing a face peering down at us, which would have been valuable in an artist's studio, as the model of the head of the impenitent thief. I thought of a pirate and a hold full of captives, and might have called out for mercy, had I not been aroused to a true sense of my situation by the husky voice of the driver, who told us, in an impatient tone, to "make ourselves scarce where we were, and let things be got to rights agin."

"Well I'm blowed!" said the judge; but why or wherefore he was so I did not hear, as I was making my way out whilst he was vouchsafing the explanation. On getting out, I found myself perched on the side of the coach which was uppermost, the vehicle lying flat in the mud on its other side, like a ship on her beam ends, with her cargo shifted. The driver, who was by this time perched on the opposite side of the hatchway, immediately put down the handle of his whip amongst those below, shouting out at the same time, "Come, be stirrin' there, will you!" The judge thereupon began to exhibit some signs of life. First raising his head, and turning it slowly round, he took the exact measure of his position, after which he brought his arms into play, and then, one after the other, recovered his legs. Having at length raised himself to a kneeling position, the driver and I got him by the collar of the coat, by means of which, with some aid from himself, we managed to elevate the "fourteen stun'" into air and sunshine. The commissioner was the next dragged out. His face, poor fellow, was somewhat scratched,

and one side of it besmeared with dirt, the judge
having pressed it into a soft pillow of mud, which had
squeezed itself in through the window. Next came
my friend with the nails in his shoes, who turned out
to be a farmer from the banks of the Miami in
Ohio. From his position we could only render him
aid by dragging him out heels foremost, which we did.
Then came the lady, of whom for a time we had lost
sight altogether. She came up much crushed and
disordered, and on being let down in the mud, frantically grasped the judge, who was still engaged in
adjusting himself, and asked if there was any chance
whatever of our getting safely to our journey's end.
After pausing for a time to consider, he replied,
gravely but kindly, that there " was a chance, but
that it was not mighty promisin'." He bade her calm
herself, however, as she would get used to such incidents in time, as he had done.

The rest of the passengers having been extricated,
the coach, but not without some trouble, was, if I
may use the expression, got upon its legs again. We
had a long ride after this ere we reached Columbus,
but it was fortunately accomplished without the
recurrence of an upset.

As we approached Columbus, the surface of the
country became much more broken and picturesque
than I had seen it at any point since leaving the
coast. The northern and western portion of the
State of Georgia, which is traversed by a spur of the
Alleganies, is generally of an undulating character,
and in many places not only hilly but mountainous.
In its rolling surface, in its rich and varied vegetation,
amongst which the magnolia, the jessamine, and the
wild vine, were conspicuous—in its pleasant prospects,

its genial airs, and its pure and lively streams, it is quite a contrast to the dreary region extending in such monotonous succession between it and Charleston.

Columbus is but a small town, and is prettily situated on the east bank of the Chatahouchee, a navigable tributary of the Apalachichola, which empties itself into the Gulf of Mexico, close to the peninsula of Florida. Like Macon, though far inland, it has thus a navigable channel to the sea. It is the frontier town of Georgia, on the west, the Chatahouchee here separating that State from Alabama. There are some pretty falls and cataracts in the neighbourhood of the town, which well repay the trouble of a visit.

I left Columbus, after a brief stay, for Montgomery. Between these two places, the country is wild but not uninteresting. On crossing the Chatahouchee into Alabama, it seemed as if I had passed from an old country into a new. And such, indeed, was the case, the western part of Georgia having been much earlier settled and much longer cultivated than the more easterly belt of the conterminous State. For some time after entering Alabama my road led through a portion of the territory which had once been the domain of the Cherokees and the Creeks, but of which they had been divested by means which the American casuist may fancy himself able to justify. Well aware that the better regions of Alabama were before me, I was not disappointed with the sample of it presented along the road between the frontier and Montgomery. The land was not of the most fertile description, neither could it be called poor. For two-thirds of the way, it was only at long intervals that anything like clearances were to be seen, and it was only in the neighbourhood of Montgomery that I came to what might be termed regular plantations, with anything like decent or comfortable habitations upon them. On these I could see the slaves at work, on either side of the road; their condition betokening, at a glance, the character of their owner, some being well clad, apparently well fed, and hilarious in their dispositions ; and others in rags, with their physical frames but poorly supported, and their spirits seemingly much depressed. For the whole way the road was excessively bad, and had it not been for a couple of days' dry weather, I do not know how we could have overcome them.

As a town, Montgomery is not calculated to leave so pleasing an impression upon the mind of the stranger as either Macon or Columbus. I stayed in it but an hour or two, during which I ascertained that it could offer very excellent accommodation to the traveller. After arriving I took the first steamer for Mobile, and found myself, in a little more than two hours after quitting the detestable stage-coach, steaming at the rate of eleven miles an hour down the winding channel of the Alabama.

Every step that we proceeded on our course to the Gulf served to develope more and more to the eye the inexhaustible resources of this noble State. Both sides of the river abounded with the evident signs of great fertility, and plantations on a scale equal to any in Georgia were passed in rapid succession. The country had not yet lost the picturesque and undulating aspect which it had assumed in western Georgia; whilst the vegetation with which the face of nature was clothed, and which was equally varied with, was, if anything, still richer than, that immediately to the east of the Chatahouchee. Montgomery is not at the head of steamboat navigation, the river being navigable for about forty miles further up to Wetumpka, where it is interrupted by falls, and between which and Montgomery the country is so broken and varied as almost to deserve to have applied to it the epithet of rugged.

It was on the Alabama that I first found myself on board one of those high-pressure steamboats, which so often prove fatal to their passengers, and which have so ominous a name to European ears. It was some time ere I could reconcile myself to my position, and for most of the voyage I kept at a respectable distance from the boilers. We had but little cotton on board, although the boats on this river are sometimes very heavily laden with that commodity, on its way to Mobile for exportation, the quantity on board increasing at almost every station at which they call between Montgomery and that city.

As the voyage from Montgomery to the coast consumes at least the greater part of two days, the steamers on the Alabama are, of course, well provided with sleeping accommodations. The saloon, which extended almost from one end of the boat to the other, was lined on either side by a double row of excellent berths, in which the passenger could do anything except sleep. For this the berths were not to blame, the cause of it being the perpetual jarring of the boat, the powerful engines with which it was provided making it vibrate at every stroke, like a harp-string on being touched. There was a crowd of passengers on board, most of whom were, to judge from appearances, highly respectable; but there were a few whose look, conduct, and demeanour, but too plainly told to what class of desperadoes they belonged. They were most respectably dressed, but kept almost constantly together, there being too many people on board to allow of their carrying matters with the high hand with which they conduct their operations on the Mississippi and some of its tributaries. They belonged to the class of professional gamblers, who form so large an ingredient in the population of the South; and, taking them altogether, they had the most sinister look about them that I had ever witnessed. It seemed to be generally understood who and what they were; and although a few conversed and played a little with them, they were prudently shunned by the great bulk of the passengers. Their gambling habits are not the only bad feature about them, it being sometimes their delight, and at other times their object, for reasons best known to themselves, to create disturbances amongst the passengers, which, in these fiery latitudes, are so often fatal to those who are implicated. When the voyage is long, and there are but few respectable people on board who can protect themselves by their numbers, a gang of these fellows are not only troublesome, but dangerous as fellow-passengers. Public opinion, however, is now, even in the South, so decidedly against them, that this great drawback to travelling in the South and West is fast diminishing.

Amongst my fellow-passengers was a young Irishman, whose ready wit, active fancy, and lively rattling conversation, went far to beguile the tedium of a long and rather monotonous sail. He had been "caught young," as he said himself, having emigrated with his parents at a very tender age to America. He was, when I met him, the travelling agent of a large mercantile establishment in New York, his occupation keeping him in almost constant locomotion, and frequently leading him to the South, with every portion of which he appeared to be well acquainted.

"You'll be going to New Orleens?" said he to me, as we were conversing together the first night in the saloon over a sherry-cobbler, previously to retiring for the night.

"That, for the present, is my destination," I replied.

"And a mighty fine place you'll find New Orleens to be," continued he; "indeed, I prefer it to all the other towns in the Union."

"That's strange," said I, "for in more than one respect its character is none of the best."

"Is it character you're speakin' off?" he rejoined; "sure there's no other town in the whole country where you'll find green peas in the month of January."

I could not but confess that in this at least there was nothing unfavourable to the town.

"And as for mint-juleps," he continued, "they begin to drink them there before winter has thought of going off for the season in the north. What think you of that?"

"That the sooner they begin they're the sooner over," said I; "besides, they have the satisfaction of beginning them in the north when you're tired of them at New Orleans."

"Yes, but you see you can enjoy that satisfaction with them, by going north with the juleps," he observed. "Nothing can be nicer than keeping on the track of the warm weather, and for weeks finding yourself only in the beginning of summer, drinking bumpers to it morning, noon, and night. Many's the time I have thus juleped it from New Orleans to Portland."

I could not but confess to the excellences of mint-juleps in hot weather, although I could not see the pleasure of being drenched with them. On observing this to him, he assured me that he was no slave to them, as he alternated pretty frequently between the julep, the cobbler, the phlegm-cutter, and the gin-sling.

" Besides," said he, " I like, when I can manage it, to take the strawberries along with them."

" What," said I, " then you have also travelled north with the strawberries?"

" That I have," he replied, "and nice companions they are, to be sure. They seemed to grow under my feet as I went along, and I have sometimes almost lived on them for days together. Yes," he continued, depositing his quid into the spittoon at his feet, " I have dined on strawberries, and taken my baccy for a dessert."

" Which could you most easily dispense with," I asked, " the strawberries or the tobacco?"

" That's as much as to say," said he, " which could you most easily give up, a luxury or a necessity?"

" Do you place either in the category of neces-saries?" inquired I.

" I look on one of them as both a luxury and a necessity," he replied; " strawberries are a luxury, but tobacco is as necessary to me as it is agreeable; I have chewed since I was knee high to a goose, and will go on chewing until I'm a gone goose."

" I wish all your countrymen," I observed, "had as ample means of appeasing their appetites as you have."

"The more fools they if they hav'n't," said he. "Why don't they come here, where they can not only appease, but also pamper their appetites? Instead of living here in plenty and quiet, they starve at home on nothing and agitation. The more fools they."

"But the majority of Irishmen who do emigrate, do not seem to improve their condition much," said I.

"Ah sure, but they do!" said he quickly. "Isn't anything an improvement upon Ireland? Besides, you'd hardly know them in the second generation. My father hadn't a shoe to his foot till he was seventeen; nor I till I was seven. He's dead and gone, and here I am. 'Faith, he would hardly know me now if he saw me. How many generations would it take to make the change in Ireland! Why, here, a gentleman can be made out of the coarsest stuff in half a lifetime."

"Then you think," said I, "that your fellow-countrymen should emigrate more with a view to the advantage of their descendants than that of themselves?"

"I mean," he replied, "that they should come here for their own, as well as for their children's benefit. If they do not much improve their own condition, that of their immediate descendants will be vastly bettered. But no Irishman need come here without finding it to his advantage. In this country the poorest man need not be for any length of time without plenty to eat, a coat to his back, shoes to his feet, and a good hat on his head; for, republican though it be, this is the only country in the world in which every man wears a crown. Fools they are, say I again, to stay at home eating one another up, when there are not mouths enough in this country to consume all that it produces."

" But," said I, " your countrymen are not so universally insensible to the advantages of emigration as you seem to suppose, as witness the shoals in which they yearly land in Canada and the United States. Thousands more would follow them if they had the means of doing so."

" Why don't the landlords help them?" he inquired. " I am sure it would be a good bargain on both sides. To the landlords, the people's room would be more agreeable than their company, whilst the parting with their landlords would not be a matter of much regret to the people."

" There would be but little love lost on either side," I replied. " Some of the landlords, however, have liberally aided in this way; but the majority have done, are doing, and will do, nothing. Irish landlordism is an enigma which nobody can solve ; a gigantic abortion, based on fallacy, and floundering between difficulty and apprehension."

" But can the government do nothing?"

"Yes," I observed, "it can and does; for it occupies its time, taxes its ingenuity, and exhausts its energies, first in devising paupers, and then in devising laws for their relief. But it takes no steps towards the eradication of the evil by a judicious and well-sustained system of emigration. It shrinks from the subject as you would from an alligator. Talk to it of emigration, and it shrugs its shoulders, hems and haws, says much, that means nothing, of difficulties in the way, interference with private enterprise, and ends by saying that it can do nothing. Not only is there a noble field in this country for our pent-up surplus population, but within a month's easy sail of our poor-houses, we have, in Canada, a rich, fertile dominion of our own, the greater portion by far of which is yet but a preserve for rabbits, deer, bears, and wolves. Yes, strange as it may appear, we have under the same flag, and at no great distance from each other, infinite poverty and in-exhaustible resources, and yet the one cannot be brought to bear upon the other with a view to its relief. Here the wilderness waits for cultivation— there the multitudes pine to be fed. Yet the poor-houses are being constantly filled, whilst the wolf and the bear are left undisturbed. At the bottom of all this there is but little foresight, and much false economy."

"But why don't the country force the subject upon the government?" inquired my companion.

"Simply because, inexplicable though it may seem, the country is not yet sufficiently of one way of thinking upon it. There is a set of men with no little influence who set their faces against emigration, calling it transportation, and insisting upon it that England is large enough to subsist not only all her present population, but many more. They forget that the question of subsistence is one of pressing urgency, and that the starving multitude cannot afford to wait until all their schemes are in operation for the better development of the country's resources. The question to decide is, not how many England could support with all her resources in full play, or with a different distribution than now prevails of the means of subsistence which she actually possesses; but has she, or has she not, for the time being, a surplus population? If so, she should, in the most advantageous way for all parties, rid herself of a present evil, whilst schemes are in preparation which, at the best, can only be productive of a future good. Besides, there are grave considerations connected with her commercial prospects which should induce England to raise up for herself markets in all her colonies. Not only in Ireland, but also in England and Scotland, there are multitudes of drones in the busy hive, who would become active honey-makers abroad. But the subject is endless, and we cannot well longer pursue it, for I see we are disturbing the sleepers around us."

This last remark was elicited by the sudden apparition of a head in a blue nightcap with a red tassel, which projected from between the curtains of one of the berths opposite me. It had two very large bright blue eyes in it, which were steadily fixed upon me whilst I made the observation, and remained so for a few seconds afterwards, making the whole scene both fascinating and ludicrous. " Young man," said it at last, opening its mouth, which was surrounded by a sandy beard, in good state for the razor, " it's mighty fine that there discoorse, and mayhap it isn't, by gum; but I'll tell you what it is, you had better adjourn the meetin', and give us the concloodin' part of the subject at breakfast, you had." It then, after spitting twice upon the floor by way of emphasis, suddenly disappeared, when the curtains resumed their former position.

" I fear," said I, speaking at the place which had just been vacated by the apparition, " we have not only to beg your pardon, but that of many others around, for any disturbance that we may have caused them; but ——"

Here I was interrupted by my fellow-delinquent, who was not disposed to be quite so complaisant in his reply; for, after sundry ejaculations, calling for direct injury to his own eyes, he asked the head where it had got " so much night-cap"—where, after certain contingencies, it "expected to go to" if it was " ill off for goose-grease;" and a variety of other questions to which it was not every head that would have quietly submitted. How long the particular head in question would have done so was problematical; but seeing the curtains of a number of other berths in motion, I drew the Irishman's attention to the circumstance, and he had good sense and good feeling enough at once to take the hint. Swallowing the remainder of his sherry-cobbler at a draught, he expressed a desire to have " another drain," but the bar having been closed half an hour previously, he was obliged to go to bed without it. In a few minutes I observed him tumbling into one of the fore berths, with everything on but his coat, after placing a spittoon in a convenient position for any purposes for which it might be required.

I remained seated for some time after he had left me, musing upon the singularity of my position. I appeared to be the only occupant of the saloon, for no other human form was visible to me. And yet I was surrounded by about a hundred people, all of whom were then packed, as it were, upon a double row of shelves, with red damask curtains in front, to conceal them from view and keep them from the dust. Most of them were asleep, as was evident from their heavy regular breathing; and this concord of respiration proceeding from so many points, made the scene all the more lonely and impressive. The machinery was busily at work under my feet, the water was gurgling past me on either side, and at each stroke of the engine the frail craft shook through her whole length, as if she were a floating earthquake. But one solitary lamp gleamed in the cabin, casting a faint yellow light about the centre, where I was seated, but leaving its distant extremities shrouded in gloom, so much so that I sometimes fancied myself a lonely watcher in a huge vault, in which the dead had been long deposited, and in which some were just awaking from trances which had closely resembled death. And all this at midnight on the devious current of the Alabama, so far from home and friends, and everything that was familiar to me! I was then in the very depths of those interminable forests, with the romantic tales of whose former occupants my youthful imagination had been so often fired; afloat on one of those streams whose marvellous extent and capabilities had so frequently excited my astonishment; and traversing the very regions in which Raleigh had sought for an El Dorado, and Soto and his followers had vainly searched for gold.

It was not long ere I yielded to the somnolent influences of the scene; and, having retired to my berth, I slept as well as could be expected of one lying, as it were, in the hopper of a mill.

Next morning I rejoined my Irish friend at breakfast, when we resumed, in a low voice, the conversation of the previous evening. Whether the head with the night-cap was or was not within hearing distance of us, was more than we could tell; for, on looking for it, we found it impossible to distinguish it, divested of its nocturnal appendage.

I remained on deck most of the day, although the

sky was clear and the sun of a broiling heat. The
level of the country was still elevated, and its surface
undulating and picturesque, the forest, amongst other
woods, containing an immense variety of laurel,
having a most refreshing look to the eye. The river,
as at Montgomery, was not of very great width, being
no broader than the Thames at high water in Bat-
tersea-reach; and so free from obstruction was its
channel, and so uniform was its depth, that although
it runs at the average rate of three miles an hour, its
current was scarcely discernible. Now it passed
through an open country, where its banks were low
and chequered by alternations of forest and plantation; then it would wind through bold and precipitous
bluffs, varying from 100 to 200 feet high; after which
it would again take a serpentine course through an
open tract, again to pass through bluffs as before.
The different settlements which were visible on its
banks were generally situated on these bluffs, the
inhabitants building their houses, as much as possible,
in upper air, to escape the malaria of the lower levels.
In the afternoon we reached Fort Claiborne, a sort of
military station on a small scale, with a little town
contiguous to it; and here I was separated from my
Irish fellow-traveller, who was to remain for a couple
of days in the town, having some business to transact
in it. He advised me, on parting, to be careful of
myself in New Orleans; and, as the sickly season was
approaching, by all means to " make myself scarce "
before catching the " fivver." He was a singular
mixture of levity and soberness, folly and good sense,
and possessed great knowledge of the country, from
which I should have profited more had we been
longer together.

A little below Fort Claiborne, a great change
becomes perceptible in the conformation and aspect
of the country.   On descending the river from that
point the bluffs are found to be less frequent and
elevated, until, at length, they entirely disappear,
where the stream debouches upon the coast region
resting upon the Gulf of Mexico.   The elevated and
rolling   country   from   which   the   traveller   then
emerges, is the scene of the last appearance of the
Alleganies, in their prolonged course towards the
south-west.   In the northern part of the State, the
mountainous range, as in Georgia, is still bold and
lofty, but rapidly subsides into detached hills, covered
with wood to the top, in pursuing its way to the
centre of the State, after which it declines into mere
undulations of the surface ; and at last, after extending in one unbroken chain from the western part of
Pennsylvania, in the neighbourhood of Lake Erie,
disappears altogether within a hundred miles of the
Gulf of Mexico.   Once in the coast region, the eye
is no longer charmed with the rich variety of vegetation which characterised the upper country, or with
its waving outlines and picturesque effects.   All is
flat, wearisome, and monotonous, as in the corresponding region on the Atlantic coast.   But the soil
in the low parts of Alabama is, on the whole, far
richer than that of a large proportion of the great
belt of land extending from the Potomac to the
Alatamaha.   Taking it all in all, Alabama is not
surpassed, in point of fertility, by any of the sister
States of the Confederation.   The rolling country
constituting its northern and north-eastern sections,
produces cotton and Indian corn in abundance, cotton
being the staple chiefly cultivated in the rich level

flats of the west and south, as it is indeed the chief staple of the whole State. Both in this State and in Mississippi, immediately to the west of it, the cultivation of the cotton plant is carried to an extent which has already rendered them most formidable rivals to the Atlantic States of the south, which so long possessed a virtual monopoly of this staple.

In the gradual subsidence of the country from the upper to the lower level, the vegetation with which it is covered undergoes a perceptible change. The live oak, the laurel, the mulberry, the chestnut, and the hickory, become less frequent in their appearance; the pine, the cedar, and the cypress gradually taking their places, and prevailing more and more as you approach the coast. The spectral outline of the one, the lank and leaning trunk of the other, and the dark sombre colour of the third, impart gloom to a scene otherwise sufficiently dreary and monotonous. Rich bottom lands, swamps, pine barrens, and small prairies, follow each other in dull succession, the only things which exist to enliven the journey being the company on board, and the activity which is sometimes visible on the plantations on either side, where hordes of negroes are at their daily task under a hot sun and a generally merciless overseer. Like all the western and southern rivers, pursuing their respective courses through the extensive flat regions, which, by their combined action for untold ages they have themselves conjured into existence, the Alabama here pursues a most serpentine course, winding and zigzagging through the level open country, as if it were loath to quit it, and bent upon irrigating it in the most efficient manner. The current, in this part of its progress, diminishes its strength, and the banks are frequently lined with long rank grass and rushes, amid which the timid alligator may be sometimes seen basking in the sun. The river was low and peaceful when I descended it, but when in flood, the Alabama is sometimes a rolling devastating torrent.

Rich and fertile as, on the whole, this region is, although interspersed with many unproductive tracts, it is not very desirable as a place of residence, inasmuch as, for several months in the year, it is visited with the same heavy curse which, from July till October, annually descends upon the tide-water region on the Atlantic. A hot sun, blazing for days, weeks, and months upon stagnant pools and putrid swamps, and a reeking fermenting earth, rich with vegetable decomposition, cannot fail to produce the noxious malaria, which prevails at all seasons of the year, to a greater or less extent, but which about the close of summer attains a virulence which renders it incumbent on all, who can, to fly from its poisonous influences. For the greater part of the year, the coast region cannot be called absolutely unhealthy ; but it is much inferior, in point of salubrity, to the middle and more elevated section of the State. Even there the people, in building their towns, find it prudent to occupy the bluffs instead of the low lands, that they may be as much as possible out of the reach of the malaria during the sickly months. In the northern and hilly portions of the State, the climate is mild, and the air comparatively pure and salubrious.

About fifty miles from the coast the Alabama unites with another river called the Tombeckbee, after which the confluent streams pursue their peaceable course to the Gulf, under the designation of the Mobile. Along the banks of this stream the pine-barrens are more frequent than along the Alabama ;

and although fertile tracts are not wanting, they are neither so numerous nor so well cultivated as on the banks of the latter river. On the forenoon of the second day after leaving Montgomery, we came in sight of the city of Mobile, and much rejoiced was I, after my long overland journey, once more to approach the coast, as it was evident that we were doing, from the many steamers which were clustered about the wharves, and the square-rigged vessels which were seen at anchor beyond.

The city of Mobile, the commercial emporium, though not the political capital of the State of Alabama, (the city of Tuscaloosa in the interior enjoying the latter dignity,) is a tolerably large and very handsome town, occupying a most advantageous situation on the right bank of the Mobile River, at its entrance into the fine, spacious, and open Bay of Mobile. The portion of the town immediately contiguous to the quays is about as unattractive as the corresponding parts of most seaport towns are found to be, the streets being, for the most part, narrow, ill-ventilated, and not over clean. Behind them, however, the town developes itself in a very different aspect, the portion of it which lies back from the river being situated on a gentle acclivity, commanding, from many points, a good view of the harbour, and affording every opportunity for the regularity of plan with which this part of it is characterised. The main streets are long and broad, well shaded by trees, and admirably paved. Nothing can be conceived cleaner and more comfortable than this section of the town, attention to cleanliness having been rendered indispensable from the fatality with which the yellow fever used to visit Mobile. A great many of its private, as well as most of its public edifices, are constructed of brick, but the bulk of the town is built of wood. Some years ago a destructive fire laid one-third of it in ashes; but it has since recovered from the effects of this terrible visitation. It would be difficult to find anywhere a more hospitable set of people than the better portion of the population of Mobile, although a large proportion of the lower orders are prone to a dissoluteness of manners equal to that characteristic of the corresponding classes of the more immoral of European capitals. The situation of the town is, on the whole, very favourable to health, from the nature of the site which it occupies, and the open, airy bay at the head of which it stands. The attention which has recently been paid to cleanliness has very much diminished the amount of disease and mortality which formerly prevailed in it. The country around is, in most directions, sandy and dry, covered with pine, and cedar, and oak, the tract immediately contiguous to the town being dotted with the villas and country residences of the wealthier class of its inhabitants.

The hotels in Mobile are on a most extensive and sumptuous scale, scarcely surpassed by any of those in New York, Boston, or Philadelphia. The population of the town may now be taken at about 30,000, of which number not more than one-half are whites, the remainder being slaves; for the free coloured population of the town is too insignificant in point of number to be taken into the account. In the character of a portion of the population, as well as in other circumstances, the stranger can see proofs of the comparatively recent annexation of this portion of the country to the Republican con-

federacy. It was only as late as 1813 that it was
transferred by Spain to the Union, about ten years
after the purchase of Louisiana from the French.
The existence of a Royal-street in Mobile, and of a
Rue Royale in New Orleans, is of itself indicative
of these two places having remained more or less
under monarchical rule until the *furor* of the American revolution was over, during the prevalence of
which every King-street, King-alley, King-court,
and King-lane within the then limits of the Union
received names more in accordance with the dominant ideas of the time.

Mobile is a place of great commercial activity,
being, after New Orleans, the most important American seaport on the Gulf of Mexico. Cotton is, of
course, the staple article of its export; its import
trade being large, but much below that which it transacts in the way of exportation. It now ships more
cotton for the North, and for Europe, than either
Charleston or Savannah, and bids fair soon immeasurably to out-distance as a commercial emporium
both of these places. The cotton shipped from Mobile is chiefly the growth of South Alabama, that is
to say, about two-thirds the entire crop of the State.
It also ships a great deal that is grown in the south-
eastern section of Mississippi, a small portion of that
State abutting, contiguous to Alabama, upon the
Gulf, but possessing no seaport town of any importance of its own. The produce of Western and
Northern Mississippi, however, as well as that of
Northern Alabama, finds its way to the ocean
through New Orleans, that city being more accessible
to these portions of the two States than Mobile.
Though far from possessing those advantages of

position which New Orleans commands to so extraordinary an extent, Mobile is most favourably situated as an *entrepôt* for both an export and import trade. I have already shown the capabilities of the Alabama, in a navigable point of view, from Montgomery to Mobile, a distance of between 300 and 400 miles. The Coossa, again, is navigable from Montgomery to Wetumpka, about forty miles further north; so that the line of internal navigation from Wetumpka to Mobile, taking Montgomery in the way, may be stated as exceeding 400 miles. The richness and capabilities of the different regions through which it flows have already been described. The other chief river of Alabama is the Tombeckbee, which is navigable for steamers of but small draught to Columbus in the State of Mississippi. Tuscaloosa, the capital of Alabama, is situated upon a tributary of this river, called the Black Warrior, which is navigable up to the city for small steamers. The district through which the Tombeckbee flows, with its branches, is if possible more fertile and better cultivated than that drained by the Alabama. Thus both these streams, rising either by themselves or some of their tributaries in the north-eastern and north-western extremities of the State, after pursuing the one a south-westerly and the other a south-easterly course, unite, as already stated, about fifty miles from the coast, into one broad deep river, at the entrance of which into the bay stands the city of Mobile. It will thus be seen how the greater portion of the exports of the State must necessarily converge upon this seaport, and how admirably it is situated for the distribution of its imports to different quarters in the interior.

The bay is shallow in the immediate neighbourhood of the town, so that the wharves are approached by vessels of but comparatively small draught. Those of larger draught can get to the town, if they take a circuitous route for the purpose of doing so; for they can ascend a channel, called Spanish River, separated from it by a low sedgy island, into the Mobile River, on which they can then drop down to the town. Few vessels of any size, however, approach nearer than six miles to the city, their cargoes being conveyed to it in barges, and the cotton with which they are laden being carried down to them in the same manner. There are sometimes from thirty to sixty vessels lying at anchor in the bay, at this distance from the town, all busily loading or disgorging their cargoes—a sight which is well calculated to impress the tourist with the commercial importance of the place. On leaving Mobile, which I did after a stay of four days in the town, I passed this anchorage in sailing down the bay, and great was my surprise, some distance further down, on finding myself at another anchorage, with an equal number of vessels in occupation of it. Only some of them, however, were either loading or unloading, the remainder, having cleared the custom-house, being ready to put to sea. If on passing the upper anchorage I was impressed with the commercial importance of Mobile, I was doubly so on witnessing this unexpected sight lower down the bay.

From Mobile at the head of the bay to the open gulf the distance is about thirty miles. The shores on either side as you descend are low, but the scene taken as a whole is not wanting in effect. The chief military defence of Mobile is Fort Morgan, situated like Hurst Castle upon a long low sandy point, separating the bay from the open sea.

There are two routes by sea from Mobile to New Orleans, one being by the Mississippi, which has to be ascended to the city; the other, by Lake Ponchartrain, which is the shorter and the safer of the two. The latter is of course the usual route for passengers. On emerging from Mobile Bay we stood out to sea for some time before altering our course, compelled as we were to do so by the shallowness of the water close to the shore. The shores of the Gulf of Mexico, almost the whole way round from Key west to Yucatan, are sandy, and the water shallow, sometimes for miles from the coast. The screen of low sandy islands which intervene between the ocean and the coast, with but little intermission, from the mouth of Chesapeake Bay to the peninsula of Florida, is prolonged along the shores of the Gulf, stretching in an almost uninterrupted chain from Pensacola to the Mississippi, from the Mississippi to the Rio Grande, and from the Rio Grande to beyond Vera Cruz. These islands seem to have been engendered by the recoil of the water, on being violently thrown by storms upon the sandy coast.

On directing our course westward for New Orleans, which is about 160 miles distant from Mobile, we kept for some miles out to sea, running a parallel course with the low shore in the distance. We soon left the coast of Alabama behind us, and approached the swampy shores of Mississippi, our course then being chiefly between them and the islands. Shortly after passing St. Catharine's Sound we entered Lake Borgue, an arm of the Gulf, on ascending which we approached a narrow passage called the Rigolet, through which we entered Lake Ponchartrain. To the tourist this lake appears merely an extensive sheet of water, with nothing to interest him on its banks, which are low, sedgy, and unvarying, like most of the coast between it and the Bay of Mobile. From the strait by which we entered it to its opposite side in the direction of New Orleans, the distance is about twenty miles, which we soon made, the steamer on board of which we were being of a very superior description. The day was excessively hot, and the lake, which was unruffled, blazed like a huge mirror in the sunshine. It was so calm that, on approaching the landing-place, we could trace the wake of the steamboat almost to the strait by which we had entered.

We landed upon one of several wooden jetties, projecting far into the lake on high wooden piles. We were then but five miles distant from New Orleans, and a train being in readiness for us, we started for the city without delay.

I was at length, then, fairly in the delta of the Mississippi, and its aspect was as gloomy and repulsive as I had been prepared to find it. The tract, through which the railway led, was as flat as a bowling-green, but seemingly saturated with water. The road led straight through a dense growth of timber, such as is found in most of the American swamps, the cypress and cedar abounding on either side, with here and there some clumps of palmettos interspersed amongst them. As we proceeded at the rate of about twenty miles an hour, the tremulous ground seemed to quiver beneath our feet. The railway is short, but its construction through such a morass must have been a work of no little difficulty. It was dusk ere we came in sight of the city, and seen from a little distance through the uncertain twilight, it looked like a dark and ponderous exhalation surging slowly from the swamps around it.

CHAPTER X.

NEW ORLEANS.

THE Crescent City, as New Orleans is not unpoeti-
cally called, not from the little reverence which is
there paid to the Cross, but from the semicircular
sweep which it takes along the curving shore of the
river, is situated on the left bank of the Mississippi,
about one hundred miles above its junction with the
Gulf of Mexico. Before adverting to the nature of
its position in a commercial or political point of
view, or to the advantages which may be incident to
it in either of these respects, it may be as well first
to give a brief description of the city itself, in its
physical and moral aspects.

The general course of the Mississippi being due
north and south, the stranger would expect to find

it, New Orleans being situated upon its left bank, on
the western side of the town.   On entering the town,
however, and making for the quays, his first impression would be that his notions of geography had been
all astray ; for he finds the river lying almost to the
east of the town, and its current flowing nearly due
north.   The fact is, that the Mississippi, whose
course has been exceedingly devious since the junction of the Ohio with it, here makes a bend to the
left, flowing eastward and then northward a little,
after which it again deflects to the right to regain
its southward course.   New Orleans is thus both
east and west of the stream, having one reach of it
to the east and one to the west.

In bending to the right, the river forms a species
of bay, in the recess of which New Orleans is nestled.
Nothing can be more imposing than its position, as
you approach it by the stream.   Almost the entire
length of the noble amphitheatric front which it presents to you is in view ; the rows of warehouses and
other commercial establishments, which follow each
other in rapid succession, extending for nearly three
miles along the margin of the river.   In front of
these, and close to the quays, or to the Levee, as the
spacious promenade dividing the city from the river
is here called, are numerous vessels of all kinds, and
bearing the flags of almost all nations.   Opposite the
upper portion of the town, the river is chiefly occupied by the barges and keel-boats which ascend and
descend the river for short distances for and with
produce, and which are also extensively used for the
purpose of loading and unloading the vessels in the
harbour.   A little below, you discern a multitude of
square-rigged vessels of almost every variety of ton-
nage, lying moored abreast of each other, like those

which occupy the Pool between London-bridge and Deptford. Below them again are scores of steamers, built in the most fantastic manner, and painted of the most gaudy colours, most of them river boats, but some plying between New Orleans and Texas. There are also tug-boats and ferry-boats to communicate with Algiers, a small town directly opposite New Orleans, to give still greater variety to this motley group of wood, paint, paddle-boxes and funnels. Still further down, and near the lower end of the harbour, are brigs, schooners, and sloops, and other craft of a smaller size, designed for, and used chiefly in, the coasting trade of the Gulf. Many of the square-rigged vessels in the upper part are coasters, trading between the Mississippi and the northern ports, their voyage partaking more of the character of the "long voyage" than the coasting one, and their size and style of building corresponding with those of the finest vessels afloat for any purpose. Mid-stream is crowded as well as the quays, some vessels dropping down with the current, and others being tugged up against it—some steamers arriving from above and some from below, and others departing upwards and downwards—ferry-boats crossing and re-crossing at short intervals—small boats shooting in different directions; and barges, some full, some empty, floating lazily on the current. On a fine morning, with the sun shining brightly on town and river, the scene is one of the most lively description.

But the bustle and activity which characterise it are not confined to the stream alone. The Levee is, if possible, more lively than the river. In front of the city, along its whole line, from the upper to the lower harbour, all seem busy and in motion. The quays are piled from one end to the other with goods and produce. Here you have pyramids of cotton bales, some ready pressed for shipping, others newly landed from above, and awaiting the process of pressure. There you have rows of sugar hogsheads, filled with the produce of Louisiana. There, again, you have bags of rice piled in huge heaps together, and barrels of pork without number, which have been transmitted from the far north-west. On this side you have flour ready for exportation to South America, and coffee just imported from Rio. Here are a variety of the products of the country designed for the European markets, and bales of manufactured goods just received from foreign ports, and now ready for distribution through the great valley. Look which way you will along this noble promenade, and the eye is met by articles of commerce, either imported or ready for export, indicating by their variety the many markets with which New Orleans is connected, and the extent of the business which it transacts. The busy throng of people well accords with the vast accumulation of merchandise. There they are, from morning till night, all active, bustling, and anxious; merchants, clerks, ship captains, supercargoes, custom-house officers, sailors, boatmen, porters and draymen. The last-mentioned are busy with their carts, removing from point to point the different articles on the quays, the piles of which are being constantly increased or diminished in size. Great is the number of these carts, and rapidly do they proceed, as if they had all been loitering and were now making up for lost time. Their constant succession in every direction, and the rattling noise which they occasion, the perpetual movement, from and to every quarter, of human beings, and the incessant hum of human voices, the ringing of steamboat bells, and the hissing of steam-pipes, the song of the sailor, and the clank of the busy crane, all combine to render the whole scene, taking river and shore together, one of intense interest and indescribable animation.

So far, however, New Orleans presents to the stranger features which are, more or less, common to all the great seaports of the country. It is only when he enters the town that he perceives the many points in which it differs from all the rest. There are in it a mixture of the new and the old, and a variety of speech, manners, and costume, which forcibly strike him ere he penetrates to any great distance into the streets. The length of the city is parallel to the river—its width, which averages about a mile, being in the direction back from the stream. The city proper, or the old portion of New Orleans, occupies the centre of its position upon the river, and extends back to the outskirts of the town, upon the swamps behind it. Here the streets are both narrow and dirty, but straight and otherwise regularly planned. The houses on either side combine to some extent the more prominent features of modern French and Spanish architecture, and are almost all covered with stucco, and painted of some lively colour, generally white, yellow, or ochre. This quarter, which is now a municipality, with a council of its own (the portions of the city on either side of it being also separate municipalities, having also their respective councils), is chiefly peopled by the descendants of the original French and Spanish colonists, who occupied it before the cession of Louisiana

to America.   With very few exceptions, the names
of all the streets are French, the two principal
thoroughfares being the Rue Royale and the Rue de
Chartres.   As you walk the streets, the Anglo-
American countenance is the exception in the stream
of faces which you meet, whilst French is the language chiefly spoken around you.   Indeed everything
in this quarter remains but little changed since the
cession, New Orleans strongly reminding one, in its
mixed population, and its diversity of dialect, manners and architecture, of the Anglo-French cities of
Montreal and Quebec.   Strange indeed has been the
destiny of France on the American continent.   From
the mouth of the St. Lawrence to the Great Lakes,
from them again to the mouth of the Mississippi, we
find memorials of her power and traces of her recent
dominion.   From point to point stretched regions
of immense extent and boundless fertility, hemming
in the British colonies between them and the Atlantic.
Along the whole of this vast and concave boundary
of " New France " the French had their forts and
strong places, and their busy trading communities.
They commanded the St. Lawrence, the Lakes, the
Ohio, the Missouri, and the Mississippi, and sometimes threatened to crush the English colonists into
the sea.   But where now is New France ?   Over
what portion of the North American territory does
the French flag now wave ?   The first serious blow to
this magnificent colonial dominion was the conquest
of Canada, confining New France to the undefined
province of Louisiana, west of the Mississippi.   This
she retained till the beginning of the present century,
when she ceded to the United States, for a pecuniary
consideration, a territory not only large enough to

enable empires to be carved out of it, but possessing, at some points, commercial and political advantages of a most important nature. She then finally retreated from the continent, since which time her colonial possessions in this quarter have been confined to a few islands in the West India seas. But at Quebec, Montreal, St. Louis and New Orleans, in Canada, Missouri and Louisiana, she has left behind her traces which still survive of her former sway. But they are being fast obliterated, particularly within the limits of the Union, where everything that is French, as well as everything that is Spanish, is being rapidly submerged by the great Anglo-Saxon inundation.

No one can enter Edinburgh for the first time without being at once struck by the decided contrast presented between the old town and the new. Standing on opposite ridges, in close and full view of each other, how different are the epochs which they indicate in the progress of humanity! The one is hoary with age, the other lightsome from youth—the one antique in its form and fashion, the other modern in its garb and aspect. Standing side by side, they make the middle age and the nineteenth century as it were to confront each other ; the narrow valley between them being all that separates the thing of yesterday from the creation of a bygone time. A contrast resembling this, but neither so striking nor complete, the tourist may witness in New Orleans. This contrast is between the old town and the American quarter. The dividing line between them is Canal-street, a broad and spacious thoroughfare, lined throughout with trees, dividing the two quarters from each other, as Tottenham-court-road separates the east from the west in London. On one side of this line the aspect of the town is totally different from its aspect on the other. It is true that Canal-street does not bring, on either side of it, such distant things near, as does the valley between the old town and the new in Edinburgh; for the old town of Edinburgh was old ere any part of New Orleans was yet new. But still the contrast is very great, as not only exhibiting a marked difference in architecture, but also a difference of race. You not only, in crossing Canal-street, seem to bound from one century into another, but you might also fancy that you had crossed the boundary line between two con-terminous nations. On the American side the streets are wider, better paved, better lighted, and better cleaned; the architecture is of the most modern style; the shops are large, showy, and elegant; the names over the doors and the names of the streets are familiar to the Anglo-Saxon; the English language is generally spoken, the French being the exception; and the costume of the residents bears a close resem-blance to that of all American southern towns. From what has already been said of the old town, the reader may easily infer how much it contrasts, in everything, with the new.

New Orleans does not present much that is striking in the way of public buildings. Being the capital of the State,* all the public offices are of course here; but they are almost all accommodated, as are the two branches of the legislature, in a large building, neither elegant nor imposing, which was once a charity hos-pital. It has for some time been intended to erect a capitol more in keeping with the importance of the city and the dignity of the State; but as yet that intention has, in being postponed, but shared the fate

---

* The seat of government has since been removed.

of the great bulk of commendable resolutions. Some
of the municipal buildings, though not very extensive, are not without merit, and the same may be said
of a few of those dedicated to commerce and its
exigencies. Decidedly one of the finest structures
in New Orleans is the St. Charles Hotel, situated in
the American quarter, and surpassing in extent and
good management, though not in exterior elegance,
the famous Astor House in New York. It was erected
by a company incorporated for the purpose, and is
conducted on a scale of magnificence unequalled even
in America, where the hotel system is carried to such
an extent. It may consequently be said to be without
its equal anywhere else. With us hotels are regarded
as purely private property, and it is seldom that, in
their appearance, they stand out from the mass of
private houses around them. In America they are
looked upon much more in the light of public concerns, and generally assume in their exterior the
character of public buildings. Thus it is with the
St. Charles, with its large and elegant Corinthian
portico, and the lofty swelling dome which surmounts
it. There are many other hotels in the city with
" marble halls," and conducted on an extensive scale;
but the St. Charles is, in true Yankee phrase, the
" cap sheaf" of the whole.

It may seem to be a contradiction in terms, but in
New Orleans the cellars are all above-ground. In
other words, the basement story of the houses is
elevated several feet above the surface, a flight of
steps generally leading to the hall-door. This con-
trivance is evidently the result of necessity, for if they
dug into the swampy ground, they would have wells
and water-pools instead of cellars.

There are some very elegant and attractive looking
residences in the immediate vicinity of the town.
They are surrounded, for the most part, by gardens,
rich with the perfume of the magnolia, and shaded
with orange groves and a great variety of other trees.
These houses are generally inhabited by the permanent residents of the place, either those who have
been born in Louisiana, or immigrants into the State,
who have been long enough within the sedgy limits
of the Delta to be thoroughly acclimated.   They are
almost all wealthy, and for the most part take a run
with their families more or less to the north, not so
much to avoid the sickly season as in pursuit of
pleasure.

Immediately behind the city the swamp extends,
in one dismal, unvarying level, to Lake Ponchartrain.
Everything attractive about New Orleans is, therefore, confined to itself.   In its vicinity there are
no "pretty spots" to tempt to a day's excursion.
Seek its environs on either side, and you find yourself
still in the swamp, still treading a spongy tremulous
soil, still amongst cane brakes and thick tangled
woods, from which, if you enter them for shelter from
the blazing sun, you are unceremoniously driven by
legions of musquitos.   It is easy to trace, at the back
of the town, the lines which new streets are intended
to pursue; the rubbish, which is elsewhere collected,
being shot in straight lines, of a regular width, into
the swamp, to secure, by-and-by, as good a foundation as possible; these lines, as they radiate in different
directions, reminding one of the incipient embankments of a railway.

One of the most remarkable objects in the *tout ensemble* of New Orleans is the Levee—which is an

embankment extending, on both sides of the river, for about a hundred miles above and about fifty below the city. Its design is to confine the Mississippi to its channel, that stream having, when in flood, rather a wayward turn about it, frequently overflowing its banks and inundating whole counties, and sometimes, tired of its former courses, cutting new channels for itself, for which it occasionally entirely forsakes the old ones. This it is enabled to do from the soft and free character of the alluvial soil through which it flows, when the current is not sufficiently rapid and unimpeded to carry off its accumulated waters. It has more than once happened, that a planter has thus been transferred over-night, with his family and property, from the left to the right bank of the river, or *vice versâ;* lying down at night, say in Mississippi, and awaking to find himself, in the morning, in Arkansas. Some might think the change not undesirable. On other occasions he has not been so lucky, the new channel not being sufficiently large to drain the old, when he has found himself suddenly isolated, and cut off from all communication with the world; an awkward position, particularly if he had not formerly been addicted to boat-building. The new channels are generally deserted when the waters subside to their usual level, but they are sometimes permanently retained.

In passing through the Delta,—an enormous triangular formation, with an area of upwards of 15,000 square miles, and which is the result of the combined action of the river and its tributaries, which are constantly carrying down from the vast alluvial regions, through which they flow, material which they deposit for the formation of new territories on the Gulf,—

irruptions by the river into the circumjacent country
are prevented by its being confined to its channel by
the Levee.   It is all the more necessary thus to confine it, as in its course through the Delta the bed of
the river is being gradually raised above the level of
the country on either side.   It has more than once
broken through this embankment, submerging and
devastating large sections of the country ; the volume
of water in the channel being so great, that the Levee,
though strong and compact, could not, at the points
to which it gave away, resist the pressure.

The process by which the bed of the river is being
thus gradually elevated is a very obvious one.   The
fine silt, which, from the junction of the Missouri
with it, so largely impregnates its waters, and gives
to it the turgid, muddy appearance which it presents,
is being gradually deposited at the bottom.   This process, however, would but very slowly elevate the channel, were it not for the annual aid which it receives
from the floods of the river ; for the material brought
down by the stream, when at its ordinary level, is
almost all by degrees forced by the current to its
mouths, where it is finally applied to the extension of
the Delta.   But when the river is in flood, it is more
than usually turgid, carrying with it an extra quantity of material, a portion of which it leaves on the
open country which it invades, but the greater part of
which is deposited upon and between its banks.   When
the river returns to its ordinary size, a portion of the
extra quantity of soil thus deposited is carried down
by it to the Gulf, but a portion of it still remains,
when the floods again appear to leave new deposits
behind them.   Thus both the banks and the channel
are being gradually raised above the surrounding level.

It follows, of course, that everything which tends to confine the river to its own bed, aids the process by which the channel is raised, inasmuch as the material is thus deposited in the channel which, otherwise, would be left upon the surrounding surface inundated by the stream. Thus the process by which it periodically elevates its banks, contributes greatly to the elevation of the bottom of the channel. And this suggests a very serious reflection in connexion with the Levee; for this result of the elevation of the river's banks will take place, whether they are naturally or artificially raised. Except when their pressure is sufficiently great to break through it, the floods for about 100 miles above and 50 below New Orleans are confined to the bed of the river, by which the process of elevating it is quickened, and more particularly as in its approach to the Gulf the strength of the current sensibly diminishes. It would seem, then, that that to which the city now looks for its protection is only a means of aggravating the evil. The Levee is now kept in repair by dues which are exclusively appropriated to it; but it must not only be kept in repair, but gradually elevated, as the bed of the river rises. The level of the city is already several feet below the surface of the river at high water, so that every year would seem to increase the disadvantages of its position. Already it is difficult, if not impossible, to drain the town into the river; but the time will yet come when it will be clearly impossible to do so. Its only resource then will be to be drained into Lake Ponchartrain. But New Orleans runs another very serious risk from this constant elevation of the channel of the river, and that is, that, some day or other, the Mississippi will desert it altogether. The higher the channel rises, the more will the current diminish in strength, and the more, consequently, in flood-time, will the waters accumulate above. So much will this yet be the case, that the want of sufficient current in the lower part of the river to drain the channel above will virtually operate as an impediment to the stream, which will then accumulate to such a degree at some point above the Levee as to enable it to break through all obstacles, and seek an entirely new channel to the Gulf. It is, therefore, not improbable that the present course of the stream may yet be traced by a long and devious ridge running across the Delta, whilst the Mississippi is finding a readier outlet through Lake Ponchartrain to the Gulf.

There are few towns on the surface of the globe possessing such a medley of population as New Orleans. There are five distinct bases to the mixed race that inhabits it — the Anglo-American, the French, the Spanish, the African, and the Indian. Not only is each of these to be found in it unmixed with any other, but they are all commingled, the one with the other, in a variety of ways and in interminable degrees. The bulk of the population, however, at present consists of Anglo-Americans and French creoles; the former having no blood in their veins but that of the Saxon, and the latter having in it a small admixture of the American and the Spanish, but none other. But the majority of the creole population are of pure French extraction, natives of Louisiana; a small proportion of them having in their veins the yet unadulterated blood of Castile, and still speaking the Spanish language; and the remainder, also a small proportion, being, as already said, a mixture of the French and Spanish blood. The African race does not preponderate in point of num-

bers in New Orleans, but it constitutes not far from
fifty per cent. of the entire population. Of these
not more than one-sixth are free blacks, no less than
two-fifths of the whole population of New Orleans
being still held in bondage. The pure Indians are
exceedingly few in number, as happily is also the
mixed breed between the Indian and the negro,
which forms so large and so degraded a proportion of
the population of the Mexican confederacy. The
mulatto, and the many shades which succeed, and
also the mixed white and Indian race, are much more
common, the latter being in smaller proportion,
however, than the former. The race partly partaking
of the blood of the aborigines is not a despised one
in America ; whilst that inheriting, in the smallest
appreciable degree, the blood of the African, is put
universally under the ban of society. Unfortunately,
even when colour ceases to designate the inheritor of
negro blood, it leaves upon the features apparently
ineradicable traces to betray it. Their antipathy is
kept alive by the whites long after every thing that
may be considered repulsive in the negro has disappeared by successive infusions of white blood into
his veins. Lovelier women than the quadroons,
those removed in the fourth degree from the negro,
are nowhere to be found. The exaggerations of the
negro form are softened down in them into those
graceful curves which give roundness and elegance
to the shape; the woolly and crispy hair is superseded
by a luxuriant growth of long, straight, and silken
tresses; the eye is black, large, round, liquid, and
languishing, whilst the huge flat features of the
negro are modified into a contour embodying rather
a voluptuous expression. The complexion is beautiful and well befitting the sunny south, a slight

shade underlying the transparent skin, whilst on the
cheek a bright carnation intervenes between the two.
Despite all their charms, however, they are a proscribed race, living only to minister to the sensualities
of those who will not elevate them to an equality with
themselves. It is astonishing to witness the degree
to which they are seemingly reconciled to their fate.
From their infancy they learn that there is but one
course of life before them, and as they reach maturer
years they glide into it without either struggle or
reluctance.

The inhabitants of New Orleans may be again
divided into its resident and its peripatetic population. The former include the creoles—few of whom,
being natives of the town, ever leave it; and the
negroes, and the mixed races, who have no option but
to remain. The latter, the transitory population, are
chiefly composed of the Anglo-Americans; a small
proportion of whom are natives of the city, and the
bulk of them abandoning it on the approach of the
sickly season. A little more than one-fifth of the
whole population thus annually migrate from the
town, the runaways returning as soon as the dangerous period for such as are unacclimated is past.
From the beginning of July, until the winter begins
to make its appearance in October, the stranger who
does not quit New Orleans must be very cautious
how he acts during the first, second, and even third
season of his acclimation. The process is one which
proves fatal to many, notwithstanding all their care,
fevers of a severe bilious type carrying hundreds off,
even when the great scourge, the yellow fever, is not
at work. There is, however, a very exaggerated
notion abroad of the unhealthiness of New Orleans.
It will have been seen that the annual migration to

escape disease is a feature as common to social life throughout the whole sea-coast region, extending from the Potomac to Florida, as it is to that of New Orleans. It is true, that in the case of New Orleans is to be superadded the almost annual visitation of the dreadful epidemic which sometimes creates such havoc in the midst of it; but even this sometimes creeps far up along the coast, proving itself as fatal elsewhere as in New Orleans. Whilst the yellow fever has been in New York and Philadelphia, there have been of late, seasons during which it has not made its appearance in New Orleans. Much is annually being done in the way of cleaning, draining, and ventilating the town, for the purpose of entirely averting it, or of modifying its virulence when it visits it. The good effects of this have already made themselves manifest, and the inhabitants are not without hope that the time is not far distant when its visitations will, instead of being regular, be few and far between. They will then only have to cope with the ordinary autumn fevers, which are as common to the whole sea-coast region as they are to the delta of the Mississippi.

The process of acclimation is undoubtedly a perilous one, but so it would be on the lower parts of the James River. There, however, parties are not compelled to undergo it; but in New Orleans the necessities of business, and the temptations which exist to induce people to run the risk, make many encounter the process, great numbers passing successfully through it. Once acclimated, no persons enjoy better health than the resident population of New Orleans; whilst the natives of the city, particularly of the Anglo-American race, are as tall, strong,

and healthy a set of men as can be found in any part
of the Union.   Much of the unhealthiness, which
would otherwise be incident to the city and the
district in the midst of which it stands, is counteracted by the keen winds which now and then sweep
down the valley from the north, not only purifying
the atmosphere in the neighbourhood of New Orleans,
but making themselves felt along the whole coast of
the Gulf of Mexico, being as well known in Vera
Cruz as in the capital of Louisiana.

   The people of New Orleans are a very pleasure-
loving people.   Americans and French, negroes, mu-
lattoes, or quadroons, as soon as the business of
.he day is over, give themselves up, more or less, to
every species of gaiety and dissipation.   The creole
population being almost entirely catholic, much of
the manners of continental Europe is visible in
New Orleans.   These were established before the
cession, and the soberer character and severer tenets
of the American and protestant population have not
yet been able to make much headway against them;
and it will be long ere the strict moral discipline of
the northern towns is introduced to any extent into
New Orleans.   A change may be effected when the
resident protestant population becomes more numerous, but not before ; for the peripatetic protestants,
who form so large a proportion of the American
population, regard their sojourn in New Orleans in
the light of a somewhat protracted visit, and make
up their minds, as most visitors do every where, to
enjoy themselves.   The consequence is, that the
gaiety and dissipation of the place are kept up by
the creoles and the floating American population, who
by their combined numbers and influence completely

overbear the resident section of the latter, who, although mingling freely in the more innocent amusements, having local reputations to sustain, keep aloof from the scenes of more questionable gaiety with which the town abounds. There are three theatres, one French and two English, which are seldom shut, and are generally well attended ; and during the winter season particularly, scarcely a night passes over New Orleans without its public balls and masquerades. Some of them, particularly in the French quarter, are the mere nuclei for every species of demoralization. They are frequently the occasion of brawls, and sometimes the witnesses of fatal collisions ; many of the men attending them being armed, the handle of the " Bowie knife," or the " Arkansas toothpick," a still more terrible weapon, being not unfrequently visible, protruding from a pocket made for it inside of the waistcoat. The greatest attendance at these scenes, and indeed at the theatres, is on Sunday.

But it is now time to advert to New Orleans in connexion with its commercial position, and the political influence incident to that position.

If we consider for a moment the different circumstances which, at any particular point, call for the existence of a large *entrepôt* of trade, we must perceive, on looking at the situation of New Orleans, that whilst some of these circumstances already exist in its vicinity, they are yet all destined to develope themselves around it to an extent unparalleled in any other quarter of the world. Wherever we find a large community with diversified wants to be supplied from abroad, inhabiting a vast fertile region, producing in superfluous abundance the articles which will be received by the foreigner in exchange, that community must have some great *entrepôt,* either on or near the ocean, to serve as the medium or pivot of its export and import trade. Behind New Orleans both these conditions exist in preeminent degree; and the city itself is the result. The Mississippi valley is a region almost illimitable in its extent and inexhaustible in its fertility, lying between the parallel ridges of the Allegany and the Rocky Mountains, and extending in a northerly and southerly direction from the 29th to the 47th parallel of latitude. This enormous region, for nearly two-thirds of its whole extent, possesses a soil fertile to a degree, and yields in abundance every variety of crop and fruit produced in the temperate zone, with many of the productions more common to the tropical regions of the globe. Its western portion, that lying between a line drawn parallel to the Mississippi, about 400 miles to the west of it, and the Rocky Mountains, is sandy, rocky, and sterile; the rest, stretching across the Mississippi and eastward to the Allegany chain, being unequalled in fertility by any other portion of the earth's surface. This great valley, in its cultivable area, is about ten times the size of Great Britain, and it now comprises within its limits eleven of the States of the Union. There is nowhere else so enormous a surface cast as it were in one mould, and forming one great system. From the Alleganies to the Rocky Mountains, and from the Lakes to the Gulf, it spreads out in one huge undivided basin, irrigated by one mighty system of rivers, and possessing but one natural outlet to the ocean. At this outlet stands New Orleans, which has thus a position in point of commercial importance unparalleled by that of any other seaport in the world.

It is more in connexion with its future prospects than its present condition that we are to appreciate the importance of the position of New Orleans. It is impossible, when one reflects for a moment upon the coming destiny of the great region which lies beyond it, to set anything like reasonable bounds to its future extent, wealth, and greatness. There can scarcely be a doubt but that it will, at no very distant period, be the greatest commercial emporium in the world. At present it is, more or less, the *entrepôt* for the trade of upwards of nine millions of people, the population of the great valley at present exceeding that number. In 1810 it did not possess half a million of inhabitants. In 1840 its population as compared with 1810 was multiplied by eighteen times. What will it be in 1870? On the lowest computation it will be twenty-five millions; but even this will only be a commencement in the work of filling it. Without having to sustain as many to the square mile as England now sustains, the valley of the Mississippi can accommodate and subsist 150 millions of people. In regarding the future of New Orleans we are entitled to look to the time when the valley behind it will teem with population. The inhabitants of the valley are, and ever will be, an industrious people. Conceive 150 millions at work in the same great basin, with a fertile soil on all hands for them to cultivate! They will necessarily be chiefly agricultural, for the main sources of the wealth of the valley are in the diversified capabilities of its soil. Throughout the whole of its northern region cereal crops are, and ever will be, produced in the greatest abundance; its middle section will yield tobacco, Indian corn, hemp, and flax, live stock, and cotton;

whilst the cotton-plant and the sugar-cane will form the staples of its productions in the south. When it is all under cultivation, who can estimate the wealth which each successive year will draw from it? There will be annually an enormous surplus for exportation, and an immense yearly void to be filled by imports. It is true that much of its surplus productions will find outlets to foreign markets in the Atlantic seaports, by means of the great lines of communication already adverted to as connecting them with the valley; but if New Orleans has to act as the *entrepôt* of one-half, or even one-third of its entire trade, it would still, in the importance of its position, vastly surpass every other mercantile emporium in the world, for it would in that case be yet called upon to act as the medium through which would be transacted the export and import trade of from fifty to seventy-five millions of people.

What renders the situation of New Orleans still more imposing, is the magnificent and bounteous manner in which nature has irrigated the valley of the Mississippi. It is not only of exuberant fertility almost throughout its entire length and breadth, and capable of sustaining an industrious population amounting to three-fourths of that of all Europe; but it is also watered by a system of streams all navigable in their channels, and the commingled waters of which pass by New Orleans in their common course to the ocean. Nature has thus, without putting man, in this favoured region, to either trouble or expense, provided him, on all hands, with highways to the sea, with the like of which no trouble and expense on his part could ever have provided him. The Mississippi itself is, as it were, the great spinal cord of this vast system of irrigation. Pursuing its long and snake-like course along the lowest level of the valley, it receives on either bank, as it rolls majestically along, tributaries almost as extensive and as lordly as itself. Amongst the chief are the Wabash, the Missouri, the Ohio, the Tennessee, the Red River, the Arkansas, and the White River, all navigable for steamers and vessels of large draught, for hundreds of miles from their confluence with their common reservoir; and one of them, the Missouri, for thousands of miles. Ascending the Mississippi from New Orleans to its confluence with the Missouri, and then ascending the Missouri to the extreme point of its navigation, the combined navigable channels of the two streams exceed in length three thousand miles! Ascending the Mississippi and Ohio in the same way, their combined navigable channels are about two thousand miles in length. The Red River itself is navigable for thirteen hundred miles above its junction with the Mississippi. These tributaries again have their tributaries, some of which are navigable for hundreds of miles; and these again theirs, navigable for shorter distances. Thus the system goes on, increasing its ramifications as it penetrates into the interior, where its remoter, minor, and innumerable branches dwindle into the proportions of streams navigable only to the barge and the flat boat. But vessels of large draught navigate the Mississippi, its tributaries, their tributaries, and the chief of their tributaries again; that is to say, vessels of large draught can, in some instances, ascend into tributaries removed in the fourth degree from the Mississippi! This noble system of rivers permeates the richest portions of the valley; its arid, or more westerly part, being but indifferently irrigated by streams which are generally shallow, and whose channels are frequently interrupted by rapids. It would almost seem as if every farmer or planter in the valley had his own land skirted by a navigable stream. When to this natural is added the artificial irrigation, which will yet connect river with river in every direction, how great will be the facilities, not only for mutual interchange, but for pouring, with a view to exportation, the surplus productions of the valley upon the ocean! It is almost impossible to set limits to the extent to which canals will yet intersect the valley. The necessity for them will be obvious, and their construction easy; for nature has already, as it were, regulated the levels, leaving man only to dig out the soil. It was, no doubt, in view of all this, as forming part and parcel of the future destiny of this great region, that De Tocqueville designated it " the most magnificent habitation that God ever designed for man."

To sum up the favourable points connected with the position of New Orleans, it may here be added, that it stands at the outlet of about 25,000 miles of inland navigation! And in this estimate those streams only are embraced which are navigable for steamboats and vessels of large draught. What will yet be the amount of produce thrown upon it through such means, existing in such a region, or the amount of imports which, by the same means, it will yet have to distribute through it, I leave the reader, if he can, to appreciate. I have said enough to make out my proposition, that there is that in the position of New Orleans, which will yet render it the greatest commercial emporium, not only in America, but in the world; for, with the wide ocean before it, and the great human hive which will yet resound to the hum of universal industry behind, what bounds can be set to its progress?

The political importance of such a position did not escape the wary and far-seeing government at Washington. Previously to the cession of Louisiana, the Americans were confined to the east bank of the Mississippi, and that only for a part, although by far the greater part of its course; its lower portion flowing, like the St. Lawrence, exclusively through the territory of a foreign power. But possessed as they were of by far the better bank of the river, which was being rapidly colonized not only from Europe but also from the seaboard States, and which, at an early time, gave evidence of what its future wants would be, at no very distant period, in a commercial point of view,—they foresaw that without a free access at all times to the ocean, the enormous section of their territory stretching from the Alleganies to the Mississippi, would be in the position of Russia, a country of immense resources, pent up, as it were, within itself, and whose only outlets to the markets of the world are by the narrow straits of the Sound and the Bosphorus, its use of these depending, to a great extent, upon the caprice of foreign powers. The policy of the Union was evidently to secure a free course to the ocean for the commerce of the valley. To leave the mouth of the Mississippi entirely within the control of another power, was to leave in its hands a most profitable possession in time of peace, and one which would exercise a most inconvenient influence in time of war. The Union, therefore, had two courses before it ; either to secure the left bank of the river, the whole way to the gulf, by virtue of which its navigation would be common to it and the colonies of France on the other bank; or, if possible, to get hold of both banks, from its sources to the ocean. It wisely played the higher game, and succeeded; the cession of Louisiana putting it in possession, not only of both banks where it had but the one before, but also of the lower part of the river, from which it was previously excluded. The necessities of the French treasury happened to coincide with the views and policy of the Federal Government; and in 1803 the flag of France was struck on the continent, leaving the Americans the undisputed masters of the valley, of the river, and of all its tributaries.

Both the political and commercial importance of New Orleans have been partly trenched upon, as already shown by the great lines of communication which have been established, to connect the valley with the Atlantic seaboard, and to bring the Atlantic cities within the category of its seaports. But for these New Orleans would have been its sole outlet to the ocean. Its northern and north-eastern sections now chiefly find their way to the seaboard and to foreign markets by the lakes, the St. Lawrence, the Erie canal, and the Pennsylvania canals and railways. But to all the region south of the Missouri on one side, and bordering the Ohio on the other, the one 1,200 and the other 1,000 miles from New Orleans, the Mississippi is still and ever will remain, if not the exclusive, the chief outlet to the ocean. The principal grain-growing region lies north of these streams, but to large sections of Iowa, Illinois, Indiana, and Ohio, the Mississippi will be the medium for the exportation of grain; particularly of such as is sent from the valley to the West India and South American markets. Whatever the eastern cities may do to convert themselves into *entrepôts* for the trade of the west, New Orleans will always share in the trade of the whole of it; whilst to a large portion of it, it will ever be indispensable. Should a separation ever occur between the eastern and western States, which the communications opened with the Atlantic render the more improbable, the importance of New Orleans to the latter could not be over-estimated. And even should there be a separation between the western States themselves, such an event would have but little effect upon the prospects of the city. But such separation is scarcely within the range of probabilities. Whether combined with the East or not, the West will ever remain united. Its interests are one—its pursuits one—its component parts occupy the same great basin, and are united together by a common interest and a common necessity. The Mississippi is the great bond between them; its tributaries are the minor ligaments which bind them together; and whatever fate may yet await the other portions of the Confederacy, there is but little doubt that the States of Wisconsin, Iowa, Illinois, Indiana, Ohio, Kentucky, Missouri, Tennessee, Arkansas, Mississippi, and Louisiana, will ever remain united together in a close commercial and political alliance.

The New Orleans of the present day is typical of the greatness of the New Orleans of a future time. It would be here out of place to enter into any elaborate statistical statements with regard to its export or import trade, either in their present development, or the rapid expansion which they have undergone during the last quarter of a century. Its chief articles of export are cotton, rice, hemp, flax, Indian corn, salted provisions, and sugar, the last mentioned commodity being now the principal product of Louisiana. Its imports, being drawn from almost all points of the globe, are too varied to be here enumerated. At the cession the trade of New Orleans was but small; already it has swelled into colossal dimensions. A glance at its population returns will show the rapidity with which it has increased; and its increase in size is the sole result of the increase of its trade; for New Orleans is not the place to which people would retire merely to live. In 1810 its population, in round numbers, was 17,000. In 1820 it had risen to 27,000, being an increase in ten years of from 60 to 70 per cent. In 1830 the returns showed a population of 46,000, or an increase, during the preceding decade, of about the same per-centage as before. But in 1840 the population had risen in numbers to 102,000, being considerably more than 100 per cent. increase during these ten years. At present the number of people inhabiting it cannot be far from 150,000. And this despite not only its insalubrity, but also the exaggerated notions which are abroad, even in America, of its unhealthiness. Considering the many disadvantages under which it labours, nothing more conclusive could be adduced than this rapid advancement, in proof of the imperious necessity, in a commercial point of view, of which it is the result. As this necessity expands with the growth of population, the accumulation of produce, and the multiplication of wants in the Mississippi valley, the city, in continued obedience to the principle which first exhaled it from the swamps of the Delta, must expand with it, attaining no final limit until the valley can contain no more, produce no more, and consume no more. The sense which its inhabitants entertain of its future increase is manifest in the scale on which they have laid out the plan of the city, providing not only for its present necessities, but for its future growth ; for each of the municipalities into which it is divided extends from the river to Lake Ponchartrain, a distance of from five to six miles. Should it ever reach the lake, its principal front will then be turned upon the gulf, when it will be flanked by two harbours, one on the river for the trade with the interior, and the other on the lake for its intercourse with the North and with foreign ports.

Many think that a healthier site might have been chosen higher up the river, which would have answered all the purposes of the present one, and made the town much more healthy. But a site so chosen would not have answered all the purposes of the present one; the object in selecting it having been to erect it upon the nearest practicable point to the sea. Had an attempt been made to build a city a little higher up, it would have had to compete with another, which, despite the disadvantages of the present site, would inevitably have occupied it. New Orleans might have been built higher up, but not lower down the river.

The South occasionally exhibits some restlessness at the extent to which the North has become its medium of communication with England. Its export trade is carried on directly with Europe, but a great proportion of its imports, particularly in the case of the southern Atlantic States, reach it through the northern ports. What it aims at is that its import should be as direct as its export trade; and more particularly that it should possess a direct mail and passenger communication with Europe. However valid the objection may be to an extensive land carriage of goods, or their separate conveyance to the South by coasting vessels, after their arrival at the northern ports, the price being in either case greatly enhanced to the consumer in the South—with regard to letters and passengers it is an objection which scarcely holds. A glance at the map will show that the shortest mathematical line which can be drawn between Liverpool and Charleston, or New Orleans, will run up the American coast to New York and Boston, and thence past Halifax and Cape Race to St. George's Channel. By the present mode of communication, New York and Boston can be much more speedily reached by the overland journey than they could be passed from either Charleston or New Orleans by sea. It may be a little more expensive, but what is lost in money is more than saved in time. Besides, hundreds, and in the case of New Orleans thousands of miles of sea are always to be avoided if possible; and more particularly when a journey by land is in the direct line of one's course. If in proceeding by land from New Orleans to New York or Boston, on his way to England, the traveller deviated seriously from his course, it might be a matter worthy of consideration whether a more direct mode of communication could not be devised. But the traveller by land from New Orleans to New York, is proceeding in the direct line to Liverpool; every step which he takes towards the north-east bringing him nearer and nearer to that port. And as to the speedy receipt of important commercial or political intelligence from Europe, no direct line of ocean communication with the South could compete with that by Boston or New York, now that the electric telegraph may be considered as finished between these ports and New Orleans. The mails too can sooner be distributed through the South, by railways and steamers from the North, than they could by such an independent communication as some aspire to establish. But, as already intimated, the question as to the direct importation of goods, or the establishment of a more direct trade with Europe, rests upon different grounds.

Before leaving the South for the Western States, a few general remarks upon the more prominent peculiarities of Southern life, as they manifest themselves to the traveller, may serve as a not inappropriate conclusion to the present chapter. There is, perhaps, no other country in the world where such a contrast is exhibited between in-door and out-door life as in America. Both in France and Italy, where the pleasures and enjoyments of life partake so much of an out-door character, men and women are, in their domestic relations, pretty much what they are found to be in the gay and giddy world without. In England, on the other hand, where the chief pleasures of life centre in the domestic circle, the traveller carries with him into the world without much of the sedateness and the reserve of home. In both cases, society partakes more or less of the same general characteristics, whether you mingle with it in the public highways or in the private sanctuaries of domestic life. But it is not so in America, where it combines, to a great extent, the more striking characteristics of life both in England and France. The equable character of the seasons, the serenity of the sky, the facilities provided both by nature and art for locomotion, and the extent to which, in the prosecution of business, mutual intercourse is carried on, all tend to draw the American more frequently from his home than the Englishman leaves his, and to cause much of his life to be passed, as in France, in the open world without. But, notwithstanding this, he still partakes largely of the domestic preferences of the Englishman. His life is therefore a kind of medium between the two; for whilst he does not live so much abroad as the Frenchman, he does not live so much at home as the Englishman. Society in America has thus two very distinct phases in which it presents itself, that which it assumes in the world without, and that which marks its in-door life. Life in the streets and on the highways is therefore but an imperfect index to American society in the proper acceptation of the term. The distinction between the two aspects which it assumes in the North is not so great as in the South, the former being in perpetual and almost universal motion, whereas the wealthier portion of the inhabitants of the latter pass much of their time in the repose and quietude of rural life. The stranger therefore, who only frequents the public places, lives in the hotels, and traverses the highways of the South, can form but a very imperfect estimate of society in that section of the country. In the South, as in the North, turn which way he will, he will find a stream of people constantly on the move. But in the North the turgid current embraces almost the entire population, whereas in the South there is a large residuum that is seldom in motion. In the North, therefore, society in its external aspect is much more pleasing

than in the South, inasmuch as its better as well as
its more indifferent ingredients mingle more frequently
together; but in its internal aspect it is less so, as
almost all carry with them into their domestic relations
more or less of the asperities of life in the outer world.
In the South, society, as the mere traveller through
the country comes in contact with it, is by no means
attractive, the better elements of social life there
mingling less frequently in the current; and for the
same reason Southern society, in the ordinary acceptation of the term, is far more refined than that of
the North, there being much less of the *brusquerie*
of outward life infused into it. If, then, that with
which the traveller meets in the steamboat, in the
market, on the street, on the railway, or in the hotel,
can convey to him but an inadequate idea of society
in the North, much less is that which he encounters
under similar circumstances in the South calculated
to produce correct impressions of Southern social
life. A stranger passing rapidly through the Southern States, and judging of American society from its
development upon the streets and highways, would
form a much less favourable idea of it than he would
of Northern society in travelling rapidly through the
North. In the South he is borne along, as he proceeds, upon a stream, possessing far less in common
with that through which it passes than the current with
which he would mingle in the North possesses of
the characteristics of the society through which it
flows. Whether on the railway, the high road, the
steamboat, and with some exceptions in the hotel,
out-door life in the South has far less to recommend
it to the stranger than it has in the North. Nowhere is society, in this its public manifestation, very
refined in America, but it certainly has a tone about

it in the North of which in the South it is deficient.
Less attention is paid to accommodation as you proceed; every thing seems filthy in the car, the steamer,
and the tavern, as compared with the accommodation
met with in the Northern States ; whilst the further
South one proceeds, he naturally looks for the appli-
ances of cleanliness in greater abundance.   Even the
travellers themselves, taking them generally, are in their
tout ensemble less attractive in their appearance, and certainly less refined in their habits, and less particular
in their manner, than their Northern fellow-countrymen ; whilst not a small proportion of those met with
in the extreme South are suspicious in their demeanour, repulsive in their looks, and equivocal in
their characters.   New Orleans, and the other towns
situated near the mouth of the Mississippi, such as
Natches and Vicksburg, are infested with characters
to whom this latter description applies ; vagabonds
who can only live in that section of the Union where
the population is as yet comparatively scanty, the
law but feebly enforced, and public opinion, even
when decidedly pronounced against them, as yet too
impotent to crush them.   These gamblers and desperadoes prey upon the unwary, and sometimes by
their mere numbers overawe, pillage, and terrify their
more sober and well-disposed fellow-travellers.   Such
a nuisance in the midst of any community becomes
at last so intolerable as to work its own cure ; and it
has reached that point in the South, the parties in
question no longer carrying it with so high a hand as
heretofore, and being compelled year after year to
envelop their misdeeds more and more in the mantle
of secresy.

The reader must not imagine that in travelling
through the South one is constantly surrounded by

these vagabonds; but they are frequently met with in groups upon the Mississippi, and the other rivers of the South, particularly those which enter the Mississippi on its west bank. There can be but little difficulty in detecting them to any one travelling with his eyes open, for their reckless look, and swaggering, insolent air, enable a man of any discernment to distinguish them at once from the rest of his fellow-travellers. Putting them, therefore, out of the question, as parties who, by his encountering them on the highways, can lead the stranger into no misconception of the character of Southern society, what he has to be guarded against is drawing his impressions of social life around him from the general character of the floating population, with whom alone he mingles. In the South particularly, one must get out of the current if he would appreciate American society aright. I had afterwards many opportunities of witnessing Southern life in all its manifestations, and can testify to the fact, that it cannot be regarded from a worse or a more unfair point of view than that from which travellers have, but too often, either from ignorance, prejudice, or caprice, alone beheld it. It is this that has given rise to so many misrepresentations of it; parties assuming to delineate society generally, when they were but depicting life as they saw it in the railway carriage, on the steamer, and in the bar-room.

END OF VOL. II.

R. CLAY, PRINTER, BREAD STREET HILL.